FACTS ABOUT
BHUTAN
THE LAND OF THE
THUNDER DRAGON

Facts About Bhutan
2nd Edition
April 2010

Text and Illustrations **copyright** (c), Lily Wangchhuk, 2010

Disclaimer:
"The contents expressed in the book are solely that of the author and by no means represent the views of the Literary and Publications Sub-Committee of the National Steering Committee for Coronation and Centenary Celebrations of Bhutan, 2008".

Cover Illustration: Painting of a dragon from **Druk Wangyel Lhakhang**
Layout and Design: **Bhutan Media Services, Thimphu, Bhutan**

Publisher:
Absolute Bhutan Books
Thimphu, Bhutan
Web: www.absolutebhutanbooks.com.bt

Printed at: Ajanta Offset & Packagings Ltd., New Delhi

ISBN 99936-760-0-4
Registration No : HS/TPHU/BICMA/1002

The author is grateful to the following agencies/organization for their assistance with information and for kindly verifying the relevant contents and chapters:

- Association of Bhutanese Tour Operators
- Austrian Coordination Office
- Anti-Corruption Commission
- Bhutan Broadcasting Services
- Bhutan Information & Communications Authority
- Bhutan Post
- Bhutan Trust Fund
- Bhutan Foundation
- Bhutan Canada Foundation
- Bhutan Nuns Foundation
- Cabinet Secretariat
- Dratshang Lhentshog
- Druk Green Power Corpn Ltd
- Druk Holding & Investments
- DSLR, Survey
- Election Commission of Bhutan
- FAO
- GNH Commission
- Helvetas
- International Finance Corpn.
- JICA
- Liaison Office of Denmark
- Ministry of Agriculture and Forests
- Ministry of Economic Affairs
- Ministry of Education
- Ministry of Foreign Affairs
- Ministry of Health
- Ministry of Home and Cultural Affairs
- National Assembly
- National Council
- National Environment Commission
- National Statistical Bureau
- National Commission for Women and Children
- NSCCC
- National Women's Association of Bhutan
- Office of Attorney General
- RENEW
- RCSC
- Royal Audit Authority
- Royal Court of Justice
- Royal Office for Media
- RSPN
- Save the Children
- SNV
- Tarayana Foundation
- Tourism Council of Bhutan
- UNDP
- UNFPA
- UNICEF
- WFP
- WHO
- WWF
- World Bank
- Youth Development Fund

The author remains grateful to the Liaison Office of Denmark, Government of Denmark for kindly supporting the first edition of the book and is thankful to Druk Green Power Corporation and Austrian Coordination Office for their support in promoting this edition.

Dear Helga,

FACTS ABOUT
BHUTAN
THE LAND OF THE
THUNDER DRAGON

With my warmed regards,

Lily Wangchhuk

Lily Wangchhuk

THIMPHU
17 Oct '10

Commemoration of Coronation and Centenary Celebrations
of the Kingdom of Bhutan, 2008

Endorsed by Literary and Publication Sub-Committee of the
National Steering Committee for Coronation and Centenary
Celebrations of Bhutan, 2008

His Majesty Jigme Khesar Namgyel Wangchuck, Druk Gyalpo signing the Constitution of The Kingdom of Bhutan, July 18, 2008

100 YEARS OF
GLORIOUS MONARCHY
IN BHUTAN

BHUTAN
CENTENARY
1907-2007

His Majesty the King Jigme Khesar Namgyel Wangchuck with His Majesty the Fourth Druk Gyalpo Jigme Singye Wangchuck at the National Day celebrations, 17th December 2007

DEDICATION

To our Beloved Fourth Druk Gyalpo

Miwang Jigme Singye Wangchuck

Without whose Wisdom, Vision and Sacrifice

This Great Nation of Ours Wouldn't be

Where it is Today

&

To the Repository of all our Hopes and Dreams

As We Move into the Future

Miwang Jigme Khesar Namgyel Wangchuck

The Fifth Druk Gyalpo

Her Majesty the Queen Mother Ashi Dorji Wangmo Wangchuck

HER MAJESTY THE QUEEN

FOREWORD

Facts about Bhutan is a meaningful tribute as Bhutan celebrates 100 years of Extraordinary Leadership by our Beloved Monarchs. We have been fortunate with the clear vision and personal sacrifices made by our Kings to bring this nation to where it is today. Bhutan is the world's youngest democracy, initiated and brought into existence by the Throne. Bhutan's environment is the envy of most nations, while our traditions and culture are vibrant and thriving, contributing to **Gross National Happiness.**

This book will benefit the reader with a comprehensive overview of Bhutan, now that our country is on the travel wish list of many people around the world. Lily Wangchhuk introduces the fabric of Bhutan in all its beauty and uniqueness through her well-researched facts and compilation of beautiful pictures. This is the first book of its kind by a Bhutanese author and I am very delighted to be presenting it to the readers with the hope that it will serve as an introduction to a very special country blessed throughout history.

Tashi Delek!

Dorji Wangmo Wangchuck
Queen of His Majesty the Fourth King of Bhutan

ACKNOWLEDGEMENT

For many years I dreamt of writing a book about Bhutan that would reveal all the amazing facets of the country. With the help of friends and support from my family, this dream was finally realized in the most historic year of Bhutan's history while the Kingdom was revelling in the celebrations of 100 years of glorious reign under the monarchs and celebrating the Coronation of His Majesty, the Fifth Druk Gyalpo.

I am deeply honoured by Her Majesty the Queen Mother Ashi Dorji Wangmo Wangchuck's kind gesture of writing a foreword for the book and for Her Majesty's valuable advice and continued support.

I would like to thank Shankar Sharma profusely for plotting the comprehensive maps exclusively for the book. I am indebted to Her Majesty the Queen Grandmother, The Friendly Planet (Michael Hawley, Christopher Newell), Robert Dompnier, Tourism Council of Bhutan, Bhutan Times Limited, Jigme Wangchuk, Leki Dorji, Ian Bell, Lydia and Tenzin Namgay for providing astonishing photographs. I am thankful to Roopa Bakshi, Tashi Phuntsho, Louise Dorji, Kunga Tshering, Sonam Dorji, Damcho Rinzin, Pek Dorji, John Chiramal, Francoise Pommaret, Chimi Wangmo, Sangay Wangchuk, Karma Galey, Pema Wangdi, Drangpon Tshering Wangchuk, Dr. Sangay Wangchuk, Dr. C.T. Dorji, Hon. Sangay Khandu, Yonten Dargye, Sonam Choden, Dr. Sonam Wangyal, Karma Tshosar, Ugyen Pelgen, Dhendup Tshering and Shahdev who helped with information and in reviewing the drafts. My sincere thanks goes to Vembu Shankar, Tulku Jamyang and Jayesh Bole who has been a great source of support.

I would also like to thank the members of the Literary and Publications Sub Committee of the National Steering Committee for Coronation and Centenary Celebrations and officials from various government agencies, international organizations and individuals in various capacities who helped me make the book a true factual compendium.

My mother's prayer has been my source of strength not only during the duration of writing the book but throughout my life which no words can measure.

PREFACE

'Facts about Bhutan' is a comprehensive book which unveils all there is know about Bhutan. A maiden venture by a Bhutanese, it reveals amazing facets about the country and provides a holistic picture of the many delightful and incredible aspects of this little known Kingdom. It will help both foreign visitors and Bhutanese discover the country's history, society, tradition, culture, people, governance, judiciary, clergy, foreign relations, economy, environment, health, education, and tourism among many other topics.

Readers will also gain a good understanding of the glorious journey the Kingdom has traversed under the monarchs over the last 100 years. Policies of the government, information about all 20 districts of Bhutan and other places of interest are vividly explained in the book and would serve as a ready reference.

To help visitors, it contains exhaustive information about visiting Bhutan supported by charts, maps and illustrations on recreation activities, monthly temperature, driving time between places and contact details of travel companies. Common phrases for conversational Dzongkha supported by illustrations will help travellers strike a bond of friendship immediately with the locals.

Encyclopedic in scope, the book's 486 pages of texts are embellished with over 700 astonishing photographs, 42 maps, 10 graphs, 8 information tables, 23 mini statistics, 30 special spotlight pages all meticulously well-researched and compiled in one. Useful addresses of diplomatic missions, agencies, associations, tour operators, hotel, books and websites related to Bhutan are listed to help readers gather additional information.

Dedicated to 100 years of Bhutan glorious journey under monarchy, the book has been published under the auspices of the National Steering Committee for Coronation and Centenary Celebrations.

TABLE OF CONTENTS

Cultural Symbols

The National Flag

The upper yellow half that touches the base symbolizes the secular tradition. It personifies His Majesty the King, whose noble actions enhance the Kingdom. Hence, it symbolizes that His Majesty is the upholder of the spiritual and secular foundations of the Kingdom.

The lower orange half that extends to the top symbolizes the spiritual tradition. It also symbolizes the flourishing of the Buddhist teachings in general and that of the *Kagyu* and *Nyingma* traditions in particular. The dragon that fully presses down the fimbriation symbolizes the name of the Kingdom, which is endowed with the spiritual and secular traditions. The white dragon symbolizes undifiled thoughts of the people that express the loyalty, patriotism and great sense of belonging to the Kingdom although they have different ethnic and linguistic origins.

The National Emblem

Within the circle of the national emblem, two crossed - *vajras* are placed over a lotus. They are flanked on either side by a male and female white dragon. A wish-fulfilling jewel is located above them. There are four other jewels inside the circle where the two vajras intersect. They symbolize the spiritual and secular traditions of the Kingdom based on the four spiritual undertakings of Vajrayana Buddhism. The lotus symbolizes absence of the defilements, the wish-fulfilling jewel, the sovereign power of the people and the two dragons, the name of the Kingdom.

National Tree : Cypress
(Cupressus Sempervirens)

National Bird: Raven
(Corvus Corax Tibetanus)

National Animal: Takin
(Budorcas Taxicolor)

National Flower: Blue Poppy
(Meconopsis Grandis)

རྒྱལ་པོའི་བསྟན་བཤུག་ལ།།

དཔལ་ལྡན་འབྲུག་ཆེན་དཀོན་མཆོག་བའི་རྒྱལ་ཁབ་ནང་།།
དཔལ་ལུགས་གཉིས་བསྟན་སྲིད་སྐྱོང་བའི་མགོན།།
འབྲུག་རྒྱལ་པོ་མཆོག་བདག་རིན་པོ་ཆེ།།
སྐུ་འགྱུར་མེད་བརྟན་ཅིང་ཆབ་སྲིད་འཕེལ།།
ཆོས་སངས་རྒྱས་བསྟན་པ་དར་ཞིང་རྒྱས།།
འབངས་བདེ་སྐྱིད་ཉི་མ་ཤར་བར་ཤོག།།

The National Anthem

In the Kingdom of Bhutan adorned with cypress trees,

The Protector who reigns over the realm over spiritual and secular traditions,

He is the King of Bhutan, the precious sovereign.

May His being remain unchanging, and the Kingdom prosper.

May the teachings of the Enlightened One flourish.

May the sun of peace and happiness shine over all people.

Prayer flags adorn the Bhutanese landscapes

Rigma Phachu Cham or the Dance of the sixteen fairies at Thimphu Tshechu

Black hat dancers spectacularly clad in colourful brocades and large hats await their turn at Gangtey Goenpa Tshechu

Ian Bell

Punakha Dzong, the Palace of Happiness

Tenzin Namgay

Ura Village, Bumthang

*Bhutan embraces democracy with the conduct of first
nationwide parliamentary elections on 24 March, 2008*

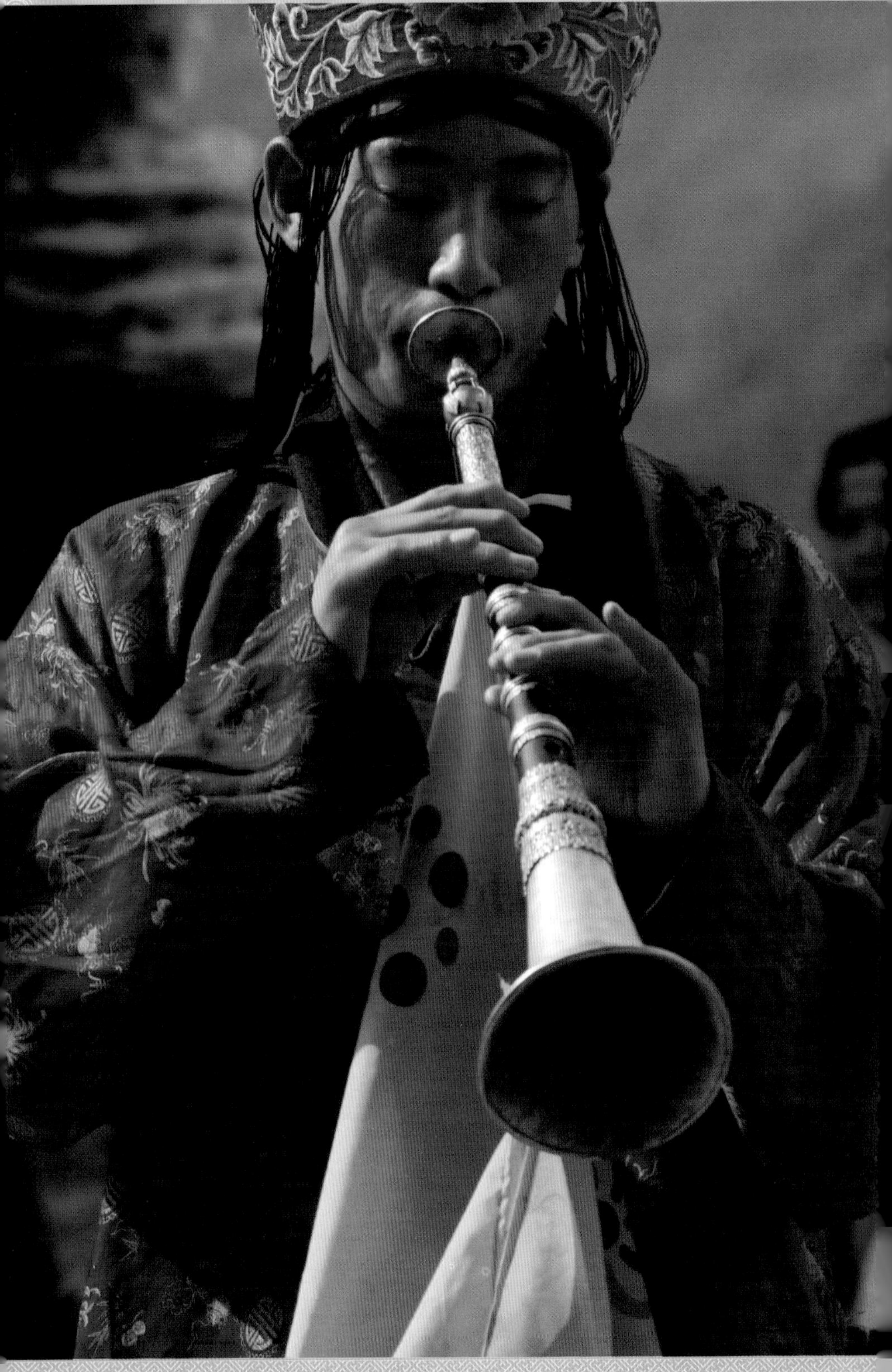

Jacaranda brightens Punakha Dzong

Ian Bell

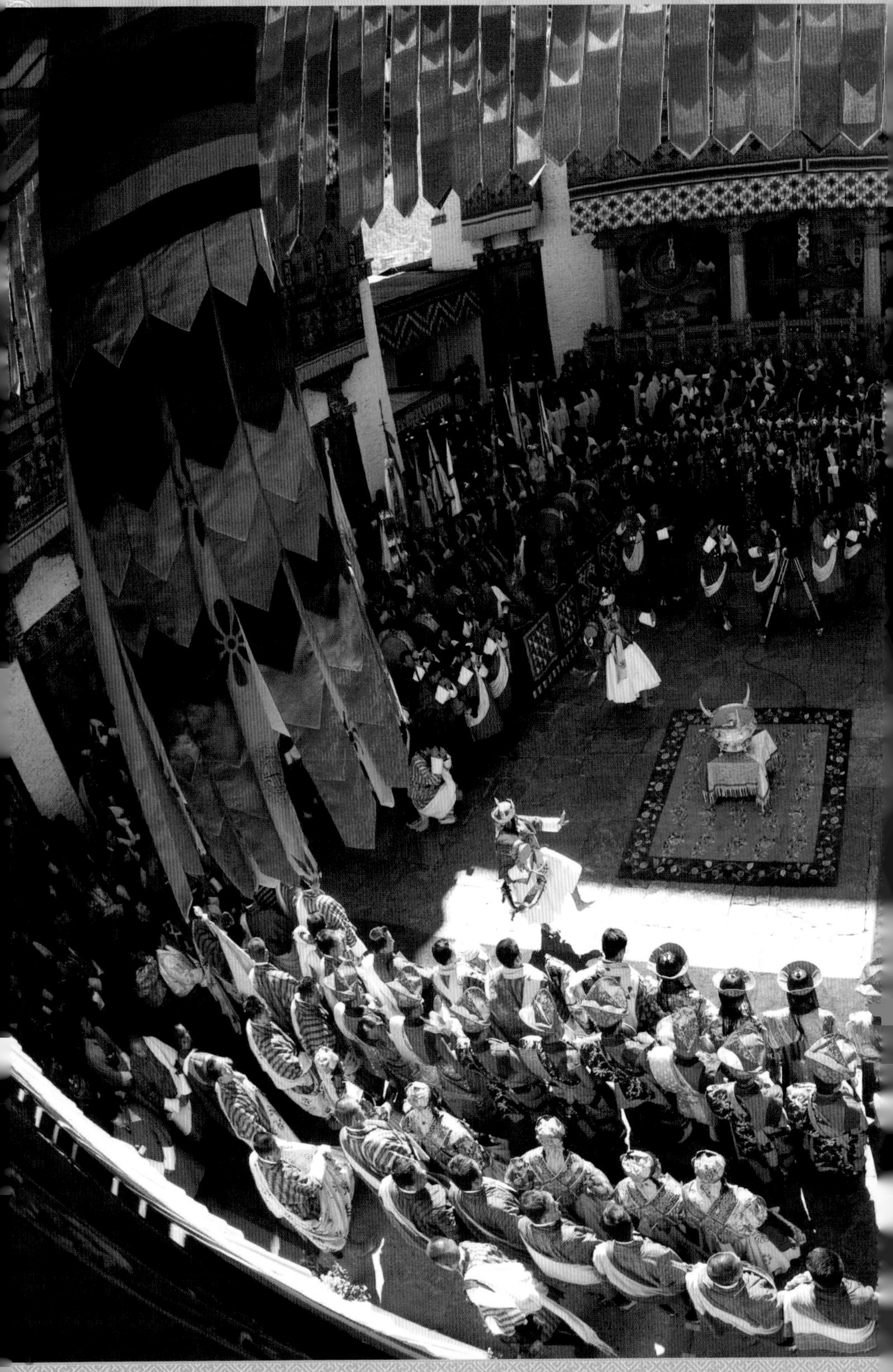

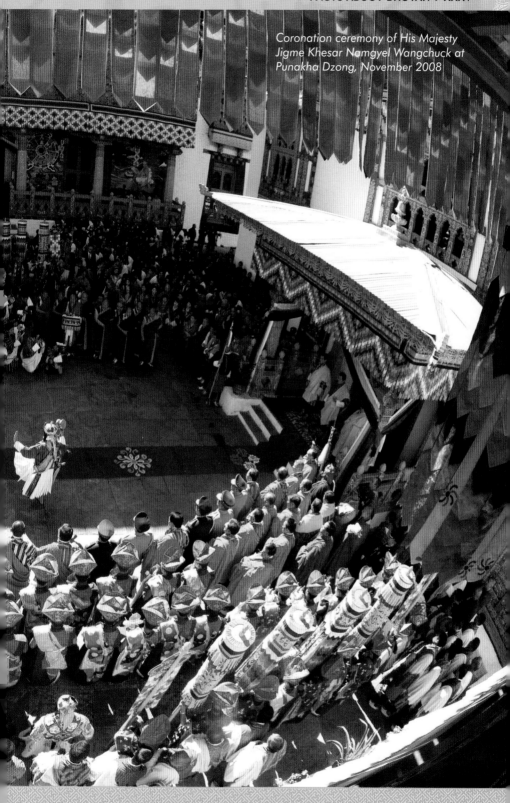

Coronation ceremony of His Majesty Jigme Khesar Namgyel Wangchuck at Punakha Dzong, November 2008

TOURISM MAP

Pg. 382

FESTIVAL MAP OF BHUTAN

Pg. 388

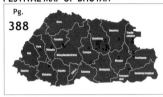

ENTRY & EXIT BY DRUK

Pg. 371

DISTANCE MAP

Pg. 374

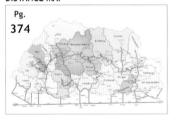

ELEVATION RANGE OF BHUTAN

Pg. 6

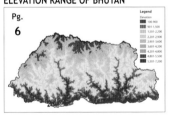

MAJOR RIVERS, GLACIER AND LAKES

Pg. 250

Profile at a glance :

Longitude : 88 45'-92 10' East
Latitude : 26 42'-28 15' North
Square Area : 38,394 sq. km
Dzongkhags : 20
Gewogs : 205
Population(2009): 683,407
Male: 357,305
Female: 326,102
Airport : 1

Map o

Gasa

Punakha

Paro

Thimphu

Wangduephodrang

Haa

Dagana   Tsirang

Chhukha

Samtse

LAND COVER MAP OF BHUTAN

Pg. 7

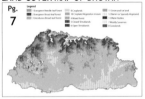

LAND USE PATTERN OF BHUTAN

Pg. 7

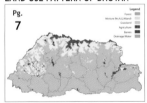

VEGETATION MAP OF BHUTAN

Pg. 6

TRANSPORTATION NETWORK OF BHUTAN

Pg. 8

LAND USE & FOREST TYPE

Pg. 242

Bhutan

Schools & Institutes : 1651
Hospitals : 30
Basic Health Units : 178
Traditional Medicine Hospital : 1
Traditional Medicine Units : 26

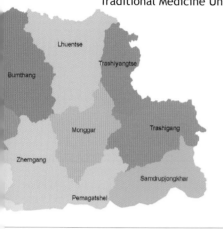

TELECOMMUNICATION NETWORK

Pg. 177

DRUKNET NATIONAL BACKBONE

Pg. 178

TASHICELL COVERAGE

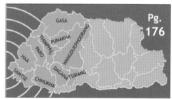

Pg. 176

PROTECTED AREAS & BIOLOGICAL CORRIDORS

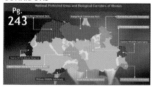

Pg. 243

DZONGKHAGWISE NORMALIZED VERY HAPPY HOUSEHOLDS

Pg. 191

FLORA AND FAUNA DIVERSITY

Pg. 244

DZONGKHAGWISE NORMALIZED HAPPY HOUSEHOLDS

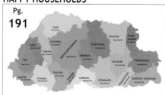

Pg. 191

MINERAL DEPOSITS IN BHUTAN

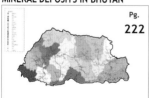

Pg. 222

CONSTITUENCIES

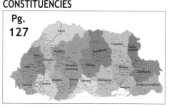

Pg. 127

ANNUAL PRECIPITATION

Pg. 270

View of Mount Jichudrake from Chebisa, Lingzhi

Chapter 1

INTRODUCTION

Bhutan - Druk Yul or The Land of the Thunder Dragon

The Kingdom of Bhutan is a landlocked nation nestled in the eastern Himalayas, bordering China to the north and India to the south. With a total area of 38,394 sq.km and aerial distance of around 350km from east to west and around 150km from north to south. Bhutan lies between 88°45' and 92°10' longitude East and 26°42' and 28°15' latitude North. It is a mountainous country except for a strip of plains in the south.

A fundamental characteristic of the country is that pronounced differences in nature and landscape come together within a small area. The valleys of Bhutan are separated by mountains ranging from 7200m to 100m from north to south and high passes ranging from 3000-3500m from west to east.

Bhutan has three distinct ecological zones with sub-tropical in the south, temperate in the middle and subalpine in the north which corresponds with three different climatic zones. The variations in climate are therefore correspondingly extreme.

The plains in the south have hot and humid summer with cool winter. The land here is covered with dense forests, alluvial lowland river valleys and the mountains rise up to 1500m.

The hills and valleys in central and eastern Bhutan are temperate and drier than the west with warm summers and cool winters. It is cut off from the foothills, by high ranges of the Inner Himalayas with a succession of valleys at altitudes ranging from 1500m to 3500 m. The hillsides are thickly forested with blue pine, conifers, oak, magnolia maple, birch and rhododendron.

The northern region with an alpine climate is perpetually under snow. Most peaks in the north are over 7,000m above sea level with the highest point being Gangkar Puensum at

7,564m which has the distinction of being world's highest mountain that has not been scaled.

Although, the country was not unified under a central authority until the 17th century, Bhutan preserved its independence from time immemorial. Bhutan followed a policy of self-imposed isolation and was largely cut off from the rest of the world until 1950s. Its formidable geographical boundaries kept out foreign authority and allowed the Bhutanese to develop a strong degree of common identity, despite ethnic and linguistic diversity. Today, unlike most countries, Bhutan has retained its integrity and distinctive way of life virtually intact.

The process of modern development in the country began only in 1961. Until then, the country possessed very little of the infrastructure that is associated with a modern nation state. The majority of the Bhutanese lived rugged lives of isolation. Bhutanese were almost totally dependent upon the land and the forests for survival, producing or collecting not only the food they required for nourishment but also the materials required for clothing. The small surpluses produced were bartered for goods like salt.

There were no roads, motor vehicles, electricity, telephones or postal services. Transport was confined to centuries old tracks. Distances that can be covered in a few hours today required days or weeks of hazardous travel and long periods of preparation.

Despite the late start towards modernization, the Kingdom has recorded many remarkable achievements in the last four decades. Today the country is connected with a wide network of roads, electricity is

Jakar Dzong, Bumthang

Tenzin Namgay, Bhutan Times Ltd.

> *Bhutan is no longer an isolated Kingdom today but increasingly forms part of the world system*

much more widely available, a modern system of telecommunications links different parts of the country and Bhutan with the outside world. The national airline, Druk Air, flies to six destinations in the neighbouring countries. The progress recorded in the economy and in terms of physical infrastructure has been matched by progress in the social sectors such as education and health.

A least developed country in the 1960s with GDP per capita of only USD 51 (the lowest in the world), Bhutan's GDP per capita as of 2008 was USD 1,852 which is one of the highest in South Asia. According to 2009 Human Development Report published by UNDP, Bhutan ranks 132 out of 182 countries with Human Development Index value of 0.619 which places Bhutan in the United Nation's 'medium human development' category of countries, one of a very few developing countries thus categorized.

A country with a mosaic of cultures, lifestyles, languages and belief systems, Bhutan's rich and unique cultural heritage has largely remained intact. Unlike many countries, traditional arts, age-old ceremonies, festivals, social conduct and structures are not remnants of a bygone age but are practiced as they were done hundreds of years ago.

With a unique development philosophy based on the principles of Gross National Happiness, Bhutan is becoming increasingly known for its visionary and dynamic leader-

ship under the monarchs. It holds uncompromising stance on environmental conservation and is known for the policy of 'high value low volume' tourism, rich tradition and cultural heritage, pristine ecology and abundant wildlife. It is a paradise of unparalleled scenic beauty with majestic virgin peaks, lush valleys, unspoilt countryside and terraced rice fields. Fascinating architecture, monumental fortresses, fluttering prayer flags, hospitable people and a devout Buddhist culture makes the Kingdom of Bhutan extraordinarily special.

BHUTAN AT A GLANCE

Total Area	: 38,394 square kilometers (350km long and 150km wide approximately)
Location	: Landlocked between China and India
Altitude	: 100m above sea level in the south to over 7,500m above sea level in the north.
Longitude	: 88°45' - 92°10' East
Latitude	: 26°42' - 28°15' North
Political system	: Democratic Constitutional Monarchy
Capital	: Thimphu
District	: 20
County	: 205
Population (2009 est.)	: 683,407 (Male 357,305; Female 326,102)
Population growth rate	: 1.8 percent (2005)
Exchange rate (Mar. '10)	: 1USD = Ngultrum 45.50
Forest coverage	: 72.5 percent of the land area
Cultivated area	: 7.8 percent of total land
Life expectancy	: 66.3 years (Male 65.7; Female 66.9)
Literacy rate	: 59.5 percent (Male 69; Female 49)
Local time	: 6 hrs ahead of GMT
Country code	: +975

Natural Resources

Minerals	: Dolomite, Limestone, Gypsum, Slate, Coal, Talc, Marble, Zinc, Lead, Copper, Tungsten, Chemical Grade Quartzite, Graphite, Iron Ore
Crops	: Rice, Maize, Wheat, Potato, Millet, Buckwheat, Orange, Apple, Cardamom, Coffee
Hydropower	: An estimated potential of 30,000 MW with mean annual energy production capability close to 120,000 GWh.

ELEVATION RANGE OF BHUTAN

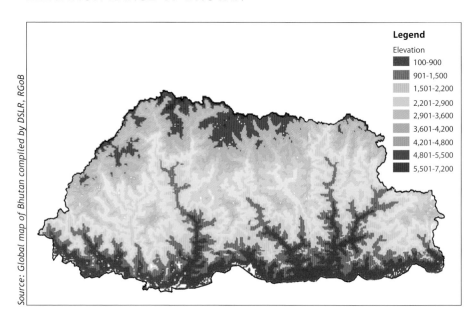

Source: Global map of Bhutan compiled by DSLR, RGoB

VEGETATION MAP OF BHUTAN

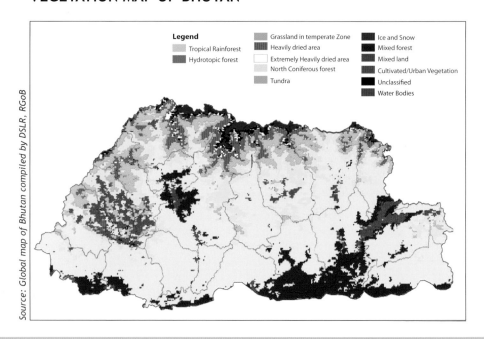

Source: Global map of Bhutan compiled by DSLR, RGoB

LAND COVER MAP OF BHUTAN

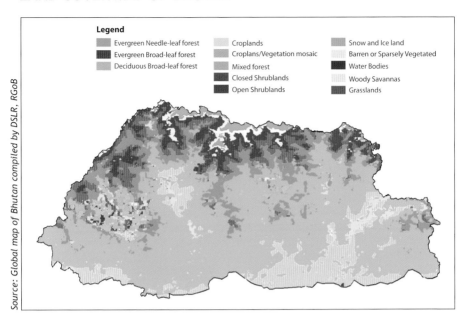

Legend

- Evergreen Needle-leaf forest
- Evergreen Broad-leaf forest
- Deciduous Broad-leaf forest
- Croplands
- Croplans/Vegetation mosaic
- Mixed forest
- Closed Shrublands
- Open Shrublands
- Snow and Ice land
- Barren or Sparsely Vegetated
- Water Bodies
- Woody Savannas
- Grasslands

Source: Global map of Bhutan compiled by DSLR, RGoB

LAND USE PATTERN OF BHUTAN

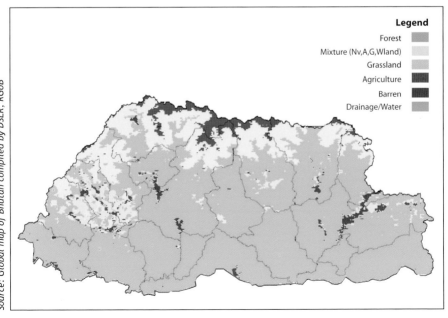

Legend

- Forest
- Mixture (Nv,A,G,Wland)
- Grassland
- Agriculture
- Barren
- Drainage/Water

Source: Global map of Bhutan compiled by DSLR, RGoB

TRANSPORTATION NETWORK OF BHUTAN

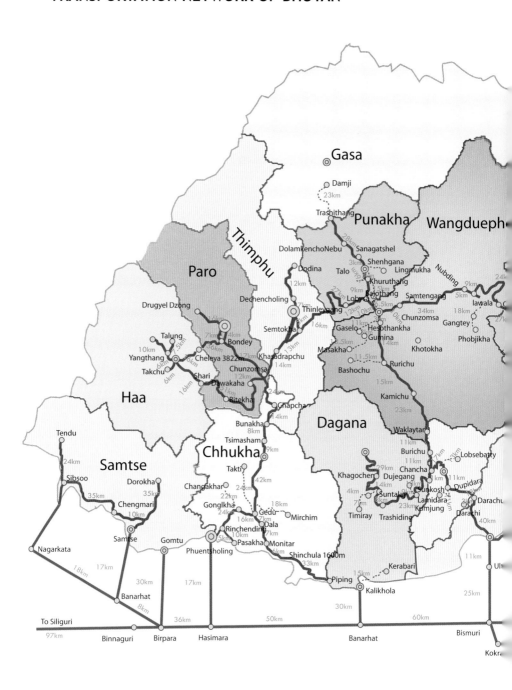

Source : Tourism Council of Bhutan, 2009

The ruins of Zongkhar Dzong

Chapter 2

HISTORY

Pre-Historic and Ancient Bhutan

Archeological artefacts reveal that Bhutan was inhabited 4000 years ago and ancient stone implements unearthed indicate settlements in Bhutan dating back to 2000-1500 BC. However, most of these records were lost to calamities; a fire in 1832 that ravaged the Punakha Dzong, the ancient capital and a massive earthquake in 1896 destroyed structures that housed the ancient records. Similarly, fire accidents in most of the Dzongs and monasteries have destroyed valuable historical documents and important religious relics and artefacts.

Notwithstanding, a few records exist and from the available *namthars* (life stories of great people or hagiography) and artefacts from ancient monasteries, the prehistoric era of Bhutan can be traced back to 500/600 AD.

Some of the early inhabitants of Bhutan practiced *Bon*, an animistic tradition that was the main religion throughout the Himalayan region before the advent of Buddhism.

HISTORY

1885
BATTLE OF
CHANGLIMITHANG
THE LAST CIVIL WAR

1904
YOUNGHUSBAND
MISSION TO TIBET

1905-6
THE KCIE &
VISIT TO INDIA

1907
CROWNING OF THE 1ST KI

1927
ADMINISTRATIVE
AND TAX REFORMS

1949
INDO-BHUTANESE FRIENDSHIP
TREATY

1953
ESTABLISHMENT
OF NATIONAL ASSEMBLY

1965
ROYAL ADVISORY COUNCIL
ESTABLISHED

1968
CEMENTING FRIEND-
SHIP WITH INDIA

1971
BHUTAN JOINS
THE UN

1985
BHUTAN BECOMES
FOUNDING MEMBER
OF SAARC

1986
CHHUKHA
HYDROPOWER PROJECT
COMMISSIONED

1991
GYT – DECENTRAL-
IZATION GATHERS
MOMENTUM

197
WORLD'S YOUNGEST I

2006
DAWN OF
NEW ERA

2007
POLITICAL
PARTIES FORMED

2007
THEIR MAJESTIES AT THE
100TH NATIONAL DAY

200
CORONATION OF T
FIFTH DRUK GYAI

TIMELINE

1910
TREATY OF PUNAKHA
SIGNED

1914
INTRODUCTION OF
MODERN EDUCATION

1927
SECOND KING CROWNED

1952
THIRD KING
ENTHRONED

1956
SERFS FREED

1958
INDIAN PM PANDIT
NEHRU VISITS BHUTAN

1961
FIRST FIVE-YEAR
PLAN LAUNCHED

1972
GROSS NATIONAL
HAPPINESS

1973
BHUTAN JOINS NAM

1981
DYT FORMED

1998
DEVOLUTION OF POWER
FROM THE THRONE

2001
DRAFTING OF THE
CONSTITUTION BEGINS

2003
MILITANTS FLUSHED OUT
OF BHUTANESE SOIL

2005
4TH KING ANNOUNCES
DECISION TO ABDICATE
THE THRONE

2008
DEMOCRATICALLY ELECTED LEADERS

ADOPTION OF THE CONSTITUTION OF
THE KINGDOM OF BHUTAN

2008

2009
ECONOMIC
DEVELOPMENT POLICY
FORMULATED

2010
BHUTAN
HOSTS THE
XVI SAARC
SUMMIT

Bhutan: Its name

The ancient names attributed to Bhutan provide a glimpse of how this cloistered nation was seen by the outside world. *Lho Mon* (Southern Land of Darkness), *Lho Tsendenjong* (Southern Land of Cypresses), *Lhomen Khazhi* (Southern Land of Four Approaches), and *Lhojong Menjong* (Southern Land of Medicinal Herbs) were the most popular names before the country was called Bhutan. The term south was used because the country was to the south of Tibet.

After the 17th century, Bhutan came to be known as *Druk Yul* or the Land of Thunder Dragon, a name derived from the Drukpa Kagyu School, one of the sub schools of *Kagyu*, Vajrayana Buddhism.

However, to the outside world the country is known as Bhutan. According to historians, 'Bhutan' may have been derived from the Sanskrit word *Bhu-Uttan* meaning 'High Land' or 'Head of India' when looked at the country from Indian plains. In another Sanskrit derivation, *Bhotsant* means 'End of Tibet' or 'Tail of Tibet' when looked down to the country from Tibetan Plateau.

Leki Dorji

Guru Padmasambhava

Advent of Buddhism

The seed of Buddhism was sown in Bhutan in the 7th century when the 33rd Tibetan King, Songtsen Gampo ordered the establishment of monasteries in the Himalayan region to subdue the evil spirits and to spread Buddhism. Of the 108 monasteries which were to be built, two major ones were built in Bhutan namely the Kyichu Lhakhang in Paro and the Jambay Lhakhang in Bumthang.

Buddhism came to Bhutan in its original form when Guru Padmasambhava, popularly known as *Guru Rinpoche* or the Precious Master visited the country in 747 AD. Guru Padmasambhava laid the foundation for the community of *lamas* (Buddhist teacher) in Bhutan and firmly established the Vajrayana form of Buddhism imbued with tantric practices. In the succeeding two centuries, Buddhism gained considerable adherents in the country.

Guru Padmasambhava is the patron saint of Bhutan and is regarded as the Second Buddha. He is still worshipped as a great historical and religious figure in Bhutan embodying almost all its religious, ethical and national legends. Since its introduction, Buddhism has played a predominant role in shaping the social, political, economic and cultural evolution of the country.

Medieval Era

During the reign of King Langdharma in Tibet from 836 to 842 AD, Buddhism was banned and religious institutions were destroyed. Following religious persecution in Tibet, many lamas came to Bhutan, particularly after the 11th century. Many of them settled in western parts of the country and established their monastic orders.

One of the most important of these lamas was Gyalwa Lhanangpa, who founded the *Lhapa Kagyu* lineage and established a system of *Dzongs* (fortresses) in Bhutan similar to Tibetan forts. In 1220 AD, Lama Phajo Drugom Zhigpo came to Bhutan, defeated Lama Lhanangpa and introduced the Drukpa Kagyu School of Vajrayana Buddhism. His sons further helped spread the tradition of Drukpa Kagyu, especially in western Bhutan. Between the 13th and 16th centuries, the Drukpa Kagyu lineage flourished and Bhutan adopted a separate religious identity.

Mebar Tsho

Ian Kean, Bhutan Times Ltd.

Over the years, many more lamas from Ralung, Tibet were invited to teach and build monasteries which contributed to the propagation of Buddhism in Bhutan. They include Ngawang Choegyal, who established several *goenpas* (monasteries) and Lama Drukpa Kunley, the divine madman, who established the Chimi Lhakhang.

Between the 11th and 16th centuries, numerous *termas* (sacred treasures) hidden by Guru Padmasambhava in caves, rocks and lakes were discovered by tantric lamas called *tertons* (treasurer revealer), as he had prophesized. The tertons were important religious figures and the best known of these was Pema Lingpa, who recovered his first treasure from *Mebar Tsho* (burning lake) in Bumthang in 1475. He constructed several monasteries in Bumthang and is an important figure in Bhutanese history. The traditions of Pema Lingpa have been passed down intact to the present day and many of the holy places, especially in his home region of Bumthang, are dedicated to him. Among the aristocratic families descended from him is the present Royal Family.

The age of Zhabdrung Ngawang Namgyal - Unification of Bhutan (1594-1651)

Until the early 17ᵗʰ century, Bhutan existed as a patchwork of minor warring fiefdoms. The political arena was fragmented with intermittent conflicts between principalities until the arrival of Ngawang Namgyal, a leader of the *Drukpa Kagyu* School of Buddhism from Tibet in 1616.

Born at Gor-gong in Tibet into a family of prince-abbots, Ngawang Namgyal was installed as the 18ᵗʰ prince-abbot of the *Drukpa* monastery at Ralung in 1606 at the age of 12. Because of theological and succession disputes surrounding his investiture, he was forced into exile to Bhutan at the age of 23.

Zhabdrung Ngawang Namgyal

Soon after his arrival, he taught Buddhism throughout western Bhutan which eventually increased his political strength. His rule was opposed by leaders of Buddhist lineages within Bhutan who formed a coalition of five lamas under the leadership of Lama Palden. Their attack was repelled which led to the eventual decrease of the influence of the rival lineages. Ngawang Namgyal further consolidated his power by establishing relations with the neighbouring Kings of Nepal, Cooch Behar and Ladakh.

After his great victory over the Tibetans in 1639, Ngawang Namgyal was recognized as the leader of *Druk Yul* and assumed the title of *Zhabdrung* (literally meaning at whose feet one submits, or the Supreme Religious Power) and became the temporal and spiritual ruler of Bhutan.

He unified the country and installed a dual system of administration. Later he nominated under him a *Desi* (civil ruler) and *Je Khenpo'* (the Chief Abbot or spiritual ruler).

He divided the country into regions under the governorship of *Chila Namsum* (later called Penlops), and appointed *Dzongpons* (provincial rulers) to administer civil affairs at the local level. Strict regulations were introduced for religious and secular officers and a judicial and revenue administration was set up.

He also constructed a number of important monasteries and *Dzongs*, religious institutions and firmly established the Drukpa Kagyu as the state religion. He thus established the foundations for national governance and a distinct Bhutanese national and cultural identity. These political and administrative achievements by Ngawang Namgyal effectively unified Bhutan as a political entity which was able to stave off Tibetan attempts for domination.

Conflict and Reconciliation

Invasions from Tibet

For the first time in several centuries, Bhutan had to contend with aggression from outside when in 1639, the King of Tsang in Tibet invaded from the north. The Tibetan-Mongol troops launched another invasion in 1647. Ngawang Namgyal personally led the successful resistance and several Tibetan officers and a large number of horses were captured. He also repelled Tibetan invasions in 1648 and 1649. Drugyal Dzong (victorious fortress) was built at the head of Paro valley in 1646 to commemorate the victory and to check further Tibetan infiltration. These battles which united the Bhutanese against a common enemy, and his success in repelling the Tibetan attacks further cemented Ngawang Namgyal's position as a undisputed ruler. The large militia, that he raised for the purpose, also gave him effective control of the country. Zhabdrung Ngawang Namgyal thus came to be known as the founder of *Druk Yul* and governed the country for 35 years.

Period of Civil Wars

After the sacred retreat of Zhabdrung Ngawang Namgyal in 1651, Bhutan was ruled by *Desis* until 1907 during

Drugyal Dzong, The Victorious Fortress

which, the country was once again torn with civil strife. Of the 54 *Desis* (excluding Additional *Desis*), who ruled the country since 1651, some important ones were the third *Desi* Chhogyal Minjur Tempa, the fourth *Desi* Gyalse Tenzin Rabgye, who ruled from 1680 to 1694 and 13th *Desi* Sherab Wangchuk. Only a few of the rulers completed their terms; 22 Desis were assassinated or deposed by their rivals. Furthermore *Penlops* (governor of a region consisting of several districts), vying for central power, plotted and fought against each other. Death and destruction marred the daily lives of people for the next two centuries.

Clash of Arms with the British in India

Prior to 1772, the British had no political relations with Bhutan. When the East India Company established its sovereignty in Bengal, the State of Cooch Behar, situated between Bengal and Assam had not become a dependency of the British Government. In 1772, Bhutan invaded Cooch Behar, overran the country and occupied the capital. In response, Khagendra Narayan, a pretender to the throne, made overtures to the British government on 5 April, 1773. He signed an agreement with the East India Company making Cooch Behar a virtual dependency of the British. He surrendered half the revenue of the state and promised payment of Rs. 50,000 for defraying the expenses of British troops sent to assist in his reinstatement in Cooch Behar.

Under this agreement, a British force was dispatched and succeeded in not only uprooting the Bhutanese from

Cooch Behar but also captured the two Bhutanese forts of Pasakha and Dalimkot in the foothills.

Alarmed by these developments, 17th *Desi* Tshenlop Kunga Rinchen at once called upon the Panchen Lama of Tibet to intercede on his behalf with the Governor-General of India, Warren Hastings. This intercession was successful and an Anglo-Bhutanese Treaty was concluded between the East India Company and Bhutan on 25 April, 1774 which provided that

The Duar Issue

The plains between the river Brahmaputra in India and the lowest hills of Bhutan were known as Duars (Indian word meaning doorway or gate). In the late 17th century, the third Desi, Minjur Tempa had annexed the western part of the Duars known as the Bengal Duars and the Bhutanese appropriated it as their territory. The eastern part, the Assam *Duars* had long been administered by a rental agreement between Bhutan and Assam.

Battle of Changlimithang, 1885

both the countries would return to the boundaries which existed before the Bhutanese invasion of Cooch Behar. This was followed by a number of British political missions to Bhutan. However, after the visit of Captain Turner to Bhutan in 1783, there appeared to have been very little contact between the governments of Bhutan and British India for almost 50 years.

By 1826 the Bhutanese effectively gained control over all eighteen Duars, eleven in Bengal and seven in Assam, a situation which became increasingly unwelcome to the British after their occupation of Assam in 1828. British annexation of the Assam Duars in 1841 was followed by 20 years of intermittent clashes at the border. The Ashley Eden mission of 1864 failed to resolve the issue and

Young Husband Mission to Tibet, 1904

the second Anglo-Bhutanese war ensued. In November 1864, the British forces swept through Bhutanese strongholds in the Bengal Duars and by March 1865, they were firmly in control of these lowlands.

The second Anglo-Bhutanese war led by Jigme Namgyal the Trongsa Penlop, finally came to an end with the signing of the Treaty of Sinchula on 11 November 1865, which carved out permanent conditions of peace and friendship between the two governments. Bhutan agreed to give up all claim to the 18 Duars. Trade between the two countries was to be open and free and mutual extradition of criminals was agreed upon. The British government, on its part, agreed to pay to the Government of Bhutan an annual sum of Rs. 50,000 in compensation for the territories ceded. Bhutan lost approximately 2,750 sq. miles comprising the whole tract known as the Assam and Bengal Duars.

The visit of Gongsar Ugyen Wangchuck as Trongsa Penlop (seated second from left) to India in 1906, at the Hasting House in Calcutta, India. Also seen in the picture is J.C. White (center) and Sikkim Chogyal Thutob Namgyal (right).

Our great Monarchs

| His Majesty Ugyen Wangchuck First Druk Gyalpo 1907-1926 | His Majesty Jigme Wangchuck Second Druk Gylapo 1926-1952 | His Majesty Jigme Dorji Wangchu Third Druk Gyalpo 1952-1972 |

Pre-Modern History

The Establishment of Hereditary Monarchy

During the 1870s, Bhutan once again fell into political instability because of power struggles between the rival valleys. External threats in the latter half of the 19th century added a new dimension to the political dilemma.

This era can be rightfully called the 'Age of Jigme Namgyal' as he was the most influential man in the country. As the 48th *Druk Desi*, Trongsa Penlop Jigme Namgyel curbed many internal feuds. Even after his resignation from the post of *Desi* in 1873, he remained the main focus of power and an advisor to the central government and carved a political niche for himself.

His Majesty
Jigme Singye Wangchuck
Fourth Druk Gyalpo
1972- 2006

His Majesty
Jigme Khesar Namgyel Wangchuck
Druk Gyalpo
(2006-present)

100 years of Glorious reign

The years following the death of Jigme Namgyal were still marred by intriques and it was against this backdrop that the need for a strong leadership emerged in the guise of Ugyen Wangchuck, the Trongsa Penlop and son of Jigme Namgyal. From his base in central and eastern Bhutan which together constituted the old *Sharchhog Khorlo Tshibgyed*, Ugyen Wangchuck defeated his political enemies and united the country after several civil

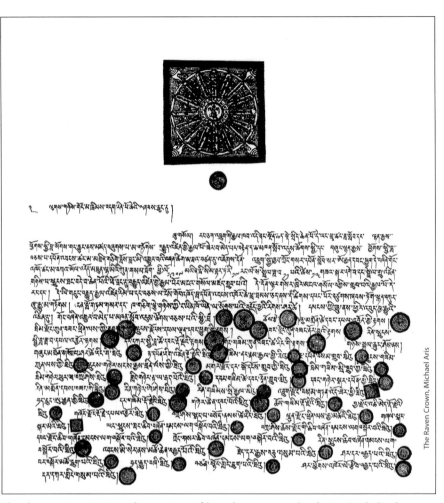

The document containing the contract of hereditary monarchy during Druk Gyalpo Ugyen Wangchuck's enthronement as King in Punakha Dzong, 17 December 1907

wars and rebellions between 1882-1885, including the decisive battle of Changlimithang in 1885.

On 17 December, 1907, Gongsar Ugyen Wangchuck was unanimously crowned as the First Hereditary King of Bhutan by representatives of the general public, the *Dratshang* (Central Monastic Body) and the *Penlops*. The establishment of monarchy ushered in an era of peace and stability and unified the country under a central authority. It also set in motion a process of contact with the outside world and laid the foundation for the country as a modern nation state. The British government promptly recognized the new monarchy, and in 1910 signed the Treaty of Punakha with Bhutan. After India gained independence on August 15, 1947, Bhutan was one of the first countries to recognize India's independence.

His Majesty Ugyen Wangchuck, in the centre, with his council of ministers, Punakha 1906. From left to right, seated: Palden Wangchuk, Kunzang Trinley, Tsewang Penjor and Kunzang Tsherin. Ugyen Dorji, stands between the last two seated on the right.

His Majesty Ugyen Wangchuck,
The First Druk Gyalpo
(1907-1926)

Era of Unification

It was under His Majesty Ugyen Wangchuck, the First *Druk Gyalpo* (King of Bhutan) that people enjoyed peace and tranquility and freedom from internal strife and external invasion for the first time since the end of 17th century. The First Druk Gyalpo Ugyen Wangchuck was instrumental in maintaining friendly relations and peace with neighbouring countries while ushering in harmony and unity within the realm. He took various measures for the development of the country and the well-being of the people. Transport and communication were improved, internal trade and commerce encouraged and land taxes and *woola* (customary service to the state for the welfare of the common people) were reduced.

His Majesty Ugyen Wangchuck also invited several Buddhist monks and scholars to the country to improve

His Majesty Ugyen Wangchuck in Bumthang with three British guests who had visited the country to attend the coronation in Punakha

> *The people of Bhutan enjoyed peace and tranquility and freedom from internal strife and external invasion for the first time after the establishment of hereditary monarchy in 1907.*

the standard of monastic education and further spread Buddhism. He instituted the training of monks in Tibet and many of them returned as scholars and contributed greatly to the improvement of monastic education in the country. During his reign, new temples and monasteries were built in different parts of the country and many old monasteries were renovated. He also opened the first school for monastic education in 1914 at Haa.

His Majesty Ugyen Wangchuck proved to be a great statesman. Despite Bhutan's inexperience in modern politics, he gained the confidence and friendship of British India. After 19 years of peaceful reign, the First Druk Gyalpo Ugyen Wangchuck was succeeded by his son, Jigme Wangchuck, as the Second Hereditary King of Bhutan in 1926.

His Majesty Jigme Wangchuck, The Second Druk Gyalpo (1926-1952)

Era of Consolidation

His Majesty Jigme Wangchuck, the Second Druk Gyalpo, inherited from his father a fledging Kingdom where powerful lords and chieftains governed according to their own rules. He was able to transform a feudal society into that of a modern state by wisely centralizing power which was the need of the time.

The Second Druk Gyalpo created an effective mechanism of tax collection, besides streamlining the types of taxes collected. He initiated land reforms and further reduced taxes to ease the hardship of the people. He abolished certain taxes paid in kind like cloth, fodder, firewood, soot, butter, etc. The taxes collected were generously used for developmental activities. He also abolished unnecessary administrative posts and reduced the power of some officers to ease the tax burden on the people.

His Majesty Jigme Wangchuck and Her Majesty Ashi Phuntsho Choden, Calcutta, India, 1935

His Majesty Jigme Wangchuck took the first steps towards modernization by sponsoring a programme of education and training of the Bhutanese abroad. He built schools, dispensaries and roads and sent many Bhutanese abroad to be trained in both traditional and western medicine.

His Majesty Jigme Wangchuck succeeded in transferring Bhutan's friendship policy from British India to independent India and signed the India-Bhutan Friendship Treaty on 8th August, 1949.

Signing of the Indo-Bhutan Friendship Treaty in Government House, Darjeeling, India, 8 August, 1949

The visit of the Second King of Bhutan, His Majesty Jigme Wangchuck, and Her Majesty Ashi Phuntsho Choden to Calcutta, India, January, 1935. Their Majesties the King and Queen are seated in the second row. The two children seated in the front are the Crown Prince Jigme Dorji Wangchuck who later became the Third King of Bhutan and Ashi Kesang Choeden Dorji who later became the Queen of Bhutan.

Her Majesty the Queen Grand Mother

His Majesty Jigme Dorji Wangchuck, The Third Druk Gyalpo (1952-1972)

Era of Modernization

The process of modern development in Bhutan started in 1961 when His Majesty Jigme Dorji Wangchuck, the Third Druk Gyalpo opened up the country to the rest of the world by ending its era of self imposed isolation.

Known as the 'Father of Modern Bhutan', Third Druk Gyalpo brought about far-reaching political, social and economic reforms. He further reduced land taxes, granted tax exemptions to the poor and abolished slavery and serfdom which had prevailed for many centuries. He initiated a plan development process in the country and instituted a modern form of governance. He also separated the powers of the different branches of the government.

In 1953, he established the country's legislature – a 130 member *Tshogdu* (National Assembly), to promote a democratic system of governance.

In 1965, His Majesty Jigme Dorji Wangchuck set up the *Lodroe Tshogde* (Royal Advisory Council), and in 1968 he formed the *Lhengye Zhuntshog* (Cabinet). He also strengthened friendship between Bhutan and India which became the backbone for Bhutan's evolution as a stable modern nation. He further enhanced the Kingdom's global role in making Bhutan a member of the United Nations in 1971, after having held observer status for three years. His Majesty Jigme Dorji Wangchuck nurtured Bhutan's identity and role in the international community.

His Majesty Jigme Dorji Wangchuck, and Her Majesty Kesang Choeden Wangchuck, looking out towards the Taj Mahal, Agra, India 1954

Royal Collection

"If I were to make a prayer, I would ask that during my son's reign the people of my country would be far more prosperous and happy than they are today."

— His Majesty Jigme Dorji Wangchuck,
The Third Druk Gyalpo

His Majesty Jigme Dorji Wangchuck with their Royal Highnesses Ashi Sonam Choden Wangchuck, Ashi Dechen Wangmo Wangchuck and Ashi Pema Choden Wangchuck

Her Majesty the Queen Grand Mother

Their Majesties the King and Queen with Prime Minister Pandit Jawaharlal Nehru and Smt. Indira Gandhi in front of Ugyen Pelri Palace at Paro, September 1958. Also seen in the picture is the Royal Grand Mother. The Crown Prince, HRH Jigme Singye Wangchuck is flanked by his two sisters HRH Ashi Dechen Wangmo Wangchuck (left) and HRH Ashi Sonam Choden Wangchuck (right) in front.

Modern History

His Majesty Jigme Singye Wangchuck,
The Fourth Druk Gyalpo
(1972-2006)

Era of Democratization

After the demise of the Third Druk Gyalpo Jigme Dorji Wangchuck, his son Jigme Singye Wangchuck ascended the throne at the age of 16 in 1972, becoming one of the world's youngest King.

During the reign of His Majesty Jigme Singye Wangchuck the Fourth Druk Gyalpo, Bhutan witnessed unprecedented development. In less than four decades Bhutan was transformed from a self contained traditional rural society into a modern nation state with a network of roads and communication facilities, free education, provision of modern health and sanitation, safe drinking water, electricity, proper system of administration and a modern trading economy with growing regional and global ties.

The Fourth Druk Gyalpo continued the reform and democratization process initiated by the Third King. In his coronation address to the nation in 1974 he stated: "The future of the nation lies in the hands of the people," a not too subtle hint at what was to come in the future. The move towards democracy was the cornerstone of His Majesty's entire reign and the political developments that took place since his accession were all targeted at empowering his subjects and enhancing their participation in nation-building.

His Majesty Jigme Singye Wangchuck defined a long-term vision of democratization and decentralization for the country and encouraged the involvement of people in their own affairs at all levels - from the national to the community level. He set up a system of government based on the political, social and development needs of the country and divided the functions of the state among the various branches of the government.

The step-by-step devolution of power to the people began with the establishment of *Dzongkhag Yargye Tshogchung* or DYT (District Development Committee) in 1981 and *Gewog Yargye Tshogchung* or GYT (Block Development Committee) in 1991.

In 1998, His Majesty Jigme Singye Wangchuck introduced significant political reform through an unprecedented Royal Edict, transferring the full executive authority to an elected Council of Ministers through secret ballot and allowing for the impeachment of the King by a two-third majority of the National Assembly.

'One of the most important responsibilities of a king is to enable the people to govern and look after the country through the establishment of a dynamic political system'

— *His Majesty Jigme Singye Wangchuck,*
The Fourth Druk Gyalpo

His Majesty Jigme Singye Wangchuck with people after a district meeting, 1997

In 1999 television and internet were formally launched which according to the Fourth Druk Gyalpo was a critical step to the modernization of Bhutan. In November 2001, the drafting of the first written Constitution was initiated, based on the principles of democracy with the separation of legislative, executive and judicial powers. The Constitution was officially endorsed on July 18, 2008.

Under the leadership of the Fourth Druk Gyalpo, Bhutan began to play a more active part in international organizations such as the United Nations, the Non-Aligned Movement, SAARC (South Asian Association for Regional Co-operation) and BIM-STEC (the Bay of Bengal Initiative for Multi-Sectoral Technical and Economic Co-operation). It also established a number of bilateral diplomatic relations, thus gradually expanding its role in international affairs. His Majesty Jigme Singye Wangchuck carefully nurtured Bhutan's socio-economic and political development giving equal emphasis to environmental and cultural preservation and good governance.

Highly revered as a visionary leader, His Majesty made human values the core of the development thrust in Bhutan. He created a development philosophy, Gross National Happiness (GNH) that is increasingly gaining international recognition.

In 2006, His Majesty abdicated the throne in favour of his son HRH Trongsa Penlop Jigme Khesar Namgyel Wangchuck and announced His Majesty's decision to introduce democracy in the country. Accordingly, democracy was introduced into the country in 2008 at the initiative of the Fourth Druk Gyalpo.

His Majesty Jigme Singye Wangchuck at Seventh NAM Summit, New Delhi 1983

His Majesty the Fourth Druk Gyalpo Jigme Singye Wangchuck crowns His Majesty Jigme Khesar Namgyal Wangchuck as the Fifth Druk Gyalpo on 6 November 2008 at Tashichhodzong, Thimphu.

The country saw in 2008 the beginning of a unique system of governance meticulously designed to represent a blend of global democratic systems and Bhutan's own traditional structures to ensure the stability of a small and vulnerable country in a fast changing world.

His Majesty Jigme Singye Wangchuck is undoubtedly one of the greatest leaders the world has ever seen. An icon of selflessness, dynamism and farsightedness with genuine love for his people, he voluntarily devolved his executive power, led the Bhutanese army to flush out the militants, resigned from Kingship at an early age and initiated a mechanism for a democratic form of government, all in the interest of his people. Ac-

"As I hand over my responsibilities to my son, I repose my full faith and belief in the people of Bhutan, who are the true custodians of our tradition and culture, and the ultimate guardians of the security, sovereignty and continued well-being of our country"

— His Majesty Jigme Singye Wangchuck, The Fourth Druk Gyalpo, December 2006.

cording to the Fourth Druk Gyalpo, no individual in Bhutan should be indispensable, not even the King. His real gift to the nation and people is a safe, secure and happy future. His Majesty Jigme Singye Wangchuck can be rightfully called the 'Father of Democratic Bhutan'.

Coronation ceremony of His Majesty Jigme Khesar Namgyel Wangchuck, 6 November, 2008.

His Majesty Jigme Khesar Namgyel Wangchuck
The Druk Gyalpo
(2006 to present)

Dawn of a New Era

Following the abdication of Fourth Druk Gyalpo His Majesty Jigme Singye Wangchuck in December 2006 at the age of 51, his son, 26-year-old Trongsa Penlop, HRH Jigme Khesar Namgyel Wangchuck, assumed the powers of the throne. Formally enthroned in November, 2008 at the age of 28, the Fifth Druk Gyalpo is a quiet and confident figure. For today's generation of Bhutanese, who are a part of the historic evolution, His Majesty Jigme Khesar Namgyel Wangchuck personifies the excitement of a new era.

The Fifth Druk Gyalpo grew up in a traditional Bhutanese environment, attending the court of his father, the Fourth Druk Gyalpo. Exposure to the traditions and disciplines of the royal household, the rich religious and cultural heritage of Bhutan and other realities of the Kingdom are considered his most valuable training as the Crown Prince. Having completed his education at home and abroad, His Majesty travelled extensively around the country and attended the government's development plan meetings, chaired by the Fourth Druk Gyalpo in every Dzongkhag.

In 2005 and 2006, he conducted public discussions on the draft Constitution and during these meetings, His Majesty met people from the most remote parts of the Kingdom and gained insights into their lives, their problems and their aspirations.

As the Crown Prince, he has also travelled abroad, officially representing Bhutan on several occasions and played an active role in numerous cultural, educational and economic organizations.

Early in his life, he developed a close rapport with the Bhutanese youth around the country, as the patron of the Scouts Association of Bhutan. Through his regular contact with youth, he came to understand many aspects of Bhutan's emerging social problems, particularly those affecting the youth. He opened Bhutan's first juvenile rehabilitation complex in Tsimalakha in 1999 and in 2004, became the Chancellor of the Royal University of Bhutan.

"Bhutan is a nation full of promise and potential. We have the security and confidence of our own culture and traditions, an unspoiled environment and most importantly, a young population full of dynamism and promise."

— His Majesty **Jigme Khesar Namgyel Wangchuck, the Druk Gyalpo.**

When His Majesty outlined the priorities of his reign in his first address to the nation on 17 December 2006, the Bhutanese gained increased confidence in his leadership when he stated, 'henceforth, our responsibilities will always be first and foremost the peace and tranquility of the nation and our Gross National Happiness'.

The Fifth Druk Gyalpo addressed the youth at several forum stressing the need for every Bhutanese to work

'... *Throughout my reign I will never rule you as a King. I will protect you as a parent, care for you as a brother and serve you as a son. I shall give you everything and keep nothing; I shall live such a life as a good human being that you may find it worthy to serve as an example for your children; I have no personal goals other than to fulfil your hopes and aspirations. I shall always serve you, day and night, in the spirit of kindness, justice and equality...*'

Coronation Address,
November 7, 2008

His Majesty Jigme Khesar Namgyel Wangchuck, the Druk Gyalpo.

His Majesty Jigme Khesar Namgyel Wangchuck is popularly known as The People's King.

Royal Office for Media

harder and strive for higher standards whether in education, business or civil service. His Majesty undertook several initiatives to prepare Bhutan for the democratic changes in 2008. He presided over the last sessions of the old parliament where electoral laws, land reform and other important issues were deliberated, and travelled extensively around the country encouraging wide participation of the people in the political process to ensure the success of democracy.

His Majesty also reformed the *kidu* (welfare) system ensuring that the plight of the underprivileged citizens were addressed without delay. In order to reach the most vulnerable people in the shortest time, His Majesty has been taking *kidu* to the people instead of people in need traveling to the capital to seek an audience with the King. His Majesty has been constantly touring the length and breadth of the country, to meet with his people and to personally grant *kidu*. The King's *kidu* or welfare system cares for the

'... My duty is to worry every single day about our people and country. And to voice these worries frankly so that we do not get carried away, get caught unaware, or become complacent...'

— His Majesty Jigme Khesar Namgyel Wangchuck, the Druk Gyalpo.

most vulnerable sections of society including, the aged, destitute, disabled, victims of natural disasters, and also students requiring financial aid to attend school.

The King passionately believes that not for a single additional day should any person suffer the pains of dire poverty, of injustice, or of neglect and disability.

His Majesty Jigme Khesar Namgyel Wangchuck is seen as a symbol of hope and promise for the nation's collective future.

Shingkhar Village in Bumthang

Robert Dompnier

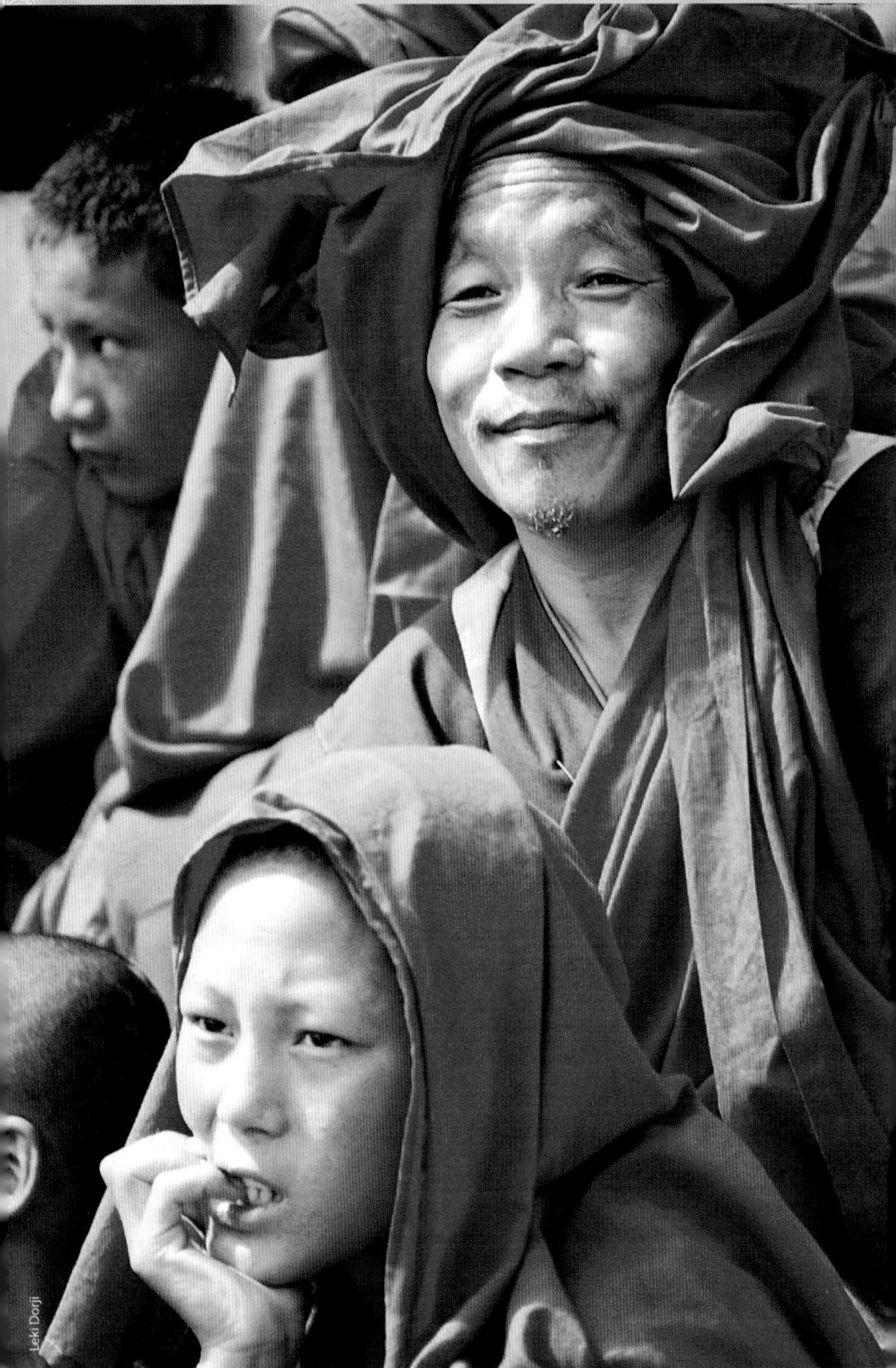

Leki Dorji

Chapter 3

THE COUNTRY AND ITS PEOPLE

Religion

With monasteries and prayer flags dotting every hill and valley, Bhutan is predominantly a Buddhist country. Bhutan is regarded as one of the Buddhist country where Buddhism has flourished uninterrupted. The *Drukpa Kagyu* and the *Nyingma* strand of Vajrayana Buddhism are widely followed in Bhutan. Vajrayana Buddhism is the later form of Buddhism that derives its origin from the *tantras* (a body of texts that emerged between the third and tenth centuries). Unlike Theravada Buddhism, which does not believe in deities, Vajrayana Buddhism recognizes the existence of numerous symbolic deities.

The influence of religion is highly visible in everyday life as it permeates every aspect of life in Bhutan. One can see a temple on almost every mountain ridge and thousands of colourful prayer flags and stupas on every mountain pass, prayer wheels and prayers carved on stones. There

is profound worship of the Buddha, Guru Padmasambhava and numerous tantric deities. Worship and faith take many forms, from daily prayers before the shrine room at home to reciting prayers with the rosary or a prayer wheel.

Bhutanese visit lamas, make offerings to monasteries, help in the repair and maintenance of religious monuments, participate in *wang* (initiation) or *lung* (a verbal transmission by a great master), put up prayer flags, go on pilgrimages and take part in religious festivals. All these are believed to add merit to one's life.

Bhutanese consult astrologers and accordingly perform rituals on all important

Bhutan's history, culture, traditions, customs and landscape bear the most venerable traces of the influences of Buddhism

The Friendly Planet

occasions such as birth, death, marriage, official functions, household ceremonies, departure on a trip or when unwell. Bhutanese tradition is thus deeply steeped in its Buddhist heritage.

Buddhism has shaped the nation's history and played a vital part in the lives of its people. Bhutanese language and literature, arts and crafts, drama, music, ceremonies and events, architecture, and basic social and cultural values draw their essence from Buddhist values.

Hinduism is practised mostly in the southern regions. Buddhism and Hinduism co-exist peacefully. Some residue of *Bon* (animism and shamanism) still exists in some pockets of the country merely as a local culture.

The spectacular Trongsa Dzong

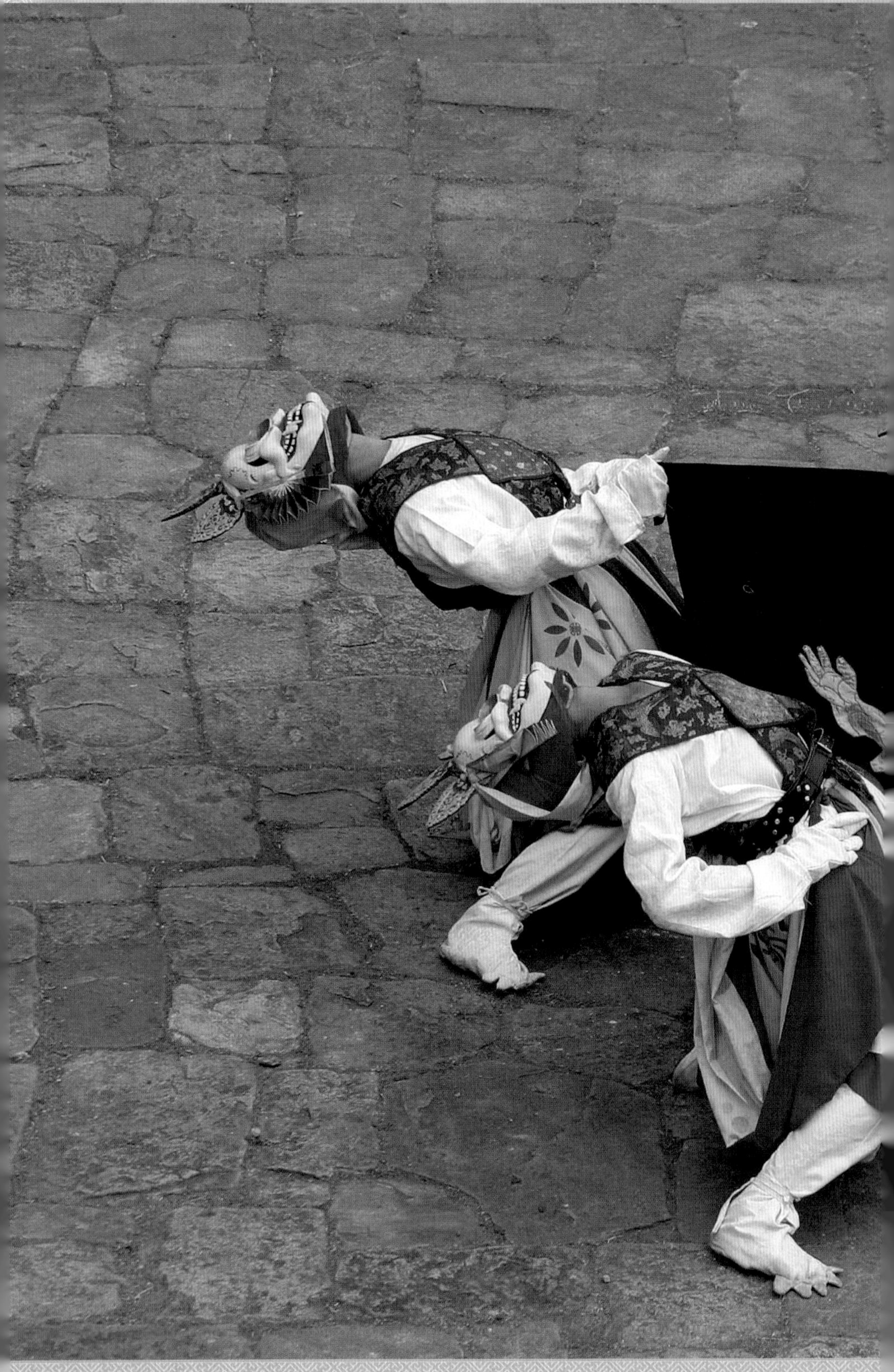

Durdag -Dance of the Lords of the Cremation Grounds

The Friendly Planet

WHEEL OF LIFE

Sidpai Khorlo or the 'Wheel of Life' represents all environments of samsara and all the beings who inhabit them. It illustrates the nature of samsara and the paths that take us and keep us bound there. The entire Wheel of Life is drawn within the clutches of *Yama*, the Lord of Death, reminding us of impermanence and showing that there is not a single being in this Wheel of Life who is outside the control of death.

The Lord of Death holds the Wheel in his mouth and embraces it with his claws, indicating that all living beings repeatedly go through the jaws of death. He holds up a mirror called the 'mirror of action' in which all the actions of living beings, virtuous and non-virtuous, are clearly reflected.

The Wheel of Life represents true sufferings and true origins, revealing how true sufferings arise in dependence upon true origins. Outside the Wheel of Life, Buddha stands pointing to a moon which shows that Buddhas are outside samsara because they have become liberated by abandoning samsaric paths and attaining true paths. The moon represents true cessations. By pointing at the moon Buddha is saying 'I have travelled along liberated paths and attained the city of liberation.'

At the centre of the wheel are three mental poisons - represented by a red cockerel (desirous attachment), a green snake (hatred and aggression), and a black pig (ignorance and confusion). These three creatures chase and bite each others tails, giving rise to the endless cycle or becoming and indicate that they are mutually dependent.

The innermost circle is surrounded by another circle that is half white and half black, indicating that after death there are two paths: the white, virtuous path that leads to the higher rebirths of humans and gods, and the black, non-virtuous path that leads to the lower realms. On the white side of the circle three *bardo* beings are drawn in the aspect of their next rebirth. One is a human, one is a demi-god, and one is a god. These *bardo* beings are upright and

2. The world of asuras (demi-gods, titans, fighting demons), suffer from competitiveness and ambition as the jealous gods strive for the realization of their desires

3. The world of pretas (hungry ghosts) is characterized by craving and enormous hunger, no matter how much they eat or drink

4. The world of hell, is characterized by the extreme suffering of the various hot and cold hells

5. The world of animals is dominated by instinct stupidity and a need to survive

6. The world of humans has constant fluctuation of pleasure and pain

There are infinite world systems inhabited by living beings, but all of them are contained within the six realms. Around the circle is a rim with twelve divisions. Inside each section is a drawing representing one of the twelve links.

ascending to the top of the wheel. On the black side of the circle another three *bardo* beings are drawn upside-down and falling. One is an animal, one is a hungry ghost, and one is a hell being.

This half-white, half-black circle is surrounded by another circle divided into six compartments representing the six realms or worlds of existence. Starting clockwise, these six worlds are:

1. The world of devas (gods) is a place of happiness and pleasure where the inhabitants are totally involved in the pursuit of pleasure

Of the six worlds of existence, Buddhism regards the world of humans as the best realm which offers the best conditions for enlightenment. A human rebirth is considered to have tremendous potential if used correctly. However human rebirths are considered very rare in occurrence as a human life is usually wasted in materialistic pursuits, and end up reinforcing undesirable emotions, thoughts, actions and deeds due to which one descends to a lower rebirth after a human life, rather than immediately going on to another human birth.

The essence of Vajrayana Buddhism

As with all forms of Buddhism, Vajrayana Buddhism believes that the consequence of deeds in previous lives, or karma, forces all beings to reincarnate. All human effort should be to attain enlightenment through which is opened the gateway to *Nirvana*, which means release from the cycle of rebirths and, therefore, the end of suffering that accompanies all existence.

Common beliefs ...

LOCHEY (household annual worship) are held each year to appease the local deities to ensure the family's welfare and well-being. They are also occasions for a family get together. A new prayer flag is unfurled each year following the *lochey*.

CHOESHAM (shrine-room) In most Bhutanese homes, there is a choesham or a quiet corner where several manifestations of the Buddha and his Dharma teachings are maintained. Every morning, the floor is swept, water offering bowls filled with fresh water, and some incense offered. Butterlamps are usually offered at night.

CHILU is a ritual performed to extend one's life and to remove any obstacles in achieving one's personal goal. An effigy of the person is prepared and burnt after the ritual is over.

KORA OR CIRCUMAMBULATION of temples, monasteries and stupas is an integral part of Buddhist ritual. Most Bhutanese circumambulate temples on auspicious days to gain merit. Circumambulation is performed in a clockwise direction for odd rather than even number of times.

CHANTING prayers on prayer beads is a common sight especially on auspicious days. There are 108 beads in a rosary which is a sacred number corresponding to 108 different manifestation of *Avalokiteśvara* (Buddha of Compassion).

BUTTER LAMPS are also commonly seen in Bhutanese homes and monasteries. The lamps traditionally burn butter, but now vegetable oil is more commonly used. Bhutanese offer butter lamps in their *choeshams* and monasteries especially on auspicious occasions to gain merit. Such merit is said to contribute to a person's growth towards liberation. Butter lamps are also offered for a deceased person to diminish the suffering of the deceased in his or her new existence.

PROSTRATION in Buddhism is used to show reverence to the Buddha, his teachings, the spiritual community and other objects of veneration. It is said, that prostrating has multiple and overlapping benefits for practitioners which includes an experience of giving and/or veneration; an act to purify defilements, especially conceit; a preparatory act for meditation, and an act that accumulates merit. There are two ways to prostrate the *kumcha* (half prostration) and *changcha* (full prostration).

Different types of Tormas offered at the altar.

Monks seen preparing ritual cakes.

Tshepamed Torma for long life

RITUAL CAKE OFFERINGS

Tormas or the ritual cakes are prepared and offered to the deities during Buddhist rituals. This offering is said to have replaced the blood sacrifices when Buddhism was introduced into Bhutan. The making of *Tormas* constitutes a very important part of any religious ceremony. They are made by male specialists with a religious background as each deity and each ritual demand different types of cake offerings.

They are usually made of wheat, barley flour or rice with ornamentation made out of butter or vegetable oil (*Dalda*), coloured with powders. These decorations which have a symbolic meaning can be supported by a wooden structure. This delicate work has to be done one day before the ritual.

The ritual cakes placed on the altar can last for several weeks. Besides *Lami Torma* which are consumed as blessings after the ceremony, most *Tormas* which used as the recipient of 'bad influences' are thrown out, away from the house.

The Phin Thom to drive away the negative energies

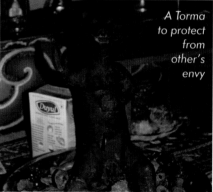

A Torma to protect from other's envy

Intricate decoration on Tormas made with butter

PRAYER FLAGS

Prayer flags adorn the Bhutanese landscapes. They are found fluttering on the mountain passes, ridges, peaks, bridges and rooftops to bless the surrounding valleys. Believed to have originated with *Bön*, there are two types of prayer flags; horizontal ones which are hung on a diagonal line over bridges or between trees or objects, and a vertical one which is mounted on a pole with *raldi* (wood carving of traditional knife) and *khorlo* (wooden wheel) on top. The prayers and images are carved on wooden blocks and printed on cloth in repeating patterns.

It is believed that the prayers on prayer flags will be blown by the wind to spread the goodwill and compassion into the all pervading space and are therefore thought to bring benefit to all. These prayer flags are therefore placed at strategic high points from which a river can be seen following a belief that the prayers will drift with the wind to the river and be carried by the river on its long journey. However, if the flags are hung on inauspicious astrological dates and direction, it is believed that they may bring negative results for as long as they are flying. Thus, astrological consultations are important to determine the direction and timing of putting up prayer flags.

While they may look similar, there are four different types of prayer flags which serve different purposes which include:

Lungdhar (wind horse flag) are usually put up in high places and is believed to carry the blessings depicted on the flags to all beings. The individual who puts up these flags are said to be blessed with good luck and the ability to achieve personal goals or objectives. The *lungdhars* are in five colours which includes blue, green, red, yellow and white representing the five elements of water, wood, fire, earth and iron respectively. The center of each print on a prayer flag traditionally features a *Ta* (horse) which carries three flaming jewels on its back. The *Ta* is a symbol of speed and the transformation of bad fortune to good fortune while the three jewels symbolize the Buddha, the *Dharma* (Buddhist teachings), and the *Sangha* (Buddhist community). Surrounding the *Ta* are various versions of writings which include mantras from three of the great Buddhist Bodhisattvas: Guru Padmasambhava, Avalokiteśvara and Manjushri. Images (or the names) of *Tak Seng Chung Duk* (four powerful animals also known as the four dignities) adorn each corner of the flag

Manidhar contains the six syllabi mantra of Avalokiteśvara. The *manidhars* are erected on behalf of a deceased person to cleanse his or her sins. They are erected in batches of 108 and invoke Avalokiteśvara's blessing and immeasurable compassion to the deceased.

Goendhar

Goendhar (deity flag) are small white flags with blue, green, red and yellow ribbons attached to their edges. They are mounted on roof tops of Buddhist homes to invoke the blessings and patronage of *Yeshey Gonpo,* the main protective deity of Bhutan. This is believed to ensure the family's welfare and prosperity. A new flag is unfurled each year following the *lochey* of the house.

Lhadhar

Manidhar

Lhadhar (god flag) are huge flags which are erected outside Dzongs and other important places. It represents victory over the forces of evil and are a bigger version of the *goendhar.*

PRAYER WHEELS

The turning of prayer wheels is a common sight throughout the country. A prayer wheel is a 'wheel' on a spindle made from metal, wood, leather, or even coarse cotton. Inside the wheel are rolled prayers. According to Buddhist tradition, spinning such a wheel will have much the same effect as orally reciting the prayers. Each time the wheel is turned, it is believed that the prayers are 'said'. While there are several different types of prayer wheels, the commonly sighted ones are the *mani lhakhor* (hand held prayer wheel), *chukhor mani (water prayer wheel)* and the *mani dungkhor (*stationary prayer wheel).

Mani Lhakhor

The *mani lhakhor*, or the hand held prayer wheel, is a cylindrical body mounted on a wooden or metal handle. The cylinder itself is weighed down with a cord or chain allowing it to be spun by a slight rotation of the wrist along with the prayer it contains.

Chukhor Mani

The *chukhor mani* is simply a prayer wheel that is turned by flowing water. The water that is touched by the wheel is said to become blessed, carrying with it a purifying power into all life forms in the oceans and lakes that it feeds into.

Mani Dungkhor
Many monasteries around Bhutan have large fixed prayer wheels
set side by side in a row. Passers by can turn the entire row of
wheels simply by sliding their hands over each one.

Culture and Society

Bhutan's rich and unique cultural heritage has largely remained intact due to its self-imposed isolation from the rest of the world until five decades ago. The lack of contact with the outside world has allowed the Kingdom to evolve through the centuries into a distinct pattern of social and economic life, religion and political institutions. Unlike many countries, traditional arts, age-old ceremonies, festivals, social conduct and structures are not remnants of a bygone age but are still practised as they were done hundreds of years ago. The society strongly follows social principles like the *Driglam Namzha* (age old social etiquette and code of conduct). With the passage of time, the Bhutanese traditional etiquette and value system has become deeply rooted in its society and has enriched the country's cultural identity.

People

Bhutan is a rich mosaic of cultures, lifestyles, languages and belief systems. This is largely because Bhutanese communities in the past settled in the valleys with limited interaction and remained isolated from one another. As a result, different dialects, customs and culture patterns came into existence. This has led to a strong sense of individuality and independence.

The majority of the Bhutanese are a homogeneous group divided into three main ethnic groups. The *Sharchops* (people from east) who speak *Tshanglakha* and live in the eastern Bhutan. The *Ngalops* (people from west) are settled in western Bhutan and they speak *Ngalopkha*, the polished version of Dzongkha. And the *Lhotshampas* (people from south) live mainly in southern Bhutan and speak *Lhotshamkha* (Nepali). There are also a number of smaller groups and communities, many with their own dialects such as *Bumthaps*, *Mangdeps*, *Khengpas* in central Bhutan, Kurtoeps in east, *Layaps* and *Lunaps* in the north-west, *Brokpas and Dakpas* in the north-east and the *Doyas* in the south-west. The ethnic divisions are however, becoming blurred with increasing inter-marriage and migration.

There is no rigid class system in Bhutan and social and educational opportunities are not affected by rank or birth. Serfdom was abolished by the Third King His Majesty Jigme Dorji Wangchuck in 1956 through a Royal Edict. Bhutanese men and women enjoy equal rights and opportunities. Both are free to choose their partners for marriage and both can file a divorce.

Monks are held in great respect and play an important part in community life. Representatives of the monk body are present at all important occasions. In the past, it was common for one son from each family to enter the monastic order, a custom that is no longer prevalent today.

The Bhutanese are by nature physically strong, friendly, hospitable, and open with a good sense of humour.

Language

Dzongkha (meaning "language of Dzong") originally spoken only in western Bhutan, became the national language in 1971 and is widely spoken throughout the country. Besides Dzongkha there are three other dominant languages which include Bumthangkha, spoken in central Bhutan, Tshanglakha, spoken in eastern Bhutan, and Lhotshamkha or Nepali, spoken in southern Bhutan. There are over 19 different dialects with very little in common. English is widely spoken in the main towns and is the medium of instruction in schools while choekey, classical Dzongkha, is used in traditional and monastic schools.

Bhutanese couple seen in the traditional attire

Bhutan Times Ltd.

Dress

The traditional dress for Bhutanese men is the gho which is a knee-length robe tied at the waist by a fabric belt known as the keyra. Women wear an ankle-length dress known as the kira, secured by a woven keyra around the waist, and fastened at the shoulders with silver brooches called koma. A long-sleeved blouse, wonju is worn underneath the kira and a jacket called tego, worn on the outside. Tshoglam or the traditional footwear for both men and women is knee high silk boots with leather soles, but these are now worn only by men on festive occasions.

On formal visits to a Dzong or an office, Bhutanese men wear a scarf called kabney. The colour of the scarf identifies the rank of a person. For instance, the King wears yellow, ministers orange, members of parliament blue, judges green, and district administrators red with a white band without fringes while assistant district administrators wear white with red band, assistant judge wear white with green band and head of county wear white with red band. The secretaries to the government wear white without fringes while the commoners wear white with fringes. Women wear a sash called rachu which is hung over their left shoulder. The colours of the sash also signifies different rank for women, as men. Citizens who have been recognized by the King for their outstanding contribution to the country are awarded the red Kabney for men and red Rachu without fringes for women.

To reinforce Bhutan's identity as an independent country, Bhutanese law requires all its citizens to wear the national dress in public areas and as formal wear.

Men's cotton and silk gho

Women's silk and cotton kira

Men's patang or sword

Coral and turquoise are popular jewellery

The colour of the band on men's traditional boots identify the rank of the person, for instance for the King its yellow, orange for minister/ deputy minister, red for senior government officials, blue for MPs and green for commoners

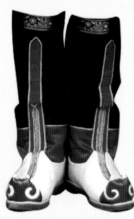

Men's traditional boots with blue band

Koma

Keyra

The favourite Bhutanese chillies are normally sun dried on windows or roofs

The green chillies are enjoyed best with cheese

The dollo (round) chillies are more popular amongst the southern Bhutanese

The doma (areca-nut) trees and betel leaf seen above is commonly grown in southern foothills

Cottage cheese

Chugo or the dried, hard cheese

Food and Drink

Rice is the staple diet in the lower regions while at higher altitudes wheat and buckwheat are the staple food. In Bumthang, *khuley* (buckwheat pancakes) and *puta* (buckwheat noodles) are also eaten along with rice. The diet also includes pork, beef, yak meat, chicken, and mutton. Traditional Bhutanese food always features spicy red and green chillies, either dried or fresh.

Most Bhutanese love spicy food. The favourite Bhutanese dishes are *ema datshi* (chillies with cheese), *shamu datshi* (mushroom with cheese), *kewa datshi* (potatoes with cheese) *phaksha laphu* (stewed pork with radish), *sikam paa* (dried pork), *norsha huentsey* (dried beef with spinach), *phaksha phin tshoem* (pork with rice noodles), *bja sha* *maroo* (minced chicken with garlic). Seasonal favourites are *nyakhachu datshi* (asparagus with cheese) *and nakey datshi* (edible wild ferns with cheese). Several Tibetan style dishes like *momos* (steamed dumplings filled with meat or cheese), *thukpa* and *bathuk* (noodles) are also popular.

The common snack food is *zaw* (toasted rice), *jasip* (beaten rice) and *gayzasip* (beaten maize). *Chugo* (hard, dried cheese) is also an all time favourite. Most Bhutanese chew *doma* (betel leaf and areca nut with a dash of lime) which is also carried by many in their pouches. The offering of *doma* to someone is an act of friendship, politeness and a mark of generosity. It is also a preferred digestif. Popular beverages include *suja* (salted butter tea), *ara* (home brewed alcohol) and beer.

A display of Bhutanese cuisine

Textiles

Textiles, Bhutan's premier art, are the product of centuries of individual creativity in fibre preparation, dyeing, weaving, cutting, stitching and embroidery. Vibrant fabrics and intricate weaves and designs are an inseparable part of Bhutan's rich culture that has evolved over the centuries. A specific design is attributed not just to a particular village but also to a home and family. Weaving is an ancient skill identified with women in eastern and central Bhutan and their designs express not just their creative talent but also their personal aesthetics. The colour combinations, sophistication of pattern, type of weave, and innovative elements determine the value of textiles. Raw silk, cotton, nettle, wool and yak hair are fibres basic to the country. However, imported fibres and dyes have become widely available and weavers have adopted these with enthusiasm, altering the palette, textures and surface qualities of the cloths produced. The complex warp-striped patterns of Bhutanese textiles are unmatched.

Bhutan's textile tradition has gone international, in recent years. The distinct technique, colour and style of indigenous Bhutanese weaving are being increasingly appreciated by textile specialists, collectors and users.

Western evening wear made from Bhutanese textiles

The Friendly Planet

Yatha, made from Yak or Sheep wool is
commonly woven in Bumthang

Common patterns of Gho and Kira

The Brokpas

The extreme north-east is a home to the Brokpas, who live in the villages of Merak and Sakten in Trashigang. Also known as the *Sagtengpa* or *Dakpa*, the Brokpas are one of the many tribal groups in the country.

The Brokpas are semi-nomads depending on yaks and sheep for livelihood. They speak a dialect called *Mira Sagtengpa* or *Bro-kad*. The Brokpa women wear their hair long and wear red and white ponchos, red jackets decorated with animal designs, and red wool capes. They also wear braided black wool jackets. The men wear, white wool trousers called *Bagar*, red wool jackets called *Nambu* and sometimes sleeveless outer garments made of leather and felt. Both men and women wear turquoise earrings. The most distinctive part of the Brokpa outfit is the unique felt hat made from yak hair. Each hat has five tail-like "spouts" that allow water to drain and the head to stay dry.

As virtually nothing grows in Merak and Sakten, the Brokpas trade with the *Tshanglas* of neighbouring villages for their necessities with butter, cheese and yak meat. In winter, they move to lower altitude valleys and they return to their homes in the summer.

The story of the Brokpa origin begins during the reign of King Songtsen Gombo in 640 AD, in the land of Komley Roksum in Tibet, where there lived a local ruler named Yezang Penpo of Tsona. According to Brokpa folklore, the King ordered his people to destroy the mountain peak that blocked the sun so it could shine brightly on his fort. After working on it in vain for several years, out of sheer desperation the people, led by a young woman called Jhomo, murdered the King and fled Tsona into Bhutan.

Those who fled Tsona was divided by Jhomo into three groups. The first group known as *Sharpa Dengze* (Eastern group) settled down in Sakten while the second and third group- the *Lhopa Dengze* (Southern group) and the *Nuppa Dengze* (Western group) settled down in Lung Zempo. However, the *Lhopa Dengze* and the *Nuppa Dengze* later moved to Sakten and started making their way to present day Merak. Over the years the Brokpa settlements in Sakten spread to areas fuelled by the search for warmer climates for agriculture and for easier access to trading.

Yak dance at a community festival, Sakten

The Layaps

The Layaps are an indigenous people inhabiting the high mountains of north-west Bhutan in the village of Laya, in Gasa at an altitude of 3,850m. Until the 1980s, the Layaps lived in complete isolation from the rest of the country, except for occasional visits to Thimphu or Punakha, which used to be a five day walk. Over the years, the Layap communities developed their own language, customs and distinct dress.

They speak the *Layapkha* which is very similar to Dzongkha. The Layap men wear the *gho*, usually black in colour with knee length leather shoes called *yue-lham*. The women wear a black ankle length skirt with a black woollen jacket. They wear their hair long and adorn themselves with silver jewellery and beads usually worn at the back. The conical bamboo hat is the most distinctive feature of the Layap women's dress.

The Layaps lead a semi-nomadic lifestyle with livelihood dependent on yaks and sheep. They barter their butter and cheese products with the people of Wangdue and Punakha with rice, salt and other daily necessities.

The Layap community is also known for their marriage custom of polyandry, although the practice is said to be in decline now. They practice a mixture of Bön and Tibetan Buddhism.

Peldon Dorji

The Lhops or the Doyas

Believed to be the indigenous habitants of western and central Bhutan, the Lhops or the Doyas are found in the low valleys of Samtse. Like other tribal groups they have also remained isolated from the rest of the country for a long time and over the years developed their distinct cultural, tradition and lifestyle.

Several Lhop communities are found living in Rangtsekha, Doga, Dorokha, Satakha, Sanglung, Lhoto-Kuchu, Lotok and Drambey, Thangtokha and Denchuka villages. The Lhops believe that their people had lived in Sibsoo, Bara, Tendu, Chengmari and in the south of the Yaba La range but had been wiped out by a terrible epidemic around the 19 century.

The Lhops speak *Lhopokha*, a Tibeto-Burman language. Both men and women wear the *Pagay*, a piece of handwoven rough white cloth. Men wear them till knee while women wear them till their ankle. The Lhops communities made their livelihood in the past by raising goats and through shifting cultivation. They are short and sturdy in appearance and both men and women have similar body stature. While they are generally around four to five feet tall, they are said to be physically fit. Lhops are generally seen as very friendly, simple, humble and loyal by nature.

Despite the influence of modernization, their lifestyle has not changed much and their unique culture and tradition remains strong and vibrant. The Lhop community is a close-knit society and marry within themselves, often among cousins. Marriages outside their community are not encouraged as it is against their ancestral tradition. As a result, every Lhop is somehow related to one another. They worship local deities called *Zhipda-Neda* and their lives are filled with religious beliefs and superstitions.

Lhop communities celebrate their Losar or New Year in September, coinciding with the first day of the eighth month of the Bhutanese calendar. Celebrations spread over five days is an occasion for families and communities to gather and usher the New Year with merriment.

Tenzin Namgay

The Monpas

The Monpa community inhabit Mangdue and Wangdue valleys in central Bhutan and are often considered the first inhabitants of Bhutan. The Monpas occupy Wangling, Jangbi and Phumzur villages in Langthil, Trongsa and Rukha village in Adha, Wangduephodrang. The two Monpa community groups are not in direct contact with each other. Other pockets of Monpa communities reside in Reti, about 20 km north of Nabjikorphu; Chungseng, about 10 km from Surey and Berti in Zhemgang, which is 15 km from Tingtibi.

The Monpas are homogenous and close-knit community who live and work in groups. It is believed that Monpas of the three villages in Trongsa are members of huge families whose members got married amongst each other. Intermarriage with outsiders is very rare which ensures that their property remains within their family. For hundreds of years they are said to have kept themselves isolated from mainstream of Bhutanese society and thus they developed distinct local culture and tradition.

Monpas were originally hunters and food gatherers, entirely dependent on the forest resources for their daily needs. They now cultivate crops and rear some domestic animals. Their staple food is maize and rice. Bangchang or the local wine, made of wheat, buckwheat, maize or some wild plants is the most popular drink amongst both adult and young children.

Their local dialect is Monkha which is significantly different from any other dialect or language in the country and is one of the endangered languages of Bhutan. The traditional dress worn by Monpa is called Pagay which are hand woven with fibres from nettle plant.

Majority of the Monpas still practice Bonism which was widely practiced in the country before the advent of Buddhism. Thus, Choesham or altars are almost absent in the Monpa households. Traditional healing practices both for human and livestock is very popular in the Monpa community.

Every twice a year they perform rituals, once in summer and once in winter, to welcome rich harvest and to please their local deities by offering their first crops and Bangchang made from first crops. It is also an occasion for the community to gather and celebrate.

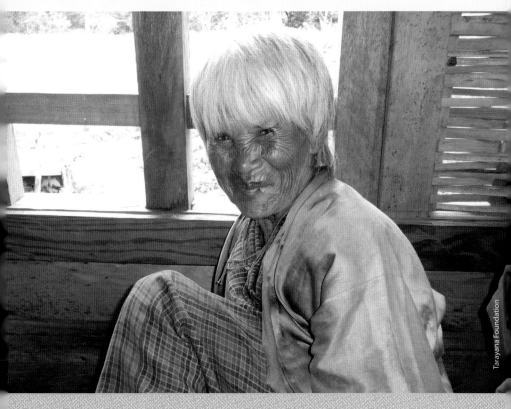

Tarayana Foundation

Tashichhodzong, Thimphu

Bhutan Times

Interior of Jakar Dzong

Architecture

Architecture is a significant feature of Bhutanese identity. Traditional shapes, colours and patterns of the Bhutanese architecture are unique. Wooden surfaces such as beams, windows and doors are normally painted with various floral, animal and religious motifs and colours, each with a special significance.

In traditional Bhutanese architecture, there is generally no planning and designing done on paper before a structure is built. The master carpenter works with the size, layout and structure of the building in his mind. In traditional constructions, nails are not used and the wood pieces are assembled by the dovetail technique. The best examples of traditional Bhutanese architecture can be seen in *Dzongs* (fortresses), *lhakhangs* (temples), *goenpas* (monasteries), *choetens* (stupas), houses and bridges.

While architectural styles vary from place to place and from different periods, Bhutanese law requires all new buildings, public and private to follow the designs and rules of traditional architecture on the exterior.

Right: Steep wooden staircase
Top Right: Traditional Bhutanese window

Traditional House

Traditional Bhutanese farm houses have a distinct character from those of other Himalayan countries. Due to the steep terrain, they are usually built as scattered houses or in clusters, rather than in rows. Traditional houses are built without the use of a single nail and all houses follow the same architectural pattern. They are normally three-storied with room for livestock on the ground floor, storage and sometimes living quarters on the second floor, while the third floor houses living quarters and the shrine-room. Between the third floor and the roof an open space is usually kept for open-air storage. Stones are used to hold down wooden shingles on the roof. The typical construction materials used in traditional Bhutanese houses are timber, stone, clay and bricks.

A traditional mud stove

A woman brewing Ara or the local alcohol

A woman winnowing grain

A traditional roof is normally seen with stones placed on top to hold the wood shingles together

A Layap woman churning milk

Dzongs

Bhutan's castle-like ancient fortresses, the Dzongs are striking landmarks in every Dzongkhag, located at strategic positions. The Dzongs are all designed as oblong or square structures enclosing a courtyard. The corners are rarely at right angles. Deviations from this pattern are generally due to the physical characteristics of the terrain. The shapes tend slightly towards a parallelogram with heavy reliance on stone walls, gently tapering from the foundations to the roof. The vertical architectural order in size and decoration serves the purpose of both defence and aesthetics. The windows at the lower levels are small and modest. The higher the floor levels the larger and more ornamented the windows become. Thus windows form the main decorative elements in the white outer walls. The core of the Dzong is always the *Utse* (central shrine), a tower like structure in the centre of the courtyard which is usually a multi-storeyed structure, square or oblong.

View of Trongsa Dzong

Monasteries

There are more than 2,000 monasteries in Bhutan. Almost every major monastery provides the spiritual centre for important festivals and ceremonies for village communities. They are also often the focal point of cultural, secular, administrative and religious events. The monasteries, though diverse in their shapes and appearance, do have certain basic features in common. Most are built like small villages consisting of two or more buildings arranged around a courtyard. The

A monastery on a cliff at Paro

Prayer flags lead the way to a monastery

A monk offering at Jigje Lhakhang, Trongsa Dzong

lhakhang is the most conspicuous place in the monastery and is isolated from other buildings. It is usually surrounded by a paved path to allow circumambulation. The door to the monastery is normally ornamented with intricate metal work or painted with religious motifs. The inside walls of the monastery are covered with paintings depicting representations of numerous deities, saints and lamas. A monastery is distinguished by a maroon band near the top of the building and some of them have a *sertog* (golden pinnacle).

Tashichhodzong courtyard at Thimphu

Choetens

Choetens or stupas are found by the thousands all over the country and many new ones are still being built today, a testimony of the profound faith people have in Buddhism. There are several different forms or styles of *choetens* and is a structure of great symbolic significance. *Choetens* are mainly built in honour of Boddhisattavas and are shaped to symbolize the five elements; Earth, Water, Fire, Air and Ether. The ground plan of the choeten is circular, around a central vertical axis making it visible from all directions.

Choeten at Khuruthang, Punakha

Druk Wangyel Choeten at Dochula has 108 choetens

Choeten De-gyad or the eight classes of stupas

Image of Dorji Jeynu Yab Yum
- the male representing strength and female representing wisdom

Bhutan's traditional cantilever bridges are built with a series of interlocking wooden structures to form a central bridge. Many of these bridges are essential passage ways for people, horses and other animals.

Cantilever Bridge at Punakha Dzong

Ian Bell

Arts and Crafts

The most exciting and vital aspects of the Bhutanese tradition and heritage are found in its arts and crafts. Much of Bhutan's spiritual and intellectual life is manifested through its arts. Bhutanese art is not primarily concerned with abstract concepts of 'beauty', but with interpretation of values and beliefs that are held by the vast majority and embody the eternal stream of life or consciousness. It is a process, deeply imbued with a strong sense of morality, with many art forms epitomizing the eternal struggle between the forces of good and evil.

Bhutanese art and crafts, particularly those that are religious in their thematic content, follow strict iconographic rules. Merit can

Chana Dorji

be earned only if the prescribed rules are strictly followed. Creative energy is used mostly in secular artistic ventures.

Bhutan is well-known for its *Zorig Chusum*, the thirteen traditional arts and crafts, which include *shingzo* (woodwork), *dozo* (stonework), *jingzo* (clay crafts), *lugzo* (bronze casting), *parzo* (wood, slate and stone carving), *lhazo* (painting), *shagzo* (leather work), *garzo* (black smithy), *troeko* (silver and gold smithy), *tsharzo* (bamboo and cane crafts), *dhezo* (papermaking), *thagzo* (weaving) and *tshemzo* (tailoring).

The skills of Bhutan's craftsmen, working with bronze, silver and other fine metals, are seen in the statues of deities, doors and pillars of temples, bells, trumpets, swords, tables, trunks and jewellery. Wooden crafts include a wealth of items from bowls to finely worked bamboo hats, baskets, butter containers and bows and arrows.

Robert Dompnier

Tashi Tagye or the Eight Auspicious Symbols

Tashi Tagye or the Eight Auspicious Symbols for good fortune, each possessing a deep symbolic meaning adorn the Bhutanese shrines and homes, monasteries, temples and the Dzongs. Originally offered by the Indian gods to Buddha Sakyamuni at the time of his enlightenment, these symbols are believed to bring luck, wealth, health and harmony.

Duk or the Golden Parasol offers protection against the sun. In like manner the Buddhist doctrine protects a person's spirit. It symbolizes preservation and protection from illness and negative forces.

The *Bumpa* or the Treasure Vase symbolizes the contents of the Buddhist doctrine treasures that will overcome all desire on the part of its believers. It represents long life, wealth and prosperity.

The *Sernya* or the Golden Fish keep their eyes wide open in spite of water, and they have the knowledge of obstacles and objectives. Similarly, the Buddhist doctrine permits the faithful to take correct actions in the world. It represents the auspiciousness of all beings in a state of fearlessness without drowning in the ocean of suffering.

The *Pelbeu* or the Glorious Knot of Eternity is a symbol of love which represents the mind and the union of wisdom and compassion.

The *Dungkar* or the White Conch symbolizes the propagation of Buddhist doctrine and awakening of sentient beings from their state of ignorance.

The *Gyaltshen* or the Victory Banner proclaims the victory of Buddhism and the victory of virtue over sin. It represents triumph and victory of good over evil.

The *Pema* or the Lotus Flower symbolizes non-attachment. As the lotus does not remain caught in the mud, so the non attached spirit does not remain caught in the life of this world. It is the symbol of purification of the body, speech and mind.

The *Khorlo* or Wheel of Life as it moves symbolizes that the Buddhist doctrine is alive and dynamic. It is the precious wheel of Buddha's doctrine.

Tak Seng Chung Druk

Tak Seng Chung Druk also known as four powerful animals, comprise of the garuda, the sky dragon, the tiger and the snow lion. These four powerful animals are depicted on the prayer flag panels in the four corners with the garuda on the top left side, the sky dragon in the top right, the tiger in the lower left side and the snow lion in the lower right. Simpler prayer flags have only the names inscribed in these corners. The four powerful animals are also seen as wall paintings and are considered highly auspicious, believed to bring good luck, prosperity, courage and harmony.

Garuda, the devourer, is the lord of birds in the Hindu and Buddhist tradition. He is the sworn enemy of all nagas or naga spirits. In Buddhist iconography, garuda has the torso and arms of a man, a horned head, and the wings, legs, and tail of a mighty bird of prey. With his vajra-like beak he bites upon a poisonous naga, and traditionally grasps two nagas' tails when he appears crowning deities' thrones and temple doorways. His practice counteracts alimental and physical poisons, obstacles, and afflictions, particularly those instigated by the nagas.

Phalluses are commonly seen painted on the exterior walls of Bhutanese homes to ward off evil spirits and negative energies.

Tshering Namdrug or the six types of long life is believed to promote well-being and longevity as symbolized by six companions - old man, deer, stork, rock, waterfall and tree.

Guardians of the Four Directions

Paintings or statues of the guardians, or Kings, of the four directions are found at the entrance to most *lhakhangs, goenpas and Dzongs* in Bhutan. The four guardians each holding different objects, are believed to guard the world against demons and earthly threats.

Chenmizang, the King of the west holds a *choeten* and a snake and is the lord of the nagas.

Yulkhorsung, the King of the east, plays the lute and is the lord of the celestial musicians.

Namthosey, the gold King of the north, holds a mongoose and a banner of victory. He is also the god of wealth and prosperity.

Phagkepo, the King of the south, holds a sword in his right hand.

Thunpa Punzhi

Thunpa Punzhi or the Four Harmonious Friends (sometimes referred to as brothers) is a story from the Jataka tales, Buddha's previous lives. This moral tale illustrates that age must be respected and also to give up self cherishing attitude and help others.

According to the story, once there lived four friends – a bird, a rabbit, a monkey and an elephant. Their mutual respect had diminished, and in order to determine who was the most senior, they discussed the age of the tree. The elephant shared the story about him being a baby when the tree was only a small bush. The monkey then related in his infancy, the tree was merely a shrub. The rabbit stated that when he was baby, the tree was flowering. Then the bird spoke, how he had once swallowed the seed and how the mighty tree actually sprouted from his droppings. The bird was then honoured as the eldest senior in rank to the rabbit, monkey and the elephant. Once again harmony prevailed in the animal kingdom.

Thunpa Punzhi is a popular Bhutanese art theme for thangkas and wall paintings. The symbol is widely used in home and workplaces as it is believed that this symbol attracts harmony to the environment and is a reminder to respect to the elders.

Rigna Ngachu Cham or the Dance of Paradise at Thimphu Tshechu

Black hat dancer at Thimphu Tshechu

Music and Dance

Bhutan's traditional culture is alive in its performing arts, such as music and dance. In addition, secular performances such as dance, songs, traditional instrumental music, drama based on biographies of religious personalities hold a special place in the lives of the people as they play an important role in national, village, or local functions and festivals.

The influence of Buddhism on Bhutanese culture is significant. Bhutanese music has traditional genres such as *Zhungdra* (traditional or classical song) and *Boedra* (folk song), and a modern genre called *Rigsar* (modern song). The reign of Zhabdrung Ngawang Namgyal (1594-1651) saw a blossoming of folk music and dance. Instruments dating to

A monk practising sacred mask dance for religious dance festival

The Friendly Planet

this time include the *lingm* (flute), *dranyen* (traditional guitar) and *chiwang* (fiddle).

Zhungdra and *Boedra* are the two main forms of traditional Bhutanese folk dance and song. First appearing in the 17th century, *Zhungdra* is an entirely endemic Bhutanese style which is characterized by the use of extended vocal tones in complex patterns which slowly decorate a relatively simple instrumental melody. Untrained singers, even those with natural singing ability, typically find it challenging to sing *Zhungdra*. This has reduced the popularity of *Zhungdra* as compared to *Rigsar*, which is the new emergent style of popular music played on a mix of traditional instruments and electronic keyboards. *Rigsar* songs first emerged in the late 1980s and are becoming increasingly popular in several dialects and languages.

Folk dances and songs are performed at all occasions, whether during annual household worship, celebrations or festivals. The dancers form a line or a circle and move in an intricate series of forward and backward steps accompanied by graceful arm movements. Each song has different steps, and is quite varied.

Folk Dance

Festivals

Bhutan is a country of festivals, both secular and religious ones. The National Day, Birthday of Druk Gyalpo, Coronation Day, New Year celebrations (a different one for each region or community) are secular festivals. The most popular religious festivals are the *dromchoe* and *tshechus* (religious dance festival) which are held annually in different parts of the country. There are many other local community festivals distinct to different villages that attract crowds from the remotest of villages. The festivals are important religious and social gatherings. It is believed, by attending them one gains merit and blessings. People turn up for the festivals in their finest clothes and jewellery.

The religious dance festivals are marked by masked dancers in striking brocade costumes. They last two to five days and take place in the courtyards of the *dzongs*, *goenpas* and *choetens*. Each dance has its own significance and is performed by monks and villagers. These festivals are held to commemorate the events in the life of Guru Padmasambhava.

There is also a display of *thongdroel* (large scroll painting) of deities and saints which is believed to liberate people just by a mere glimpse of it.

The most popular festivals that attract foreign visitors are held in Paro during spring and in Thimphu and Bumthang during autumn. The *tshechu* at Bumthang is well-known for taking place almost entirely during the night and includes exotic fire dances which are intended to help childless women conceive.

Yak dance at a community festival, Sakten

The main form of dance at *tshechus* is the *chham* or sacred masked dance. These dances are religious and symbolize the destruction of evil spirits. The tradition of *chham* was begun by Buddhist masters, including Terton Pema Lingpa in the 15th century and by Zhabdrung Ngawang Namgyal in the 17th century.

Bhutan's national sport, Archery

The Friendly Planet

Traditional Sports

The people of Bhutan are sports lovers. Traditional sports and games form an essential part of national culture. Traditional games and sports such as archery, *degor* (somewhat like discus), *pungdo* (shotput), *khuru* (dart), *soksum* (javelin) and *keshi* (wrestling) form an integral part of Bhutanese life.

Archery, the national sport, is a competitive and favourite recreational sport for young and old alike. It differs from Olympic standards in terms of target distance and atmosphere. There are two targets placed 140m apart and teams shoot from one end of the field to the other. Each member of the team shoots two arrows per round.

Traditional Bhutanese archery is a social event and competitions are held regularly between individual teams, organizations, villages and towns. The tournament begins with traditional ceremony of abundance known as *Zhugdrel Phunsum Tshogpa* and traditional breakfast. There is plenty of food and drinks with singing and dancing. Women decked in their finest clothes are cheer leaders for the teams at major tournaments. They dance and sing between play and perform brief routines during the shooting. Archery is considered to be an art, mastered to attain physical dexterity, mental strength and above all, the highest spirit of competition.

Khuru is a dart game which is an equally popular outdoor team sport. The heavy wooden darts, pointed with a 10cm nail, are thrown at a paperback-sized target 10 to 20m away. Another popular traditional sport is the *degor*. A round, flat stone is tossed at a target and the winner is the one closest to the target. *Pungdo*, the Bhutanese version of shotput, played with heavy round stones is also popular.

Bhutan and Montserrat at 'The Other Final,' Thimphu

Robert Dompnier

In 2002, Bhutan's national football team played against Montserrat in a game dubbed 'The Other Final.' At the time Bhutan and Montserrat were the world's two lowest ranked teams. The match held in the capital's Changlimithang National Stadium, took place on the same day Brazil played Germany in the World Cup Final. Bhutan won 4-0.

Khuru is a popular out door game

The Friendly Planet

Modern Sports

Modern Sports such as football, golf, tennis, basketball, table tennis, badminton, volleyball and taekwondo, are encouraged. Cricket has gained popularity in recent years while football has always been popular. Bhutan as a member of International Olympic Committee (IOC), Olympic Council of Asia (OCA), and South Asian Olympic Council (SAOC), participate regularly in the South Asian Federation (SAF) Games, Asian Games and Olympic Games. Besides these major international and regional games, different National Federations also participate in the International Sports Championships, Grand Prix and World Cups organized by different countries around the world.

There are currently 15 National Federations affiliated to the Bhutan Olympic Committee which includes Amateur Athletics Federation, Archery Federation, Bhutan Basketball Federation, Badminton

Federation, Boxing Federation, Body Building and Weight Lifting Federation, Cricket Association, Football Federation, Golf Federation, Shooting Federation, Table Tennis Federation, Tennis Federation, Volleyball Federation, Taekwondo Federation and Indigenous Games and Sports Association.

With increasing awareness of the importance and benefits of sports and physical fitness, Thimphu has also seen a growing number of fitness and yoga centers.

Cinema

Since the production of first Bhutanese feature film, 'Gasa Lamai Singye' by Ugetsu Communications in 1988, Bhutanese cinema has come a long way with the production of over 160 films and 390 music albums as of 2009. The country's first block buster was 'Jigdrel' which was released in 1998. Within two decades, Bhutanese films have won international film awards and nominations at Venice, Telluride, Toronto and Cannes. It also won eight major documentary awards at Tokyo, New York, Seoul, Munich, Trento, Basel, Kaula Lampur and Tehran.

The National Film Awards, instituted since 2001 has played an important role in recognizing and rewarding professionals in the film industry. The Motion Picture Association of Bhutan (MPAB) established since 1999 which comprises of producers and professionals in the film industry strives to promote Bhutanese cinema.

Bhutan at Sydney Olympics, 2000

Bhutan at regional games in Dhaka

Lhaki Dolma and Chencho Dorji won the best lead actress and actor for their performance in, 'Seday' in the 8th National Film Award held in 2009.

Art by Kama Wangdi

Contemporary Art

Contemporary Art in Bhutan is promoted by VAST Bhutan (Voluntary Artists' Studio, Thimphu). It is a non-governmental and non-profit organization that was established in April, 1998 by a group of professional artists to provide an opportunity to the Bhutanese youth to participate and develop their potential talents as well as share social responsibilities through artistic explorations.

VAST offers classes for all ages on basic drawing, sketching, water-colour, oil painting, computer aided designing and traditional painting techniques. It also organizes regular exhibition, art shows, talks, camps and field trips to relevant institutions besides inviting internationally acclaimed artists to conduct art classes and exchange ideas. Till date, more than 1500 students have received basic training in art.

Art by Dorji Gyeltshen

Art by Kama Wangdi, co-founder of VAST Bhutan.

His Majesty Jigme Khesar Namgyel Wangchuck, the then Trongsa Penlop, discusses the draft Constitution with the people

I am happy to mention that, by the year 2007, Bhutan will no longer be among the countries categorized by the United Nations as least developed countries. While other countries have taken hundreds of years to reach their present level of development, for us in Bhutan, we have achieved tremendous socio-economic development in every field in the 44 years since we first started implementing development programmes. How much our country has developed and how the lives of our people have changed and improved during this period in our own lifetime is there for all of us to see.

This unprecedented progress has been possible due to the sound policies followed by the government and sustained efforts of our people. The government and people of Bhutan can be truly proud of this great achievement.

While drafting the Constitution of our country we have attached the highest importance to ensuring the security and sovereignty of our nation and the interest and kidu of our people. The highest importance was also given to ensuring that the new political system will be able to serve the national interest of the country and fulfill our people's aspirations. The Constitution has been framed with the sole objective of ensuring the long-term interest of our country and people.

During my consultations on the Constitution in the different Dzongkhags, the main concern of our people is that it is too early to introduce parliamentary democracy in Bhutan. As our people know, Dzongkhag Yargye Tshogdus were established in 1981 when we first started the policy of decentralization. Thereafter, Gewog Yargye Tshogchungs were introduced 10 years later in 1991. Furthermore, under the policy of greater empowerment of the people, administrative and financial powers were also given to the Dzongkhag Yargye Tshogdus.

During the next two years in 2006 and 2007, the Election Commission will educate our people in the process of parliamentary democracy and electoral practice sessions will be conducted in all the 20 Dzongkhags. After 26 years of the process of decentralization and devolution of powers to the people, I have every confidence that our people will be able to choose the best political party that can provide good governance and serve the interest of the nation. I would like our people to know that the first national election to elect a government under a system of parliamentary democracy will take place in 2008.

— Druk Gyalpo Jigme Singye Wangchuck
Address to the Nation, National Day,
Trashiyangtse, December 17, 2005

Chapter 4

GOVERNANCE

Political transition: 100 Years of Monarchy to Democracy

The political system of Bhutan changed dramatically when in April, 2008, Bhutan became a democracy after hundred years of monarchy. On 17 December 2005, the Fourth King, His Majesty Jigme Singye Wangchuck, announced his abdication from the throne in favour of his son and heir-apparent, Trongsa Penlop Jigme Khesar Namgyel Wangchuck. Even more significantly, the Fourth Druk Gyalpo declared that Bhutan would become a democracy and that the general elections would be held in 2008. He was steadfast about his decision even as his people begged him to reconsider, voicing their concerns and fears about a new system they were skeptical about. The general perception was, the hereditary monarchy has worked well for the country and there is no need for any change.

What is unique about Bhutan's transition to democracy is that unlike other countries where democracy was often achieved with bloody rebellions and warfare, in Bhutan it was initiated from the throne itself. It was introduced at a time of unprecendented peace, stablity and prosperity, and against the will of the people who literally worshipped

Contrary to most countries where monarchy is only a symbolic institution, the Bhutanese monarchy has always been the leading force of change and unity

His Majesty Jigme Khesar Namgyel Wangchuck, King of Bhutan in the center with His Majesty Jigme Singye Wangchuck, Fourth King of Bhutan and His Holiness Tulku Jigme Chhoeda, Spiritual Leader of Bhutan at Punakha Dzong, 31 October 2008

their wise and visionary monarchs. His Majesty Jigme Singye Wangchuck said:

'It is my duty, as the King, to strengthen the nation so that the people can develop in security and peace, and the nation becomes more prosperous and secure than before. During the past years of my reign, I have made constant efforts to em-power the people by delegating au-thority, resources and responsibility to them. Reforms on decentraliza-tion and devolution of power have been quiet but continuous'.

In 2008, with the completion of the National Council and National Assembly elections and adoption of the Constitution, Bhutan made a smooth transition to democracy spearheaded by the dynamic His Majesty Jigme Khesar Namgyel Wangchuck, the Fifth Druk Gyalpo and the first democratically elected Parliament.

The Constitution of Bhutan

Bhutan adopted its first written Constitution on 18 July, 2008 ushering in a new era in the history of Bhutan. The Constitution was signed by His Majesty the King and other designated representatives of the people in the *Kuenrey (main shrine)* of Tashichhodzong. The signing of the Constitution formalized the return of power to the people that had been vested in the First Druk Gyalpo a century ago.

On 4 September 2001, the Fourth Druk Gyalpo Jigme Singye Wangchuck commanded the Council of Ministers, the Chief Justice and the Chairman of the Royal Advisory Council to draft a formal Constitution for the Kingdom of Bhutan. Accordingly, under the Royal Command, the Constitution Drafting Committee, comprising thirty nine members with the Chief Justice, Lyonpo Sonam Tobgye, as its Chairman and eminent representatives of the clergy, government, and the people drafted a written Constitution.

Safeguarding the security and sov-ereignty of the nation, ensuring the well-being of the Bhutanese people, and the establishment of a demo-cratic political system that will best serve the interest of Bhutan were the chief objectives that prompted the Fourth Druk Gyalpo Jigme Singye Wangchuck to initiate the draft-ing of a written Constitution. In the words of the Fourth King, *"the ba-sic purpose of the Constitution is to ensure the sovereignty and security of the nation and the well-being of the Bhutanese people for all time to come. The political system of the country must evolve so that the peo-ple would continue to enjoy peace and prosperity, justice, and the fun-damental rights which have always been enshrined in the Bhutanese system."*

The draft Constitution, which was released on 26 March 2005, was distributed to every citizen in the country in both Dzongkha and Eng-lish. The provisions of the draft Con-stitution was aired on the radio as well as on television. Panel discus-sions on the various Articles were held. The Fourth Druk Gyalpo him-self led nationwide consultations with the people in seven Dzongkhags

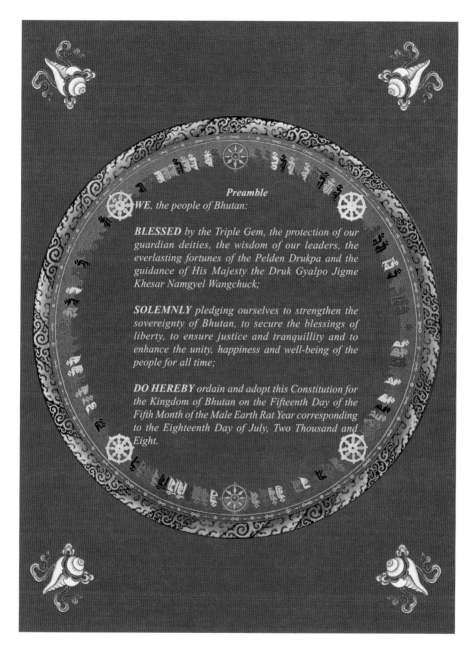

Preamble
WE, the people of Bhutan:

BLESSED by the Triple Gem, the protection of our guardian deities, the wisdom of our leaders, the everlasting fortunes of the Pelden Drukpa and the guidance of His Majesty the Druk Gyalpo Jigme Khesar Namgyel Wangchuck;

SOLEMNLY pledging ourselves to strengthen the sovereignty of Bhutan, to secure the blessings of liberty, to ensure justice and tranquillity and to enhance the unity, happiness and well-being of the people for all time;

DO HEREBY ordain and adopt this Constitution for the Kingdom of Bhutan on the Fifteenth Day of the Fifth Month of the Male Earth Rat Year corresponding to the Eighteenth Day of July, Two Thousand and Eight.

The Preamble of The Constitution of The Kingdom of Bhutan

'The Constitution must ensure the well-being of the country, serve the needs of the people and fulfil their aspirations. Bhutan is extremely fortunate today, because we have the time and opportunity to achieve this cherised goal.'

-His Majesty Jigme Singye Wangchuck, the Fourth Druk Gyalpo

The Constitution Drafting Committee

while His Royal Highness the Crown Prince, now the Fifth Druk Gyalpo, held consultations with the people in the remaining 13 Dzongkhags to create awareness and to provide an opportunity for people to express their views and submit their recommendations to further refine the draft Constitution of Bhutan.

The Constitution was drawn up from several sources, most important of which was the command, vision and policy directives of the Fourth Druk Gyalpo Jigme Singye Wangchuck. Other sources include Royal Decree and addresses, historical documents and laws codified by Bhutanese ancestors and leaders and the laws enacted by the National Assembly, including the *Thrimzhung Chhenmo* (Supreme Law). It also has cross-references to the Constitutions of 20 other countries and various inter-

national conventions, political and Buddhist philosophies.

According to the Constitution of Bhutan, the King of Bhutan will remain as Head of State but will retire at the age of 65. The powers of the King have also been drastically reduced. The legislature will have the authority to force abdication with a three-quarters majority vote. All of the above clauses were included in the Constitution, after much debate and on the insistence of the Fourth Druk Gyalpo. The Constitution guarantees fundamental rights to every Bhutanese citizen.

The Bhutanese Constitution seeks to ensure the progress of Bhutan as a nation by establishing a dynamic system of governance which will uphold the true principles of democracy while strengthening sovereignty, security, peace and prosperity.

STATE STRUCTURE

Political Parties

The first parliamentary elections in 2008, was contested by two political parties — the People's Democratic Party or PDP (founded on March 24, 2007) and Druk Phuensum Tshogpa or DPT (founded on July 25, 2007). The DPT led by Jigmi Yoezer Thinley was elected to power with a landslide victory on 24th March, 2008 to form the national government. The PDP won just two of the 47 seats to form the opposition.

The Executive

The *Lhengye Zhungtshog* (Cabinet) was established in 1968 by the Third Druk Gyalpo. It used to be presided over by the King and comprised His Majesty's representatives, Ministers, Deputy Ministers, the Royal Advisory Councillors, selected government Secretaries and other senior officials nominated by the King.

Today, the King of Bhutan is the Head of State and the executive power is exercised by the *Lhengye Zhungtshog* which is headed by the Prime Minister and his Cabinet. The Cabinet is collectively responsible to the Druk Gyalpo and the Parliament. It is responsible for assessing the state of affairs arising from development in the state and society and from events within the country and abroad; defining the goals of state action and determining the resources required to achieve them; reviewing government policies and ensuring their implementation through issuing directives and representing the government. It is mandated to promote good governance based on democratic values and principles enshrined in the Constitution.

Lyonchhen Jigmi Yoezer Thinley being sworned in as the first democratically elected Prime Minister of Bhutan, 9 April 2008

Bhutan's first democratically elected
Parliamentarians with His Majesty the King

The Legislature

Parliament

Bhutan's Parliament comprises *Gyalyong Tshogde* or the National Council (equivalent to the Upper House) and *Gyalyong Tshogdu* or the National Assembly (equivalent to the Lower House).

The Parliament is vested with all the legislative powers under the Constitution. It ensures that the government safeguards the interests of the nation and fulfills the aspirations of the people through public review of policies and issues, bills and legislations and scrutiny of state functions. It also ratifies all International conventions, treaties, protocols and agreements.

The Parliament meets twice a year. However, if important and emergency matters so require, special sessions may be convened by the Speaker. The duration of a Parliament is governed by the nature and scope of the points for discussion received from the people. A session normally lasts about three to five weeks.

Parliament in session, June 2008

The National Council

The *Lodroe Tshogde* (Royal Advisory Council) was established in 1965 by the Third Druk Gyalpo to advise the King and government ministers and to supervise the implementation of programmes and policies laid down by the National Assembly. The Royal Advisory Council had nine members which includes six elected representatives of the people, two elected representatives of the clergy and one government nominee who usually became the Chairman of the Council. The Royal Advisory Council was dissolved in August 2007.

In the new dispensation of the state structure, the *Gyalyong Tshogde* or the National Council is a legislative body and also the House of Review on matters affecting the security and sovereignty of the country and the interests of the nation and the people. It is responsible for reviewing the functioning of the executive and the National Assembly, reviewing and commenting on legislative proposals, or bills and national policies, plans and programmes being implemented by the government.

The National Council consists of 25 members formed by 20 members elected by the electorate of the 20 Dzongkhag and five eminent persons appointed by the King. The Chairperson and Vice Chairperson are elected by the National Council from among its members.

The National Council members are not affiliated to any political party. The minimum qualification required to serve as a member is a formal Bachelors Degree or equivalent from a recognized University.

Honourable democratically elected members of the first National Council:

Front row: (Left to Right) Tshewang Lhamo, Pema Lhamo, Dr. M. K. Rai, Jigme Wangchuk, Jigme
              Rinzin, Dr. Jakar Dorji, Justin Gurung, Sangay Zam, Sonam Yangchen
Middle Row: Sonam Dorji, Naichu, Rinzin Rinzin, Tshewang Jurme, Thrizin Namgye Penjore,
              Sangay Khandu, Kezang Namgyel
Last Row: Karma D. Wangdi, Tshering Dorji, Sonam Kinga, Ugyen Tshering

The National Assembly

The *Gyalyong Tshogdu* (National Assembly) was established in 1953 by the Third Druk Gyalpo. It consisted of 150 members comprising 10 elected ministers, 10 representatives from the *Dratshang* (clergy), 106 elected representatives of the people including six Royal Advisory Councillors and 24 nominated representatives of the government. All the members served for a term of three years. The erstwhile National Assembly was dissolved in August 2006.

The *Gyalyong Tshogdu* or the National Assembly consists of 47 members elected by the people from the 47 constituencies in the country. The members serve a five-year term. The National Assembly's main function is to enact, amend or repeal laws, and approve the national budget. It is also responsible for approving the Five-Year Plans which are formulated by the government in consultation with the people through the Dzongkhag *Tshogdu* (District Council), *Gewog Tshogdu* (County Committee) and *Thromde Tshogde* (Municipal Committee).

The National Assembly also deliberates on issues that affect the security and well-being of the country, promotes the welfare and happiness of the people and advises the government on all matters of national importance. Decisions are passed by a simple majority. Any Bhutanese citizen above 25 years of age with a minimum qualification of a formal Bachelors Degree or equivalent from a recognized University can vie for the membership of the National Assembly. The Speaker and Deputy Speaker are elected by the National Assembly from amongst its members.

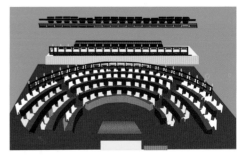

Seating arrangement of the Parliament

CONSTITUENCY MAP

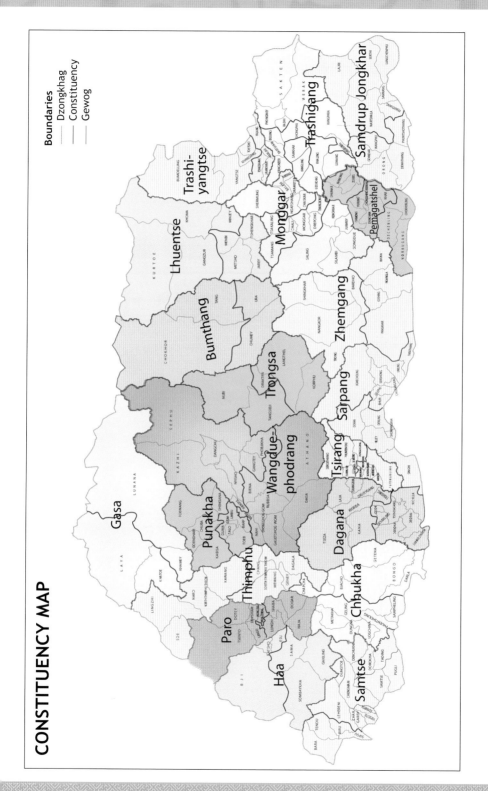

Boundaries
— Dzongkhag
— Constituency
— Gewog

The Bhutanese System of Governance

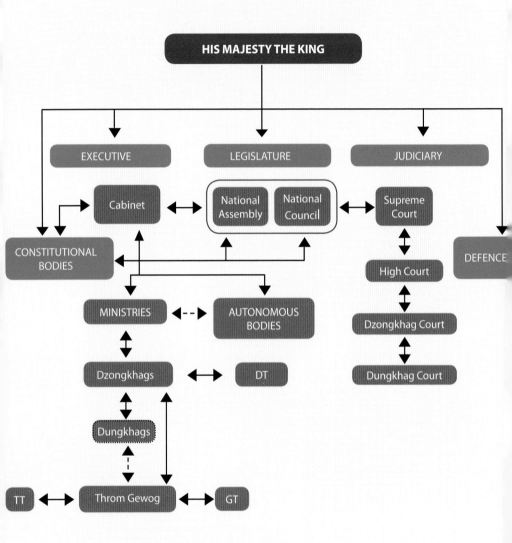

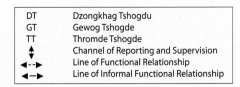

DT	Dzongkhag Tshogdu
GT	Gewog Tshogde
TT	Thromde Tshogde
↕	Channel of Reporting and Supervision
◀--▶	Line of Functional Relationship
◀—▶	Line of Informal Functional Relationship

DEMOCRATIC BHUTAN'S NEW LEADERS

PRIME MINISTER

Lyonchhen Jigmi Yoezer Thinley is the country's first democratically elected Prime Minister who was elected from Nanong-Shumar Constituency in Pemagatshel. As the founding President of the Druk Phuensum Tshogpa (DPT), he led his party to a landslide victory in Bhutan's first ever national elections held in March 2008, winning 45 out of 47 seats. He completed his schooling from Dr. Graham's Homes in Kalimpong, India, and graduated with a Bachelors (Honours) Degree from St. Stephen's College, Delhi University, India. Thereafter, he obtained a Masters Degree in Public Administration from Pennsylvania State University, USA.

In a career spanning 34 years, he has served as the Joint Secretary in the Ministry of Communications; Zonal Administrator for the six eastern Dzongkhags; Secretary of the Royal Civil Service Commission; Secretary of Home and Cultural Affairs and Permanent Representative of Bhutan to the UN in New York and Geneva. He further served as the Minister for Foreign Affairs and the Minister of Home and Cultural Affairs. He also served as the Head of Government (Prime Minister) from 1998-99, and again from 2003-04, when the post was held on an annual rotational basis by the Cabinet Ministers.

Lyonchhen is presently the Chairman of the National Environment Commission, the Chairman of the Ugyen Wangchuck Institute of Conservation and Environment (UWICE) among others. He is also an International Counsellor for the Asia Society, New York; Member of the SNV International Advisory Board, and the President of Maha Bodhi Society of India.

He has published many essays and papers on a wide range of topics and has spoken at many conferences, meetings and seminars including numerous times at the United Nations General Assembly. He is a strong advocate of the philosophy of GNH, an alternative development model conceived by Fourth Druk Gyalpo. He is also very committed to conservation of environment and has been promoting ecoliteracy throughout the schools in Bhutan.

Amongst the various awards received by him, Lyonchhen was conferred the Druk Wangyel Medal which is the highest civilian decoration, by His Majesty the Fifth Druk Gyalpo in 2009. He also received the Distinguished Alumni Award Pennsylvania State University, USA and HR Strategic and Iconic Leader Award at the World HRD Congress 2010.

'As democracy's first government, you have the responsibility of setting the right examples, laying strong foundations and promoting the best practices of democracy. We, the people and King, have complete confidence and faith in the new government. As long as you work to serve the country and people, you will have our full support. If you should falter in your service to the nation, then the duty to counsel you also rests with the people and King.'

— His Majesty Jigme Khesar Namgyal Wangchuck, the King of Bhutan at the opening ceremony of democratic Bhutan's first Parliament's first Session, Thimphu, May 10, 2008

Leader of the Opposition

The Leader of the Opposition is *Dochok Gothrip* Tshering Tobgay. He graduated with a Bachelor of Science in Engineering from the University of Pittsburgh, Pennsylvania, USA. Later he obtained a Masters Degree in Public Administration from the Kennedy School of Government, Harvard University, USA.

He began his career as a Pogramme Officer with the Technical and Vocational Section of the Department of Education in 1991. He has served as the Director of the National Technical Traning Authority and later as the Director of the Department of Human Resources before he resigned to join politics. He was the founding member of the Thimphu Youth Centre and Education Staff Welfare Scheme. He also served as the Board Member of Royal University of Bhutan, Council for Higher Education and Bhutan Board of Examinations.

Dochok Gothrip Tshering Tobgay was elected from Sombaykha Constituency in Haa.

Chairperson of the National Council

The Chairperson of the National Council is *Thrizin* Namgye Penjore. He was elected as a National Council member from Punakha and was elected as the Chairperson of the National Council through a secret ballot on April 29, 2008. He graduated with Bachelors Degree in Commerce from Sherubtse College, Bhutan and later obtained a Masters Degree in Business Administration from MP Birla Institute of Management Studies in Bangalore, India.

He has worked as an Officer on Special Duty for the Penden Cement Authority Limited; Manager for the Tashi Group of Companies and General Manager of the Forestry Development Corporation and Bhutan Power Corporation.

Thrizin Namgye Penjore was elected from Punakha.

Deputy Chairperson of the National Council

The Deputy Chairperson of the National Council is Hon. Sonam Kinga. He graduated with a Bachelors (Honours) Degree in English from Sherubtse College, Kanglung, Bhutan, I.B (Diploma), Lester B. Pearson College, Canada and Masters Degree in Area Studies from Kyoto University, Japan.

He started his career as a Senior Research Officer with the Centre for Bhutan Studies. He also served as Senior Program Officer, Save the Children US, Thimphu; Publication Officer, CAPSD, Ministry of Education, RGoB and the Editor for Bhutan Observer (private newspaper). He has many academic achievements to his credit and has authored a number of books.

Hon. Sonam Kinga was elected from Trashigang and was elected as the Deputy Chairperson of the National Council of Bhutan in November 2009 following resignation of Dasho Karma Ura.

SPEAKER NATIONAL ASSEMBLY

The Speaker of the National Assembly is *Tshokpon* Jigme Tshultim. He graduated with a Bachelors Degree in Arts from St. Joseph College in Darjeeling, India, and underwent Post Graduate Studies in Public Administration at the University of Manchester, UK. He has served the government for 32 years and held various senior positions such as the Managing Director of Tourism Corporation; District Administrator in Paro, Samtse and Monggar; the Chief of Protocol in the Ministry of Foreign Affairs and Ambassador of Bhutan to Bangladesh and concurrently accredited to Pakistan, Maldives, Sri Lanka and South Korea. He was awarded the Red Scarf and the title of *Dasho* in 1997 by His Majesty the Fourth Druk Gyalpo. *Tshokpon* Jigme Tshultim was elected from the Radhi-Sakten Constituency in Trashigang.

DEPUTY SPEAKER, NATIONAL ASSEMBLY

Tshokpon Wogma Yangkhu Tshering Sherpa is the Deputy Speaker of the National Assembly. He graduated with a Bachelors Degree in Dzongkha from Sherubtse College, Kanglung, Bhutan and served as a Dzongkha teacher for more than fifteen years before he resigned to join politics.

Tshokpon Wogma Yankhu Tshering Sherpa was elected from Kikhorthang — Mendrelgang Constituency in Tsirang.

HONOURABLE MINISTERS, ROYAL GOVERNMENT OF BHUTAN

The Minister of Works and Human Settlement Lyonpo Yeshey Zimba is responsible for Department of Roads, Department of Urban Development and Engineering Services, Standard and Quality Control Authority, Construction Development Board and National Housing Development Corporation. He studied Economics at St. Josephs College, Darjeeling, India where he also received both silver and gold medals for excellence in studies, character and leadership. Lyonpo received his Bachelors and Masters Degree from the University of Wisconsin-Madison, USA. He served as the Managing Director for the Royal Monetary Authority; Director for Trade and Industry and two terms as Prime Minister. He was conferred the Red Scarf in 1991 and the Orange Scarf and title of Minister in 1997 and was also awarded the Druk Thugsey by the Fourth Druk Gyalpo. Lyonpo Yeshey Zimba was elected from South-Thimphu Constituency.

The Minister of Economic Affairs Lyonpo Khandu Wangchuk is responsible for the Department of Energy, Department of Geology and Mines, Department of Industry, Department of Trade and Tourism Council of Bhutan. He received his Bachelor (Honours) Degree from St. Stephens College, University of Delhi, India. He started his career as a Trainee Officer in the Ministry of Foreign Affairs in 1974.  During his 26 years of service with the government, he served in many senior positions which includes, Managing Director of Industrial Development Corporation; Director of Department of Trade and Commerce; Managing Director of Food Corporation of Bhutan; Director General of Agriculture; Secretary of Agriculture and Royal Civil Service Commission; Deputy Minister of Agriculture; Ministry of Trade and Industry and Minister of Foreign Affairs. He also served two terms as a Prime Minister in 2001 and 2006. He was conferred the Red Scarf in 1987, the Orange Scarf and title of Minister in 1994. Lyonpo Khandu Wangchuk was elected from the Lamgong-Wangchang Constituency in Paro.

 The Minister of Finance Lyonpo Wangdi Norbu is responsible for Department of National Budget, Department of National Properties, Department of Budget, Department of Public Accounts, Department of Revenue and Customs, and Directorate of Lottery. He graduated with a Bachelors Degree in Economics from University of Western Australia in 1976. Lyonpo has taken specialized mid-term trainings in finance including programming and policies at Public Accounts and Audit in London, and the IMF in Washington DC. He was conferred the Red Scarf in 1998 and the Orange Scarf and the title of Minister in 2003. Lyonpo Wangdi Norbu was elected as a National Assembly member from Bartsham-Shongphu Constituency in Trashigang.

The Minister of Foreign Affairs Lyonpo Ugyen Tshering is responsible for the Department of Bilateral Affairs, Department of Multilateral Affairs, Department of Protocol and Bhutanese Missions and Embassies abroad. With a Bachelors Degree in Arts from the University of California at Berkeley, USA, Lyonpo began his career in the Planning Commission in 1978. He has served as the Permanent  Representative of Bhutan to the United Nations in New York; Foreign Secretary, Cabinet Secretary and Minister of Labour and Human Resources. He was conferred the Red Scarf in 1998 and the Orange Scarf and the title of Minister in 2003. Lyonpo Ugyen Tshering was elected from North Thim-Throm Constituency in Thimphu.

The **Minister of Health** Lyonpo Zangley Dukpa is responsible for the Department of Public Health and the Department of Medical Services. He has a Masters Degree in Education from Bristol University, United Kingdom. Lyonpo began his career as a teacher and served as the first Bhutanese Principal of Sherubtse College in Kanglung; Deputy Director of Ministry of Education and as District Administrator of Chhukha and the first Vice-Chancellor of the Royal University of Bhutan. He was conferred the Red Scarf and the title of *Dasho* in February 1994. Lyonpo Zangley Dukpa was elected from Khar-Yurung Constituency in Pemagatshel with the highest percentage of vote (93.7 percent).

The **Minister of Education** Lyonpo Thakur Singh Powdyel is responsible for the Department of Adult and Higher Education, Department of School Education and Department of Youth and Sports. Currently Lyonpo is the Chairperson of National Commission for Women & Children and National Commission for UNESCO. He graduated with a Masters Degree in English from North Hills University  in Shillong, India, and earned his PGCE from the Institute of Education, University of London, United Kingdom. He started his career as a teacher and served as a lecturer and Vice Principal of Sherubtse College in Kanglung and as Director of the Centre for Education Research. He was a visiting Professor to the Graduate School of Asian and African Studies at the Kyoto University in Japan. Lyonpo Thakur Singh Powdyel was elected from Dorokha-Tading Constituency in Samtse.

The **Minister of Home and Cultural Affairs** Lyonpo Minjur Dorji is responsible for the Bureau of Law & Order, Royal Bhutan Police, Department of Civil Registration & Census, Department of Immigration, Department of Culture, Department of Disaster Management, Department of Local Governance, Commission for Religious Organizations and the Administrations of all 20 Dzongkhags. He received Bachelors Degree in Commerce from University of Delhi, New Delhi, India and Post Graduate Degree in Auditing from the Canadian Comprehensive Auditing Foundation (CCAF), Canada. Lyonpo had also undergone trainings on Indian Administrative Service (IAS) at Lal Bahadur Shastri National Academy of Administration, Mussoorie, India and Indian Audit and Accounts Service (IA&AS), Staff College in Shimla, India. He started his career as a Trainee Officer. He later served as Assistant Auditor General and Dzongdag of Mongar and Trashigang Dzongkhags. Lyonpo Minjur Dorji was elected from Kanglung-Samkhar-Udzorong Constituency in Trashigang.

The **Minister of Information and Communications** Lyonpo Nandalal Rai is responsible for Bhutan Infocomm and Media Authority, Department of Civil Aviation, Department of Information and Media, Department of Information Technology and Road Surface and Transport Authority. He graduated with a Bachelors Degree from Jawaharlal Nehru University, New Delhi, India and Masters Degree in Science from the University of Madras, India. Lyonpo also obtained a number of specialized trainings from the Indian Military Academy, Dehradun, India, College of Military Engineering, Pune, India and Defence Services Staff College, Wellington, India between 1976 till 1990. He joined as a Cadet Officer and was commissioned as Second Lieutenant in Royal Bhutan Army (RBA) in 1976. He served in various capacities as Company Commander (RBA), Sport Officer (RBA), Training Officer (Militia, Security Forces) and as Chief Administrative Officer in the RBA. Lyonpo Nandalal Rai was elected from Shompangkha Constituency in Sarpang.

The **Minister of Agriculture and Forests** Lyonpo Pema Gyamtsho is responsible for Council for Renewable Natural Resource (RNR) Research of Bhutan, Department of Agriculture and Park Services, Department of Forestry Services, Bhutan Agriculture & Food Regulatory Authority, Department of Livestock, Druk Seed Corporation, Food Corporation of Bhutan, Natural Resources Development  Corporation Limited, and National Biodiversity Center. Lyonpo has a Masters Degree in Agricultural Science from New Zealand and Ph.D from the Swiss Federal Institute of Technology in Switzerland. He has worked in various fields such as rural development, planning, project management, and research both within and outside Bhutan. Lyonpo Pema Gyamtsho was elected from Chhoekhor-Tang Constituency in Bumthang.

The **Minister of Labour and Human Resources** Lyonpo Dorji Wangdi is responsible for Department of Employment, Department of Human Resources, Department of Labour and Department of Occupational Standards. He graduated with Bachelors Degree in Commerce from Sherubtse College, Kanglung, Bhutan and later obtained a Masters Degree in Business Administration from Maastricht School of Management, Netherlands. Lyonpo has worked for four years as Assistant Planning Officer in the Ministry of Planning; two years as a Programme Officer in the Ministry of Finance and seven years as Deputy Cabinet Secretary in the Cabinet Secretariat. Lyonpo Dorji Wangdi was elected from Panbang Constituency in Zhemgang.

Local Government

There is local government in each of the 20 *Dzongkhags* or administrative districts, which oversees the grassroots development programme. Each Dzongkhag is divided into several *Gewogs* (county) while the larger Dzongkhag are divided into sub-districts called *Dungkhag* (sub-division of a district), headed by a *Dungpa* (head of sub-divisions).

The lowest level of administration is the Gewog which is made of *Chiwogs* (group of households) There are 205 Gewogs and each is headed by a *Gup* (head of a county) who is elected by the people. The Dzongkhags are under the charge of a Dzong*da* (district administrator) responsible for civil administration and development activities. Each Dzongdag is assisted by a *Dzongrab* (deputy district administrator) and various sector officials who are responsible for planning, development and civil administration.

The local government comprises of the *Dzongkhag Tshogdu* (District Council), *Gewog Tshogde* (County Committee) and *Thromde Tshogde* (Municipal Committee) which are supported by administrative machinery staffed by civil servants. The election of the members of the local government are governed by the provisions of the Election Act of Bhutan.

The Dzongkhag Tshogdu is the highest decision-making body in the Dzongkhag and comprises the *Gup* and *Mangmi* (elected representative of the county, also the deputy *Gup*) as the two elected representatives from each Gewog, one elected representative to represent the *Dzongkhag Thromde* and one elected representative to represent the *Yenlag Thromdes* (satellite towns).

The *Gewog Tshogde* is the highest decision-making body in the Gewog and it comprises the *Gup* and *Mangmi*, who are elected by the people and *Tshogpas* (*chiwog* representatives) Both the Dzongkhag *Tshogdu* and Gewog Tshogde are not law making bodies and does not have legislative functions, while it may formulate rules and regulations consistent with national laws.

The Thromde Tshogde is headed by a *Thrompon* (municipal administrator), who is directly elected by the voters of the Dzongkhag Thromde. The powers and functions of the Thrompon are defined by law passed by the Parliament.

The local governments are mandated to provide democratic and accountable government for local communities; ensure provision of services to communities in a sustainable manner and encourage the involvement of communities and community organizations in matters of local governance.

The programme of administrative and political decentralization has, since 1981, enhanced democratic powers, social responsibilities, transparent processes and decision-making at the grassroots level. It has created a development planning in which the needs and aspirations of local communities are expressed through their elected representatives.

A local village

The Friendly Planet

GNHC

Training on planning and prioritization for Gewog functionaries conducted by Gewog Administration Officers at Nichula, Dagana

Judiciary

Bhutan's overall policy aims at maintaining peace and tranquility in the Kingdom through effective administration of justice and easy access to faster, responsive, and user-friendly courts. The courts seek to uphold the rule of law and promote due process, fair trail, judicial review and transparency in the system. There has been a concerted effort to strengthen infrastructure and provide court specific facilities, while technology is being harnessed to increase the efficiency and improve cost effectiveness to instill public confidence, a strong sense of security and guarantee to the Bhutanese people the promise of "Thrim gi wog, dhagzhen ayer meth da-ngyom" (Equal justice under law), irrespective of differences in language, religion, race, class or status.

Judicial power is vested in the courts of Bhutan. Thrimchee Lyonpo (Chief Justice of Bhutan) as primus inter pares (the first among equals) functions as the administrative head of the Judiciary and also presides over court hearings. The judicial system of Bhutan comprises the Nyentho Thrimkiduensa (Supreme Court), Dzongkhag Thrimkiduensa (District Court) and Dungkhag Thrimkiduensa (Sub-Divisional-Court). The courts other than the Dungkhag Thrimkiduensa have both Appellate and Original jurisdiction. All courts in Bhutan are courts of general jurisdiction, which deal with both civil and criminal cases. His Majesty the King in the exercise of His Royal prerogatives may grant amnesty, pardon and reduction of sentences.

With the establishment of the High Court in 1968, consisting of the Chief Justice and five Thrimpons now known as Drangpons (Judges), and Thrimkiduensa (abode of justice - courts) in all 20 Dzongkhags and 15 Dungkhags, the Judicial system has been separated from the executive and the legislative branches of the government. The court in each Dzongkhag and Dungkhag is headed by a Drangpon and assisted by Drangpon Rabjams (assistant Judges). Minor disputes, however, continue to be settled by Barmis (mediators) at the Village level based on the traditional concept of Nangkha Nangdig (mediation) as a form of 'alternative dispute resolution'.

The laws of the country has been codified in the Thrimzhung Chhenmo (Supreme Law), which was enacted by the National Assembly during several sessions in the 1950's, and several subsequent Acts passed by the National Assembly. Bhutan's legal system is based on the code laid down by Zhabdrung Ngawang Namgyal. The traditional Buddhist precepts have been significantly maintained in the legal processes and later legislations while at the same time incorporating good practices from other systems to keep pace with the rapid socio-economic development of the country.

The Supreme Court is the highest court in the country. Drangpons of the Supreme Court are appointed by the King in consultation with the National Judicial Commission (NJC) while the High Court Drangpons are appointed on the recommendation of the NJC. The Supreme Court, based in Thimphu, is an appellate court which hears appeal cases from High Court. Given that most users of the court are pro se litigants, the Bhutanese court system has adopted both the adversarial and inquisitorial methods of adjudication.

Judicial Reforms

Institutional reforms include the appointment of efficient Drangpons, the abolition of the post of *Thrimtsap* (acting Drangpon), establishment of Dungkhag Thrimkiduensa, and the conduct of a series of workshops, seminars and trainings. The annual National Judicial Conference was introduced in 1976 and a separate judicial cadre in 1990. The NJC was established in 2003 under a Royal Degree and the enactment of the Judicial Service Act (2007) ensures the independence of the Judiciary. Financial and administrative powers have been decentralized from the High Court to the Lower Courts.

Under the Royal Command, the Civil and Criminal Procedure Code and the Penal Code, was drafted and enacted by the National Assembly in 2001 and 2004 respectively.

The Penal Code of Bhutan (2004) is a systematic collection of legal provisions laying down penalties for various kinds of offences or transgressions. In preparing the Code the drafters in an effort to keep the essence of the Code "Bhutanese in nature" drew from the Dharmapada, existing laws (piecemeal legislations) and regulations and also from western jurisprudence, whenever necessary and appropriate. The Penal Code is therefore, in consonance with religion, tradition, international laws and incorporates standards and concepts of modern social defense. Extra mural treatments like civil commitment in a hospital, psychiatric centers or other institutions for rehabilitative treatment; compensation to victims of crimes, and value based sentencing and community service or conditional discharge on probation have been effectively covered in the Penal Code.

High Court, Thimphu

Lily Wangchuk

The country's first Supreme Court Judges

Chief Justice

Justice Rinzin Gyaltshen

Bhutan's first Chief Justice is Lyonpo Sonam Tobgye. With a Degree of Doctorate of Laws (LL.D) (Honoris Causa), NALSAR University of Law, Hyderabad, India he has won many awards and honours and has served in several important posts. He began his career in 1971 as *Ziminangma* to His Majesty the Third Druk Gyalpo. He later served as Chamberlain for His Majesty the Fourth Druk Gyalpo. He also served as the Justice for the High Court; Auditor General, Secretary of Royal Civil Service Commission and Chief Justice of the High Court until 2010.

Lyonpo Sonam Tobgye was the Chairman of the Drafting Committee of the Constitution of Bhutan and was responsible for amendment and enactment of several Acts of Bhutan. He was conferred the Red Scarf in 1974, title of Deputy Minister in 1991, Orange Scarf and title of Minister in 1998. He is a proud recipient of many prestigious awards including "*Medaille d' Honneur*" (Court de cassation, France) and Druk Wangyel from His Majesty the King of Bhutan in 2008.

He was elevated as the Chief Justice of the Supreme Court on 21 February, 2010.

Justice Rinzin Gyaltshen with a background in Diploma in Development Administration, South Devon Technical College, Torquay, UK has served over 39 years with RGoB. He began his career as a Staff Officer for Bank of Bhutan in 1969. He later served as the Under Secretary and Deputy Secretary for Royal Advisory Council (RAC); Deputy Administrator for Samtse; Administrator for Sarpang and Trashigang; Joint Secretary for the Ministry of Home and Cultural Affairs and Chairman of the RAC. He was conferred the Red Scarf and title of *Dasho* in 1987.

He was member of the Constitutional Drafting Committee. He also played a key role in drafting the National Council Act. As the nominee of His Majesty the Fourth Druk Gyalpo, he was one of the Chief negotiating members with the militant leaders of ULFA, BODO and KLO and Member of the Bhutan-Nepal (JVT) talks.

Justice Dasho Rinzin Gyaltshen is a proud recipient of Premature Grade Promotion from His Majesty the Fourth Druk Gyalpo and His Majesty the Fifth Druk Gyalpo's Coronation Gold Medal in 2008. He was elevated as the Justice of the Supreme Court on 21 February 2010.

Justice Tshering Wangchuk

Justice Rinzin Penjor

Justice Tshering Wangchuk graduated from St. Stephen's College, University of Delhi, India with a Bachelor (Honours) Degree in History. He also obtained Certificate in Human Rights from the René CASSIN International Institute of Human Rights, Strasbourg, France, LL.B from Campus Law Centre, University of Delhi, India and LL.M (International & Comparative Law) from George Washington University, Washington D.C., USA.

He began his career as a Trainee Officer with High Court in 1987 and served as Judicial Officer, Senior Section Officer of the Criminal Section for the High Court; Judge for Samdrup Jongkhar Dzongkhag and Justice of the High Court. He also served as Second Lieutenant in the Royal Bhutan Army.

He has also been involved in drafting and reviewing several Bills and preparation of the Judiciary Strategic Master Plan. Justice Tshering Wangchuk is a recipient of His Majesty the Fifth Druk Gyalpo's Coronation Gold Medal in 2008 and was elevated as the Justice of the Supreme Court of Bhutan on 21 February 2010.

Justice Rinzin Penjor graduated with a Bachelor (Honours) Degree in Commerce, University of Delhi, India. He also obtained LLB from University of Delhi, India and LL.M (Corporate Law), Dalhousie University, Halifax Novascotia, Canada.

He began his career as a Senior Section Officer for the High Court in 1989. He also served as Second Lieutenant in Royal Bhutan Army. He has served as a Judge for various District Courts including Tsirang, Trongsa, Sarpang and Punakha until he was promoted as the Attorney General in 2008.

He had also been involved in drafting and reviewing of numerous Bills and Acts besides several policy documents. He has authored a book titled, 'Vicarious Liability of the Director of a Company' while pursuing his Law Masters at Dalhousie University. Among the militia officers, he is one of the recipients of Druk Yugyal medal from His Majesty the Fourth Druk Gyalpo. Justice Rinzin Penjor is a recipient of His Majesty the Fifth Druk Gyalpo's Coronation Gold Medal in 2008 and was elevated as the Justice of the Supreme Court of Bhutan on 21 February 2010.

Constitutional Bodies

There are four Constitutional Bodies, comprising the Anti-Corruption Commission, the Royal Audit Authority, Election Commission of Bhutan and the Royal Civil Service Commission.

The Anti-Corruption Commission

The Anti-Corruption Commission (ACC) established on 31 December, 2005 by a Royal Decree. With the adoption of the Constitution of the Kingdom of Bhutan in 2008, ACC became an independent authority responsible for taking necessary steps in preventing and combating corruption in the country.

It is headed by a Chairperson and two Commissioners, whose term is for five years or until attaining the age of sixty-five, whichever is earlier.

Drawing its power from the Anti-Corruption Act (2006), ACC has three main functions: to prevent corruption by addressing systemic flaws, to create public awareness on corruption through education and advocacy and to investigate corruption.

ACC has prepared the National Anti-Corruption Strategy which has been approved and adopted by RGoB in 2009. It serves as the framework to mainstream anti-corruption programmes and activities into the functions of government agencies.

ACC Chairperson

Dasho Neten Zangmo is the Chairperson of the Anti Corruption Commission. She received her Bachelors Degree in Civil Engineering from India Masters Degree in Technical Education from the United Kingdom.

She began her career as a National Service Trainee in 1985. She also served as a Lecturer and later as the Vice Principal of Royal Bhutan Polytechnic at Rinchending; the Principal of Royal Technical Institute at Rinchending; the Principal of Royal Bhutan Polytechnic at Deothang; Joint Director, Technical & Vocational Education Section, Ministry of Education & Health; Director for Planning Commission; Cabinet Secretary and Foreign Secretary. In 2006, she was elevated to the position of the Chairperson of the newly formed Anti-Corruption Commission.

She was awarded the Red Scarf and title of *Dasho* by His Majesty the King in 2008.

"It is very important to ensure that corruption does not take hold in Bhutan"

— *His Majesty Jigme Khesar Namgyal Wangchuck*
the King of Bhutan

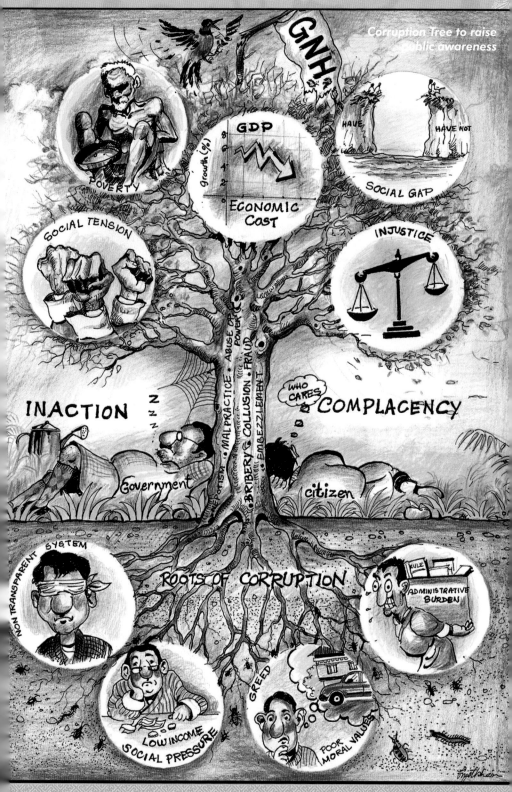

Corruption Tree to raise public awareness

The Royal Audit Authority

The Royal Audit Authority (RAA) is an independent authority headed by the Auditor General, whose term of office is five years or until attaining an age of sixty-five years, whichever is earlier. The RAA is responsible for auditing the accounts of all departments and offices of the government including all offices in the Legislature and the Judiciary, all public authorities and bodies administering public funds, the police and the defence forces as well as the revenues, public and other monies received and the advances and reserves of Bhutan. The RAA functions in accordance with the Audit Act.

In-house training of auditors

Inauguration of the Royal Audit Authority office, Thimphu

Auditor General

The Auditor General of Bhutan is Hon. Ugen Chewang. He received Bachelors Degree in Commerce from Punjab University, Punjab, India; Masters Degree in Business Administration in Management from Syracuse University, USA and Comprehensive Auditing from CCAF, Canada. He started his career as a Trainee Officer for the Royal Audit Authority in 1979.

Between 1979 - 2000 he served in several important positions with the Royal Audit Authority such as the Assistant Audit Officer; Assistant Director; Deputy Chief Auditor; Chief Auditor; Assistant Auditor General and Deputy Auditor General.

In 2000 he was appointed as the Director of National Pension & Provident Fund. In 2006 he was elevated to the position of Auditor General.

During his 31 years of service with the Royal Government of Bhutan, he also served as the Board Director of Penden Cement Authority Ltd, Bhutan National Bank Ltd, Royal Insurance Corporation of Bhutan, Druk Satair Corporation Ltd. He was also Member of Good Governance Committee and Pay Revision Committee.

He is currently serving as the Member of Accounting Standards Board.

Election Commission of Bhutan

The Election Commission of Bhutan (ECB) was established on 16 January, 2006. It is responsible for the preparation, maintenance, and periodical updating of electoral rolls, the election schedule, and the supervision, direction, control, and conduct of elections to Parliament and local governments, as well as holding of National Referendums, in a free and fair manner.

The ECB is independent and consists of a Chief Election Commissioner and two Election Commissioners, whose term of office is five years or until they attain the sixty five years of age. whichever is earlier. The ECB functions in accordance with the Election Act.

Citizens waiting in the queue to cast their vote

Chief Election Commissioner

Bhutan's Chief Election Commissioner is Dasho Kunzang Wangdi. He graduated with Bachelor (Honours) Degree in English from St, Stephen's College, University of Delhi, India and Masters Degree in Public Administration (MPA) Pennsylvania State University, USA. He started his career as a Trainee with the Ministry of Development in 1974. He later served as Asst. Protocol Officer, Ministry of Foreign Affairs; Trainee Officer, Personnel Officer and Under Secretary for Department of Manpower and Statistics; Dy. Director, Dy. Secretary for RCSC; Director for Ministry of Trade & Industries; Director for Royal Institute of Management and the Auditor General for Royal Audit Authority.

He played an important role in a number of national and international organizations such as the ASOSAI, INTOSAI, INTOSAI IT Audit Committee, Good Governance Task Force and ILO, APSDEP. He has also been involved in reviewing and drafting several Acts and policy documents.

Dasho Kunzang Wangdi is currently the Chairman for Delimitation Commission & Validation Committee of RUB, President, RSPN and TOSA-OY and the Board Director for the CBS. He was awarded the Red Scarf and title of *Dasho* by His Majesty the Fourth Druk Gyalpo in 2001. He also received the prestigious Druk Thuksey medal from His Majesty the King in 2008 in recognition for successful conduct of the First Parliamentary Elections and His Majesty the Fifth Druk Gyalpo's Coronation Medal in 2008.

His Majesty with RCSC Chairman and Commission Members, 6 March, 2009

The Royal Civil Service Commission

The Royal Civil Service Commission (RCSC) is responsible for promoting and ensuring an independent and apolitical civil service that will discharge its public duties in an efficient, transparent and accountable manner. The RCSC consists of a Chairman and four other Commissioners, who serve a term of five years or until attaining the age of sixty-five, whichever is earlier. The RCSC is mandated to ensure that civil servants render professional service, guided by the highest standards of ethics and integrity to promote good governance and social justice, in implementing the policies and programmes of the government.

Some publications by RCSC

Chairman RCSC

The Chairman of the RCSC is Lyonpo Thinley Gyamtsho. He received a Bachelors Degree in Commerce & Administration from Victoria University of Wellington, New Zealand.

He started his career as Trainee Officer in 1976 with the Ministry of Trade & Industries (MTI). He later served as the Under Secretary and Dy. Secretary with the MTI; Joint Director and later Director for Department of Education; Director, Department of National Budget & Accounts, Ministry of Finance; Director General and later Secretary of Department of Education. He later served as the Deputy Minister for the Royal Civil Service Commission; Minister for Home and Cultural Affairs and Minister of Education until his resignation in 2008.

In 1991, he was awarded the Red Scarf and the title of *Dasho* by His Majesty the Fourth Druk Gyalpo. He was further awarded the Orange Scarf and the rank of Deputy Minister in 1998 and rank of full Minister in 1998 by His Majesty the Fourth Druk Gyalpo.

Lyonpo is a member of many international and national organizations. He has also authored several publications since 1970s till date.

Lyonpo Thinley Gyamtsho is a recipient of many prestigious awards which includes Coronation Centenary Gold Medal by His Majesty the Fourth Druk Gyalpo in 1999 and Coronation Gold Medal by His Majesty the King in 2008.

Office of The Attorney General

The Office of the Attorney General is headed by the Attorney General who is appointed by the Druk Gyalpo by warrant under His Hand and Seal, on the recommendation of the Prime Minister. The Attorney General is accountable to the Prime Minister and holds Office for a term of five years.

It is the duty of the Attorney General to aid and advise the Royal Government of Bhutan upon legal matters, prosecute and defend the cause of the State, and discharge other functions in pursuit of justice. For this purpose, the Attorney General has the right of audience in all Courts of Law in Bhutan and represents the Royal Government of Bhutan in any Court of Law outside the Kingdom of Bhutan.

The Inauguration of the Office of the Attorney General.

Attorney General

The Attorney General is Hon. Phuntsho Wangdi. He graduated with a Bachelors (Honours) Degree in English from Delhi University, India. He later received the PG Course in National Laws from Royal Institute of Management, Bhutan, LL.B from University of Mumbai, India and LL.M from the University of Adelaide/ Mannheim (Australia and Germany).

He started his career as the Judicial Officer with the High Court in 1995 and rose to the position of Assistant Attorney General in the Office of the Attorney General (erstwhile Office of the Legal Affairs) in 2000. During his service he was involved in investigating various civil and criminal cases and prosecuted many high degree criminal cases. He also represented the government at various international forums. He was also involved in reviewing and drafting numerous laws, rules and regulations and provided legal opinion on various national and international issues to RGoB. Hon. Phuntsho Wangdi was elevated to Attorney General on 15 March, 2010.

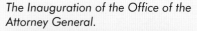

His Holiness the Je Khenpo, Trulku Jigme Chhoeda blesses the people

Chapter 5

THE CLERGY

The Monastic Body

The monastic body was instituted by Zhabdrung Ngawang Namgyel with 30 monks in the 17th century. With the support from the government, the *Zhung Dratshang* or central monastic body today comprises of *Pung-Thim Gayduen Dratshang* (Punakha and Thimphu central monastic bodies), *Rabdey* (district monastic bodies), *Shedra* (center for higher learning), *Goenday* (monastery) and *Lobdra* (monastic school). The current strength of the monastic body is about 7,027 registered monks. There are also large number of monks and nuns either pursuing studies or religious practices with various religious centers, monastic schools and institutions.

At the head of the central monastic body is the Chief Abbot known as *Je Khenpo*, equal in rank to His Majesty the King in the civil office. The *Je Khenpo* is chosen from among the high-ranking monks. The position is granted on merit, and typically is given to the most respected monk in the monastic body. The position of *Je Khenpo* is thus never held by a child but always by a seasoned monk. The *Je Khenpo* who is responsible for many liturgical and religious duties across the country, is assisted by five high ranking monks called the *Lopen Ngap* or the Five Masters. These *Lopens* who are each in charge of different areas of responsibility are equal in rank to the government ministers.

The *Rabdey* or district monastic communities in the Dzongkhag is headed by an abbot known as *Lam Neten* and buddhist colleges and meditation centers are headed by principals and meditation masters.

Though the monastic establishment does not form part of the political structure of Bhutan, it has a vital role to play in the socio-cultural life of the people. The present *Je Khenpo*, His Holiness Tulku Jigme Chhoeda assumed office in 1996 as the 70th *Je Khenpo*.

The main shrine at Tashichhodzong, Thimphu

Robert Dompnier

In the last 14 years, His Holiness has played an instrumental role in further promoting Buddhism in the country. He has not only addressed spiritual needs of the people through his personal tours throughout the country blessing, providing oral transmission and teachings in the remotest of villages but has brought about positive changes in the role and functioning of the monastic bodies. The monastic community now no longer remains within the confines of the Dzongs but actively participates in social work and in the improvement of the lives of the people. They have started attending various international religious conferences, seminars and workshops. Within the country, several workshops on religion and health have already been held with the direct involvement of the monks and other prominent religious figures. The monastic bodies regularly performs special prayers for the well-being and prosperity for the entire country and all sentient beings. The monks also continue to visit households to perform religious rites, special rituals and reading of sacred texts wishing for the recovery of sick patients, prosperity and well-being of the household, long life, or regaining fortune as well as rituals for purification and death, thereby playing an important role in the daily lives of the Bhutanese people.

The central monastic body resides in Thimphu during summers and moves to Punakha in the winter.

A little monk in meditation

Ian Bell

Chapter 6

WOMEN, CHILDREN AND GENDER

The status of women and children

Bhutanese women enjoy a relatively high status compared with women in the South Asian region. Instances of female infanticide or malnutrition, dowry deaths, and other discriminatory social malpractices are virtually unknown and unheard of. There is no significant preference for male child over the female among most sections of the population and sex-based abortions are unknown in Bhutan.

In the field of education, the enrolment of girls in primary schools is among the highest in the SAARC region as well as in the developing countries. Maternal and child health has been accorded high priority by the government. Effective service delivery and aggressive advocacy campaigns in areas of safe motherhood, concept of small family, women empowerment, adolescent reproductive health and prevention of STD/HIV diseases have also contributed to the health of women and children.

The 'head of household' concept is a relative one. Household decision-making depends on the capability of individuals and there are no fixed gender-based roles. In the case of divorce, laws provide for fair sharing of property for spouse and child support. Love marriages are common in urban areas today while the tradition of arranged marriages is prevalent in some rural areas.

Bhutanese women do not face any institutionalized form of discrimination - politically, socially, economically or legally. Law treats women and men equally and many of its provisions protect the rights and interests of women and children. Nevertheless, despite equal opportunities enjoyed by women and men alike, there are gender gaps particularly in governance and decision making positions due to cultural, social, religious and economic barriers faced by women as elsewhere in the developing countries. To address the gender gap, the government is now moving from a gender neutral position to a gendered approach in the formulation and implementation of its plans, policies and programmes.

Bhutan is party to the Convention on the Elimination of all Forms of Discrimination Against Women (CEDAW) and the 1995 Beijing Platform for Action. Bhutan is also signatory to all SAARC Conventions and is an active member of the formulation of the SAARC Gender Database (SGDB) which will have a larger implication in developing policy and programme in gender equality and women's empowerment.

Bhutan has committed to undertake a series of measures to end discrimination against women in all forms and in various areas such as education, employment, health, political and public life, marriage and family life. The National Plan of Action on Gender (NPAG) is expected to provide the guidelines in sectoral gender mainstreaming during the Tenth Five Year Plan (2008-2013).

Bhutan was also one of the first countries to show its support by ratifying the Convention on the Rights of the Child (CRC) without any reservations on 23rd May 1990. Bhutan is also party to the Stockholm Agenda and Yokohama Congress on commercial sexual exploitation of children. The country remains committed to provide the best opportunities for each and every Bhutanese child.

A Layap girl

Robert Dompnier

His Majesty the Fourth Druk Gyalpo, Their Majesties the Queen Mothers and Their Royal Highnesses, the Princes and Princesses are seen celebrating the National Day with the people

In 2009, His Majesty the King Jigme Khesar Namgyel Wangchuck, under an on-going land reform project, granted around 9,287 acres of land to 7,947 households. After the country was hit by an earthquake in 2009, His Majesty personally visited the affected areas and assisted around 6,241 households and granted around Nu. 87.5 million to those affected families who were further provided with free of cost CGI sheets and timber to reconstruct their homes.

His Majesty consoles the earthquake affected family in Walakthang, Monggar, 19 October 2009 assuring them of a new house.
Seen in the background are the army personnels bringing down the damaged house, to be reconstructed.

Chapter 7

THE ROYAL FAMILY: MAKING A DIFFERENCE

The Royal Family of Bhutan is the embodiment of benevolence for the Bhutanese. They play a pivotal role in the society making a great difference in the lives of the people.

The Fourth Druk Gyalpo His Majesty Jigme Singye Wangchuck has always interacted very freely and closely with the Bhutanese from all walks. His Majesty's regular visits to rural and remote areas has enabled him to witness the ground realities for himself and envision policies to address the needs of the society. His Majesty's selfless nature was manifested when he led the flush out operations against the Indian rebels from the Bhutanese soil in 2003.

Since the coronation in 2008, His Majesty the King Jigme Khesar Namgyel Wangchuck has traversed, often on foot, the length and breadth of his country including the remotest and inaccessible area visiting homes, discussing problems and needs while sharing meals with people in their homes.

The present Queen Mothers of Bhutan have been pioneers in the establishment of non-governmental organizations and play a pivotal role in addressing a range of social issues. Women and children's issues and rights, poverty alleviation, juvenile delinquency, youth unemployment and counselling are areas in which the Queen Mothers have played a crucial role. Their Majesties the Queen Mothers and members of the Royal Family interact very closely and openly with people from all walks of life, during several visits to different and remote parts of the country each year. This enables them to understand the ground realities for themselves and design need-based and relevant developmental programmes and projects. They also actively support fund-raising initiatives, both within the country and abroad. Their Majesties are supported by other members of the Royal Family, which includes the Princes and Princesses in gracing many occasions of varying degrees of importance.

ROYAL FAMILY

The Royal Family is the epitome o

HRH Prince Khamsum Singye Wangchuck with His Majesty the Fourth Druk Gyalpo

HRH Princess Kezang Choden Wangchuck ▶

HRH Princess Sonam Dechan Wangchuck launching an ECB publication in Paro, 2009

HRH Princess Dechen Yangzom Wangchuck consoling fire victims at Paro

HRH Prince Ugyen Jigme Wangchuck with Her Majesty the Queen Mother Ashi Tshering Pem Wangchuck

MAKING A DIFFERENCE

utanese identity, unity, solidarity, progress and happiness.

HRH Prince Jigyel Ugyen Wangchuck being welcomed
as His Majesty's Representative to the Sports Fraternity, August 2009

HRH Princess Eeuphelma
Choden Wangchuck

HRH Prince Jigme Dorji Wangchuck
addresses the people of Gasa

◀ HRH Princess Chimi Yangzom Wangchuck

From Left:
HRH Princess Chimi Yangzom Wangchuck
HRH Princess Dechen Yangzom Wangchuck
HRH Princess Kezang Choden Wangchuck
HRH Princess Eeuphelma Choden Wangchuck
HRH Prince Ugyen Jigme Wangchuck
HRH Princess Sonam Dechan Wangchuck
HRH Prince Jigyel Ugyen Wangchuck
HRH Prince Khamsum Singye Wangchuck
HRH Prince Jigme Dorji Wangchuck

Tarayana Foundation

The Tarayana Foundation was established in 2003 by Her Majesty the Queen Mother Ashi Dorji Wangmo Wangchuck, to address problems of the vulnerable individuals and communities in the country.

With a vision aimed at a happy and prosperous Bhutan, Tarayana works towards helping the vulnerable and the disadvantaged help themselves with several initiatives and activities. True empowerment of rural self-help groups bring confidence and growth in the villages.

Under the leadership and guidance of the President, Tarayana has helped provide shelter to the homeless; food to the hungry; medicine to the sick and education to poor children who could not afford to go to school. As the Patron of the Foundation, Her Majesty continues to meet and interact with communities isolated in the remote pockets of Bhutan during periodic monitoring visits.

These royal visits are vividly described in Her Majesty's book titled 'Treasures of the Thunder Dragon'.

Tarayana currently implements seven core programmes and several small projects in rural communities. The Foundation is assisted by volunteers from all walks of life in implementing their community development activities. Youth engagement in social service is ensured through a very vibrant system of Tarayana school clubs spread throughout the country. The members of these clubs take on the outreach programme into local communities learning to be part of the solution to local problems. The Board of Trustee under the leadership of Her Majesty, provides oversight and gives direction to the programmes implemented. Institutional linkages have been established to help keep the volunteer spirit alive.

Funding for Tarayana activities come from individual donations, project type grants and some fund raising drives.

Her Majesty the Queen Mother Ashi Dorji Wangmo Wangchuck has walked the length and breadth of the country meeting community in remotest parts of the country

Her Majesty the Queen Mother Ashi Tshering Pem Wangchuck places priority in guiding the youth along the right trail and preparing them to be responsible citizens

Youth Development Fund

In 1999 the Fourth Druk Gyalpo Jigme Singye Wangchuck declared that a national organization should be established to support youth development in Bhutan. Shortly thereafter the Bhutan Youth Development Fund (YDF) was launched under the leadership of Her Majesty the Queen Mother Ashi Tshering Pem Wangchuck on 16 June 1999.

With a vision to provide a better today and brighter tomorrow for the youth of Bhutan, the YDF as a leading organization is dedicated towards making every youth a leader. Through strategic programmes, advocacy, and partnerships, the YDF works to ensure that all youth in Bhutan have an equal chance to develop their full potential.

Her Majesty as the President has pioneered youth development programming across the country through a more human development of young people and their families. Under Her Majesty's leadership the organization has evolved into one of the most active members of Bhutanese civil society. Her Majesty is the driving force behind the organizations growing network and links which stimulates YDF's cause with greater efficiency and resources.

The YDF has an array of programmes which promote youth leadership and empowers young people through educational and employment prospects. Further support expands into areas of special needs education and substance abuse education, prevention and treatment. The YDF has also established many facilities for their beneficiaries; there is a youth hostel in Phuentsholing, a rehabilitation centre and youth development center in Thimphu, and a vocational training center for girls in Punakha.

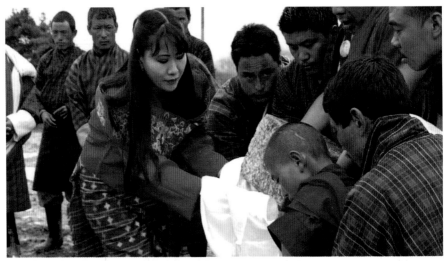

Her Majesty Ashi Tshering Yangdon Wangchuck, the compassionate Queen Mother who upholds religious tradition and culture

Bhutan Nuns Foundation

The Bhutan Nuns Foundation (BNF) is a non-profit organization founded by Her Majesty the Queen Mother Ashi Tshering Yangdon Wangchuck in March, 2009. As monastic life is an integral part of Bhutanese culture, the BNF was established to help improve the well-being and education of nuns in Bhutan to enable them to contribute to the cultural and spiritual values of the larger society. Her Majesty has been playing a key role in promoting nuns education by supporting nunneries in the country since 1995.

Despite the important role of nuns in the society, almost all of Bhutan's nunneries are faced with poor living conditions and provide little to no basic education. Thus, with a vision to enhance Bhutanese society by empowering girls and women through education and economic self-sufficiency, the objective of BNF is to ensure nunneries maintain adequate, healthy living conditions and provides a relevant and useful education for girls and women.

Following the conduct of baseline research in 2006, the BNF will implement a systematic programme to improve the living conditions and provide practical education at nunneries throughout the country. This will include infrastructure development or refurbishing of sleeping quarters, bathrooms, kitchens, libraries and classrooms. It will also provide adult literacy and practical, self-sufficiency skills training and supplies, books and other learning materials.

Under the guidance of Her Majesty, the Foundation seeks to help make nunneries leading agents and self-reliant institutions for women. According to BNF concept paper, it is committed towards women's education and empowerment as a way of enhancing their capacity to support society in its search for Gross National Happiness.

RENEW

RENEW which stands for 'Respect, Educate, Nurture and Empower Women' is the first organization of its kind in Bhutan, dedicated to the relief and empowerment of disadvantaged women and adolescent girls. Disadvantaged women are often victims of domestic violence, sexual violence, and other forms of violation against them. Her Majesty the Queen Mother Ashi Sangay Choden Wangchuck, recognizing the need to promote gender equality, conceptualized the organization in 1999. Formally established in 2004, RENEW campaigns to prevent family violence and caters to the needs of victims and survivors of gender based violence. It is striving towards forging a better understanding of gender inequalities at all levels of society. RENEW actively advocates against domestic violence of women and children.

Her Majesty the Queen Mother is also the Goodwill Ambassador of the United Nations Fund for Population (UNFPA) and has travelled across Bhutan, meeting and talking to people regarding population issues. Her Majesty initiated the Multi Sectoral Task Force (MSTF) in all the 20 Dzongkhags to carry forward the advocacy she had initiated on population education, HIV/AIDS and reproductive health. This has resulted in remarkable reduction of family size and greater awareness of family planning and HIV/AIDS.

Her Majesty the Queen Mother Ashi Sangay Choden Wangchuck, the UNFPA Goodwill Ambassador has taken the lead as a prime advocator for reproductive health and campaigns to prevent domestic violence.

The National Women's Association of Bhutan

The National Women's Association of Bhutan (NWAB) was established on 9 April, 1981 by a resolution passed by the 53rd session of the National Assembly. It was first established as an NGO with a responsibility to improve the socio-economic conditions of women throughout the country. The primary role of the association was structured on forward looking strategies for the advancement of women adopted at the UN conference in Nairobi in 1985 and the Convention on the Elimination of all forms of Discrimination Against Women (CEDAW). In 1990 NWAB was identified as the national body dedicated to the advancement of women.

Under the leadership of Her Royal Highness Ashi Sonam Choden Wangchuck, NWAB is engaged in promoting the socio economic status of disadvantaged women and raising awareness on women's issues. With a network of volunteers in nearly all 20 Dzongkhags in the country, NWAB is striving to promote socio-economic conditions of disadvantaged women through promoting economic opportunities, developing capability and raising awareness of the rights and potential of women.

HRH Ashi Sonam Choden Wangchuck with NWAB volunteers

His Majesty the Fourth Druk Gyalpo, His Majesty the King, Their Majesties the Queen Mothers and members of the Royal Family are the embodiment of benevolence for the Bhutanese and interact very closely and openly with people from all walks of life.

Chapter 8

INFORMATION AND MEDIA

Media in Bhutan is a fairly young development. The concept of the media, as a player in the growth of a modern society began in the mid 1980s, with the establishment of the first Bhutanese newspaper, Kuensel and the Bhutan Broadcasting Station. In the late 1990s, ICT was introduced and electronic media was added to the list followed by television few years later. Today, Bhutanese media has grown considerably in all its forms – print, broadcast, film, music and internet.

Until recently, Kuensel was the only available print media. However, with increasing literacy and changing social needs, a number of private newspapers and magazines were launched. Bhutan Times and Bhutan Observer were licensed in 2006; Bhutan Today in 2008; Business Bhutan and The Journalist in 2009. Magazines range from entertainment to news magazines such as Druk Trowa, Drukpa, Bhutan Window and Yeewong.

All newspapers are published in English and Dzongkha. Except for Kuensel and Bhutan Today, the rest are weekly editions.

Radio is the most effective media in the country and reaches by far the largest audience. Bhutan Broadcasting Service (BBS) is the national public service broadcaster. BBS Radio (then known as Radio NYAB) was started in November 1973 by young volunteers belonging to the National Youth Association of Bhutan. In 1986 with the commissioning of a 10 KW short-wave transmitter and a small broadcast studio, Radio NYAB was renamed as Bhutan Broadcasting Service. BBS radio broadcasts for 24 hours in 4 languages (Dzongkha, Sharchop, Lhotshamkha and English), on both shortwave and FM frequency as well as online.

In the last few years, three private FM Radio Stations i.e. Kuzoo FM, Radio Valley and Centennial Radio, were established. While, the FM services and shortwave services of the BBS reach the entire country, Kuzoo FM radio services are available in 18 Dzongkhags while Radio Valley and Centennial Radio services is currently available only in Thimphu. These new radio services have created a platform for people voice their concerns and are already addressing a range of social issues.

Television has only been introduced since 1999. BBS TV is the only television channel that caters local news and programmes in Bhutan. BBS TV was launched on 2 June 1999. Described as the most important event in the history of electronic media in Bhutan, the BBS launched its satellite television service in February 2006. BBS TV is now available in almost 40 Asian countries – from Turkey in the West to Indonesia in South East Asia.

BBS TV broadcasts for five hours daily in Dzongkha and English. The same is rebroadcast the next morning. Three additional hours of entertainment programmes and live music request shows are broadcast on weekend afternoons. On 18 September 1992, the Fourth Druk Gyalpo issued a Royal Edict delinking the BBS from the Ministry of Communications to give it the flexibility to grow in professionalism and to enable it to be more effective in fulfilling its important responsibility towards the society.

Cable television services are available in 19 of the 20 Dzongkhags and about 40 different channels are provided by the cable TV operators. While the film industry is still in its

BBS news reader on air

infancy, the number of Bhutanese films has been increasing with more people venturing into the industry.

Internet services is provided by Druknet (government-owned) and three private companies, TashiCell, Drukcom and Samden Tech. Landline is provided by the government owned Bhutan Telecom, which also provides cellular services. TashiCell is the only private cellular service provider. As of March 2010, Bhutan has over 6,484 Internet subscribers, 26,348 landline subscribers, and more than 324,052 mobile phone subscribers.

As the Constitution of Bhutan provides for establishment of freedom of expression and freedom of the media, Bhutan's media policy is the development of a free and responsible press in a competitive environment. The government emphasizes that the media must continue to grow in professionalism to fulfill its role to; Inform, Educate and Entertain'.

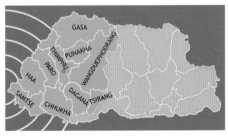

GASA

PUNAKHA

THIMPHU

PARO

HAA

WANGDUEPHODRANG

DAGANA

TSIRANG

SAMTSE

CHHUKHA

▓ *TashiCell Network coverage*

NETWORK

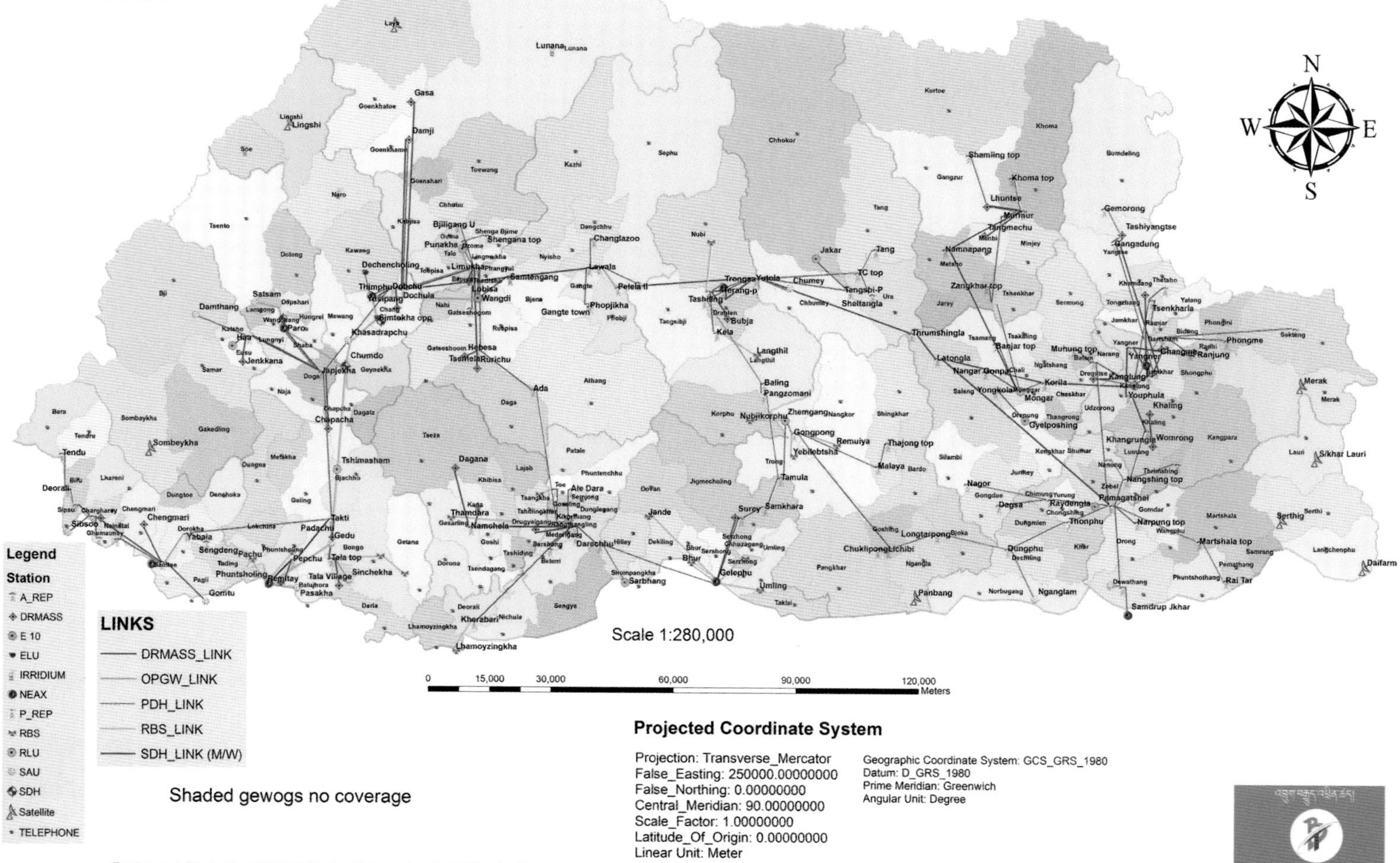

Legend
Station
A_REP
DRMASS
E 10
ELU
IRRIDIUM
NEAX
P_REP
RBS
RLU
SAU
SDH
Satellite
TELEPHONE
LINKS
DRMASS_LINK
OPGW_LINK
PDH_LINK
RBS_LINK
SDH_LINK (M/W)
Shaded gewogs no coverage
Scale 1:280,000
0 15,000 30,000 60,000 90,000 120,000 Meters
N
W
E
S
Projected Coordinate System
Projection: Transverse_Mercator
False_Easting: 250000.00000000
False_Northing: 0.00000000
Central_Meridian: 90.00000000
Scale_Factor: 1.00000000
Latitude_Of_Origin: 0.00000000
Linear Unit: Meter
Geographic Coordinate System: GCS_GRS_1980
Datum: D_GRS_1980
Prime Meridian: Greenwich
Angular Unit: Degree

Design and Printed by: GIS Unit Bhutan Telecom Limited, Thimphu Bhutan

DRUKNET NATIONAL BACKBONE

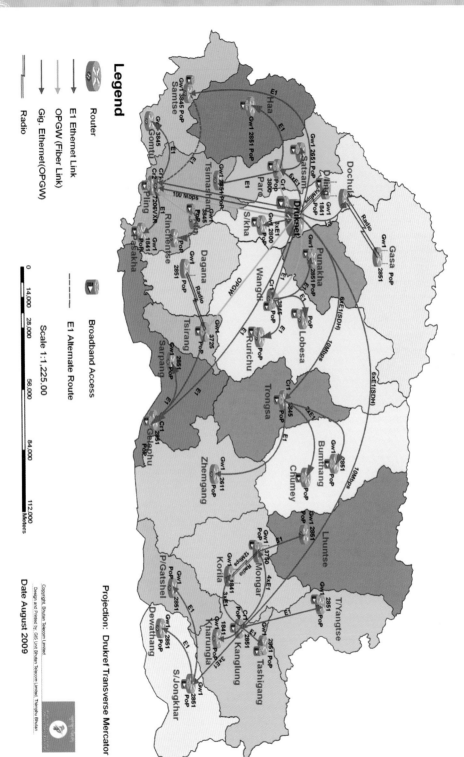

Legend

Router

Gig. Ethernet(OPGW)

OPGW (Fiber Link)

E1 Ethernet Link

Gig. Ethernet(OPGW)

Radio

Broadband Access

E1 Alternate Route

Scale 1:1,225.00

| 0 | 14,000 | 28,000 | 56,000 | 84,000 | 112,000 |
Meters

Projection: Drukref Transverse Mercator

Date August 2009

Copyright, Bhutan Telecom Limited

Design and Printed by: GIS Unit Bhutan Telecom Limited, Thimphu Bhutan

BHUTAN MEDIA FOUNDATION

The Bhutan Media Foundation was established in 2010 to support the wholesome development of mass media so that it can carry out its roles and responsibilities in the interest of democracy. The Foundation is expected to support the media in enhancing skills through scholarships, internships and training, strengthening media executive management and leadership skills. It will also support the sustainability and growth of newspapers and broadcast stations, journalists associations and press clubs. It will further invest in the future readership of the print media by striving to provide subscription grants of all newspapers to the schools and colleges in the country. In addition, it will also support the promotion of national language in the media and civic education programs in the media. All licensed mainstream media agencies (newspapers and broadcast stations) in operation are eligible for membership.

The Foundation is endowed with a seed grant of Nu 15 million from His Majesty the King.

His Majesty with representatives of the print and broadcast media at Lingkana Palace: 21 February 2010 - Coinciding with His Majesty's 30th birthday anniversary, His Majesty the King issued a Royal Charter formally establishing the Bhutan Media Foundation.

Postage Stamps

Bhutan's postage stamps is an unusual contributor to the country's foreign exchange.

Until 1962, there were no regular postage stamps in Bhutan. From earliest times, when messages had to be carried between *Dzongs*, runners made their way on foot across the rugged mountains, as they still do today in some remote villages which are not yet accessible by road.

Under the first Five Year Development Plan (1961-66), a modern internal postal service was organized. A postal agreement with India, providing an international link-up, was concluded in September, 1962 and the first postage stamps were issued the following month. The first three post offices were set up in Phuentsholing, Thimphu and Paro. Today, there are over 93 post offices consisting of four GPOs, 43 post offices and 46

community mail offices throughout the country.

Since the release of its first international postage stamp in 1962, Bhutanese stamps have established a reputation in the international market for the thematic value and technical excellence and its wide variety of exotic innovative stamps. On them are depicted an outstanding range of subjects covering portraits, flora, fauna, pictures of historical Dzongs, landscapes on silk, metal, three-dimensional images to CD ROM on Bhutan's monarchy, environment coronation and democracy. Today, Bhutan has become world-renowned in the philatelic community. The stamps of Bhutan have served as silent ambassadors and as emblems of goodwill.

His Majesty Jigme Khesar Namgyel Wangchuck, the Druk Gyalpo with the people enjoying a sporting event at National Day Celebration

Tenzin Namgay, Bhutan Times Ltd.

Bhutan's traditional values a[re] based on compassion, toleran[ce] and wisdom

Chapter 9

GROSS NATIONAL HAPPINESS

"Gross National Happiness is far more important than Gross Domestic Product"

— His Majesty Jigme Singye Wangchuck,
The Fourth Druk Gyalpo

Over the years, Bhutan has culti- vated a unique approach to devel- opment with its national philosophy anchored on the principle of Gross National Happiness (GNH) which was promulgated as the country's philos- ophy of economic and social develop- ment by the Fourth Druk Gyalpo, His Majesty Jigme Singye Wangchuck in 1972. It refers to a set of social and economic interventions that evalu- ate societal change in terms of the collective happiness of people and that lead to the adoption of policies aimed at that objective. Premised on the belief that all human beings aspire happiness in one way or an- other, the concept promotes collec- tive happiness of the society as the ultimate goal of development.

According to GNH, true development of human society takes place when material and spiritual advancement complements or reinforces each oth- er. In other words, it states that the means must always be considered in terms of the end and, therefore, every step in material development and change must be measured and evaluated to ensure that it will lead to happiness, not just more develop- ment. The philosophy therefore, at- tempts to harmonize economic prog- ress with the spiritual and emotional well-being of the people.

Bhutan believes that the holistic de- velopment of the individual and so- ciety can be achieved only through a sustainable balance between the economic, social, emotional, spiri- tual and cultural needs of the peo- ple. Development initiatives based on GNH values are therefore not re- stricted to the present population of any given society; it includes future generations and other societies, in- deed all sentient beings. GNH emphasizes that the country's current pursuit of development should not cause misery to future generations, other societies, or to other sentient beings, as understood in the Buddhist concept.

GNH has been Bhutan's overarching development philosophy that has guided the country's development policies and programmes. Guided by this policy, the country has made rapid development in a short period of time. Achievements have come with very minimal impact on its culture and environment. The government of Bhutan implemented these policies through strict adherence to the four pillars of GNH which includes equitable and sustainable socio-economic development; preservation and promotion of its culture; conservation of environment and promotion of good governance. Operation of each of these pillars to Bhutan's policy making is briefly stated below:

Equitable and Sustainable Socio-Economic Development: GNH emphasizes the importance of sustainable and equitable development. Establishment and delivery of health, education, agriculture and other economic services are guided by these two conditions of sustainability and equity. Hydroelectric power, a key source of investment and revenue for the government, has been identified as a target industry over extractive and environmentally damaging industries, such as mining or the utilization of forests.

Equity has been at the core of the Bhutan's development approach. Despite the country's difficult ter-rain and the scattered nature of population distribution, the benefits of development, both quantitatively and qualitatively, have been distributed evenly across all sections of the society.

Preservation and Promotion of Culture: GNH recognizes that the moral and ethical framework for one's thoughts and actions are shaped by culture. This pillar aims at strengthening the institutions of family and community; the spirit of volunteerism, tolerance and cooperation; the virtues of compassion, altruism, honour and dignity, which seem to be a contributing factor to Bhutan's low crime rate.

Culture also provides a framework where an individual's or society's psychological and emotional needs are addressed. By preserving local, regional and national festivals, the government attends to these needs and provides a forum for maintaining social networks and promoting the conviviality of public culture. Bhutan treasures the extended family network as the most sustainable form of social safety net. To prevent possible family disintegration or nuclearization, the government makes conscious efforts to revive and nourish the traditions and practices that bond families and keep communities resilient and thriving.

Conservation of environment: The country's environmental policy is predicated on the Buddhist perspective that human beings and nature not only live symbiotically but are inseparable from each other. According to this perspective, nature is a partner in existence; a provider of sustenance, comfort and beauty; and home to millions of life forms that possibly would have been one's parents, friends, siblings in one's timeless existence. Conservation of environment continues to be the Government's priority. Currently 72.5 percent of the country's are is under forest cover, 26 percent of the area is declared as protected areas and the state has decreed to maintain 60 percent of its area under forest cover for all times to come.

Good Governance: In order for any state to materialize a public good such as collective happiness, it must attune its system of governance towards it. Intensive efforts have therefore been made to ensure good governance as it is the main source of progress and happiness. The country has therefore has pursued a number of initiatives to facilitate the people's capacity to make choices through various decentralization programmes. In 1981, district administrations were made entirely responsible for implementation of most of the development programmes, in 1991 block development committees were created to plan and oversee implementation of development programmes, in 1998 block level plans were formulated and His Majesty the Fourth Druk Gyalpo issued a Royal Edict dissolving the long-existing Cabinet and directed the National Assembly to elect the Council of Ministers. Bhutan launched parliamentary democracy and adopted its first written Constitution in 2008. Thus, fostering people's capacity to make choices through various decentralization programmes has been the continuous efforts made by the government towards promoting GNH.

Methodology

To guide the country in making its development efforts more holistic and harmonious in its goals and means, a pilot survey was carried out between 2006 – 2008 in 12 of the 20 Dzongkhags. This resulted in GNH index and a set of indicators that can be utilized to assess the happiness and general well-being of the Bhutanese population more accurately and profoundly than a monetary measure. This is intended to inform the Bhutanese people and the wider world about the current levels of human fulfillment in the country and how these vary across Dzongkhags and across time, and will also inform government policy.

The GNH indicators include the nine core dimensions which are regarded as components of happiness and well-being in Bhutan covering Psychological Well-Being; Time Use, Community Vitality; Culture; Health; Education; Environmental Diversity; Living Standard and Governance.

Psychological Well-Being includes satisfaction with all elements of life, life enjoyment, and subjective well-being. With collective happiness as the main goal, it will guide in measuring the success of the state in providing appropriate policies and services. The indicators include general psychological distress rate, prevalence rates of both negative emotions (jealousy, frustration, selfishness) and positive emotions (generosity, compassion, calmness), spiritual activities like meditation and prayers, and consideration of karmic effects in daily life.

Time Use analyzes the nature of time spent and type of activity within a

24-hour period. It acknowledges the value of non-work activities such as sleeping, personal care, community participation, education and learning, religious activities, social and cultural activities, sports and leisure and travel that can add diversity and contribute to higher level of happiness. The indicators consists sleeping hours and total working hours.

Community Vitality focuses on the strengths and weaknesses of relationships and interactions within communities. It examines the nature of trust, belongingness, vitality of caring relationships, personal safety and volunteering. The indicators cover family vitality, safety, reciprocity, trust, social support, socialization and kinship density.

Cultural Diversity and Resilience focuses on the diversity and strength of cultural traditions. It takes into account the nature and number of cultural facilities, language use patterns and diversity, and participation in community festivities and traditional recreations. The indicators which estimate core values, and perception of changes in values and traditions include dialect use, traditional sports, community festival, artisan skill, value transmission indicator and basic precept indicator.

Health assesses the health status of the population, the determinants of health and the health system through information on self-rated health, disabilities, body mass index, number of healthy days per month. It also covers the prevalence of knowledge about HIV transmission, breast feeding practices and barriers to health services in terms of walking distance to the nearest health facility. The indicators consists health status, knowledge and barriers to health.

Education assesses the effectiveness of education in working towards the goal of collective well-being. It looks at a number of factors such as participation, skills, among others. The indicators cover education attainment, national language and folk and historical literacy .

Ecological Diversity and Resilience is intended to describe the impact of domestic supply and demand on Bhutan's ecosystems. The indicators include ecological degradation, ecological knowledge and afforestation.

Living Standard covers the basic economic status of the people. It assesses the levels of income at the individual and household levels, sense of financial security, room ratio, food security and house ownership. The indicators cover economic hardships and consists of income, housing, food security and hardship.

Good Governance evaluates how people perceive various government functions in terms of their efficacy, honesty, and quality. It includes human rights, leadership at various levels, performance of government in delivering services and controlling inequality and corruption, peoples trust in media, judiciary, and police. The indicators cover government performance, freedom and institutional trust.

While the concept and implementation of GNH continue to evolve, concrete steps, such as operationalization of the GNH Index, will continue to build potential and relevance of the concept to everyday socio-economic decision-making.

State of Happiness

In a survey conducted in the country to measure the level of happiness in 2005, 45.2 percent of Bhutanese reported being very happy, 51.6 percent reported being happy and only 3.2 percent reported not being happy. According to the Happy Planet Index estimates, the average level of life satisfaction in Bhutan is within the top 10 percent of nations worldwide, and certainly higher than other nations with similar levels of GDP per capita, and the happiest nation in South Asia. Bhutan ranks 13th out of 178 countries in the world in the international ranking of happiness.

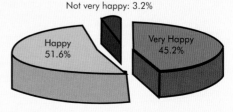

Not very happy: 3.2%

Happy 51.6%

Very Happy 45.2%

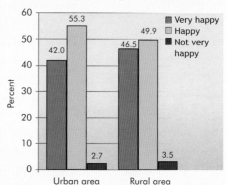

State of happiness by area of residence

Legend:
■ Very happy
□ Happy
■ Not very happy

Urban area: 42.0, 55.3, 2.7
Rural area: 46.5, 49.9, 3.5

State of happiness	Persons			Percent		
	Urban area	Rural area	Both area	Urban area	Rural area	Both area
Very happy	16,086	40,861	56,947	42.0	46.5	45.2
Happy	21,191	43,849	65,040	55.3	49.9	51.6
Not very happy	1,034	3,094	4,128	2.7	3.5	3.2
All states	38,311	87,804	126,115	100.0	100.0	100.0

Source : Fact Sheet, Population and Housing Census of Bhutan, 2005

Dzongkhagwise Normalized
Very Happy Households of Bhutan

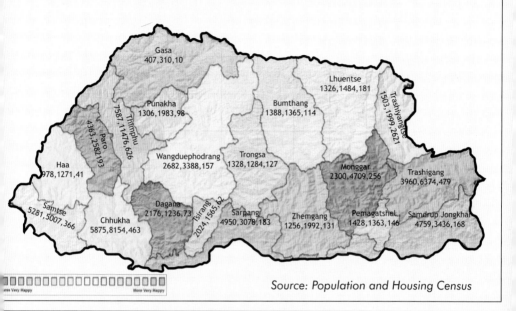

Source: Population and Housing Census

Dzongkhagwise Normalized
Happy Households of Bhutan

Source: Population and Housing Census

Chapter 10

BHUTAN AND THE WORLD

Foreign Policy

Bhutan strives to promote goodwill and cooperation with nations, foster respect for international law and treaty obligations, and encourage settlement of international disputes by peaceful means in order to promote international peace and security. The country also continues to develop and maintain friendly relations with all countries in the region and beyond and plays an active role as a responsible member of the international community.

The foreign policy of Bhutan is based on the principles of peace, prosperity and friendship with all nations. The Fourth Druk Gyalpo, His Majesty Jigme Singye Wangchuck describes the country's policy as being three-fold:

'Firstly, we are committed politically to a strong and loyal sense of nationhood, to ensuring peace and security of our citizens and the sovereign territorial integrity of our land. Secondly, to achieve economic self-reliance and the capacity to begin and complete any project we undertake, and thirdly to preserve the ancient religions and cultural heritage that has for so many centuries strengthened and enriched our lives.'

The objectives of Bhutan's foreign policy is therefore to enhance and maintain national security; promote world peace and security by engaging in meaningful dialogue with the international community; promote and contribute towards international understanding and cooperation as well as international peace and security on the basis of peaceful co-existence; develop and expand mutually beneficial bilateral, regional and multilateral economic and trade cooperation and contribute towards the development of a dynamic and a sustainable economy through mobilization of external resources.

The overall foreign policy objectives have been fulfilled by keeping Bhutan's friends and development partners regularly informed of the developments in the country through the country's diplomatic missions and embassies. The government also promotes visits at various levels, organizes international seminars, conferences, cultural and religious exhibitions on Bhutan, and actively participates in bilateral and multilateral meetings, including at the summit levels.

Foreign Relations

Following a period of self-imposed isolation, Bhutan opened its doors to the outside world by joining the Universal Postal Union in 1961 and became a member of the United Nations in 1971. Bhutan fully subscribes to the charter of the United Nations and accordingly has continued to play a committed role in all international affairs.

Since 1970s, Bhutan's international relations have increased both in scope and content. Bhutan has diplomatic relations with 24 countries.

	India	1968
	Bangladesh	1973
	Kuwait	1983
	Nepal	1983
	Maldives	1984
	Denmark	1985
	European Union	1985
	Netherlands	1985
	Norway	1985
	Sweden	1985
	Switzerland	1985
	Finland	1986
	Japan	1986
	Republic of Korea	1987
	Sri Lanka	1987
	Pakistan	1988
	Thailand	1989
	Austria	1989
	Bahrain	1992
	Australia	2002
	Singapore	2002
	Canada	2003
	Belgium	2009
	Brazil	2009

The main objective of Bhutan's establishment of diplomatic relations with other countries is to maintain close and friendly relations with all countries, particularly its neighbours. The cooperation that develops from these links has resulted in financial and technical support for the Kingdom's development. Bhutan maintains diplomatic missions in New Delhi, Dhaka, Kuwait, Bangkok and Brussels, and Permanent Missions to the United Nations at New York and Geneva.

The Ambassadors of the Kingdom of Bhutan are accredited to other countries as follows:

1. Ambassador in Dhaka: Maldives, Pakistan, South Korea and Sri Lanka
2. Ambassador in Delhi: Nepal and Japan
3. Ambassador in Geneva: Austria and Norway
4. Ambassador in Bangkok: Singapore and Australia
5. Ambassador in Kuwait: Bahrain
6. Ambassador in New York: Canada
7. Ambassador in Brussels: Denmark, Netherlands, Finland and Sweden

Bhutan and the United Nations

Bhutan was admitted as a member of the United Nations on 21st September 1971. This reaffirmed its status as a sovereign, independent country and laid the foundations for cooperation with the UN and its specialized agencies.

For Bhutan, the UN is extremely important both politically as well as economically. Politically, as an organization based on the principle of sovereign equality of its members, it provides a forum in which Bhutan can express its views and concerns on a wide range of issues on the international agenda. Economically, the UN and its specialized agencies are an important source of financial and technical assistance for socio-economic development in Bhutan. Assistance from the UN and its specialized agencies has played a vital role in the process of modernization in Bhutan since 1973. Bhutan's Permanent Missions to the UN in New York and Geneva are the channels through which Bhutan's foreign policy objectives vis-à-vis the UN and it subsidiary bodies and specialized agencies are implemented.

Over the years, Bhutan's status as an active and responsible member of the UN has gained prominence through its involvement in the numerous bodies of the UN. Bhutan has served on many important posts such as the Vice President of the UN General Assembly (New York), President of the Trade and Development Board, UN Conference on Trade and Development (UNCTAD, Geneva), three terms as member of the UN Commission on Human Rights (Geneva), two terms as member of the Economic and Social Council (ECOSOC, 1993-1995 and 2002-2004), Executive Board of UNICEF and WHO, Chairman of the Third Committee during the 50th Anniversary Celebrations of the UN (New York, 1995).

Bhutan joins the United Nations, 1971

Bhutan joins the community of nations with the hoisting of flag, New York 1971

UN System

Bhutan is a member of the following UN and Related Organizations

I	UNITED NATIONS AND RELATED ORGANIZATIONS	ADMISSION
1)	Universal Postal Union (UPU)	1969
2)	United Nations Capacity Development Fund (UNCDF)	1970
3)	United Nations	1971
4)	United Nations Conference on Trade and Development (UNCTAD)	1971
5)	United Nations Development Fund (UNDP)	1971
6)	Group of 77	1971
7)	United Nations Economic & Social Commission for Asia & the Pacific (ESCAP)	1972
8)	United Nations Childrens' Fund (UNICEF)	1974
9)	World Food Programme (WFP)	1976
10)	International Fund for Agricultural Development (IFAD)	1978
11)	United Nations Population Fund (UNFPA)	1979
12)	Asian Reinsurance Corporation (ARC)	1979
13)	International Monetary Fund (IMF)	1981
14)	World Bank - International Bank for Reconstruction and Development (IBRD)	1981
15)	International Development Association (IDA)	1981
16)	Food and Agriculture Organization of the United Nations (FAO)	1981
17)	World Health Organization (WHO)	1982
18)	South East Asia Regional Organization of WHO (SEARO)	1982
19)	United Nations Education, Scientific and Cultural Organization (UNESCO)	1982
20)	United Nations Industrial Development Organization (UNIDO)	1983
21)	Asian Pacific Postal Union (APPU)	1983
22)	Trade and Development Board of UNCTAD	1985
23)	International Telecommunication Union (ITU)	1988
24)	International Civil Aviation Organization (ICAO)	1989
25)	World Intellectual Property Organization (WIPO)	1994
26)	UN-World Tourism Organization (UN-WTO)	2003
27)	International Finance Corporation	2003

Source : Ministry of Foreign Affairs, RGoB

Bhutan is a member of the following International Organizations

II OTHER INTERNATIONAL ORGANIZATIONS	ADMISSION
1) Colombo Plan	1962
2) Non-Aligned Movement	1973
3) South Asian Co-operation Environment Programme (SACEP)	1982
4) Asian Development Bank	1982
5) World Fellowship of Buddhists	1984
6) South Asian Association for Regional Corporation (SAARC)	1985
7) International Centre for Integrated Mountain Development (ICIMOD)	1985
8) International Organization of Supreme Audit Institutions (INTOSAI)	1987
9) Association of Development Financing Institutions in Asia and the Pacific	1988
10) Office International Des Epizooties (OIE)	1990
11) Asian Institute of Transport Development	1991
12) International Telecommunications Organization (INTELSAT)	1992
13) International Plant Protection Convention (IPPC)	1994
14) Global Environmental Facility (GEF)	1995
15) Asia and Pacific Seed Association (APSA)	1996
16) Asian Broadcasting Union (ABU)	1997
17) Constitution of the Asia-Pacific Telecommunity (APT)	1998
18) Animal Production and Health Commission for Asia and the Pacific (APHCA) (applied for membership)	2000
19) Asian Pacific Institute for Broadcasting Development	2000
20) Asian Clearing Union	2000
21) Asian Organization of Supreme Audit Institutions (ASOSAI)	2000
22) Road Engineering Association of Asia and Australasia (REAAA)	2002
23) World Road Association (PIARC)	2002
24) World Customs Organization	2002
25) World Meteorological Organization	2003
26) Regional Intelligence Liaison Officer (RILO) for Asia & Pacific Region	2003
27) Asia Pacific Education & Training Institute in Tourism (APETIT)	2004
28) BIMST-EC	2004
29) Association of Government Accounts Organization of Asia (AGAOA)	2004
30) Asian Cooperation Dialogue	2005
31) International Standardisation Organization (ISO)(Correspondent member)	2005
32) Asia Pacific Rural & Agricultural Credit Association (APRACA)	2005
33) International Criminal Police Organization (INTERPOL)	2005
34) Global Tiger Forum	2005

II OTHER INTERNATIONAL ORGANIZATIONS	ADMISSION
35) South Asian Forum for Infrastructure Regulation (SAFIR)	2006
36) International Electrotechnical Commission (IEC) ACP	2006
37) Asian Disaster Reduction Center (ADRC)	2007

Bhutan is a member of the following International Sports Organizations

III INTERNATIONAL SPORTS ORGANIZATIONS	ADMISSION
1) International Olympic Committee	1983
2) Olympic Council of Asia (OCA)	1983
3) South Asian Sports Federation (SASF)	1983
4) International Amateur and Asian Amateur Athletic Federation	1983
5) International Archery Federation and Asian Archery Federation	1983
6) International Boxing Federation and Asian Boxing Federation	1983
7) International Basketball Federation and Asian Basketball	1983
8) International T.T. Federation and Asian T.T. Federation	1983
9) International Volleyball Federation and Asian Volleyball Federation	1983
10) International Tennis Federation and Asian Tennis Federation	1985
11) World Taekwondo Federation and Asian Taekwondo Union	1985
12) Association of National Olympic Committee (ANOC)	1988
13) FESPIC Games Federation	1988
14) University Games Federation (FISU)	1988
15) Asia Pacific & Oceana Sports Assembly (APOSA)	1990
16) International Badminton Federation and Asian Badminton Fed.	1997
17) Asian Golf Union	1998
18) International Football Federation and Asian Football Confederation	2000
19) International Cricket Control Board	2001
20) Asian Cricket Control Board	2002
21) International Shooting Sports Federation and Asian Shooting Sports Federation	2002

Source : Ministry of Foreign Affairs, RGoB

Bhutan and SAARC

On December 8, 1985 in Dhaka, Bhutan joined its South Asian neighbours Bangladesh, India, Maldives, Nepal, Pakistan and Sri Lanka to establish the South Asian Association for Regional Cooperation (SAARC) with the formal adoption of its Charter. Afghanistan joined as the eighth member in 2007. In view of the resurgence in South Asia, nine countries have become Observer Members of SAARC which includes Australia, China, Iran, Japan, Republic of Korea, Mauritius, Myanmar, US and EU.

The Kingdom attaches great importance to SAARC and since its inception has firmly supported and promoted its activities and worked towards making South Asian Region self reliant. Consistent with its policy of developing friendly relations with all neighbouring countries, SAARC provides a useful platform for Bhutan to enhance cooperation at regional level. In this respect, it has complemented Bhutan's bilateral and multilateral relations with the member states of SAARC. Over the years Bhutan has taken major responsibilities which has led to the establishment of the SAARC Forestry Centre and the SAARC Development Fund Secretariat in the capital.

Bhutan hosted the XVI SAARC Summit for the first time in April 2010 with 'Climate Change' as the main theme.

*The leaders of the SAARC countries at the Fifteenth SAARC Summit
(Colombo, Sri Lanka, 2-3 August 2008)*

Bhutan and BIMSTEC

On 8 February 2004, Bhutan joined her regional neighbours Bangladesh, India, Myanmar, Nepal, Sri Lanka and Thailand as a member of BIM-STEC (The Bay of Bengal Initiative for Multi-Sectoral Technical and Economic Cooperation).

BIMSTEC provides Bhutan with a platform to interact and engage in meaningful cooperation with other sovereign nations. The country's membership in BIMSTEC facilitates its efforts to gradually integrate the country's economy with regional as well as global markets and closer economic cooperation with South Asian and South East Asian neighbours.

Out of 14 areas of cooperation, Bhutan is the lead country for culture. The BIMSTEC Cultural Observatory will be established in Bhutan.

Bhutan and Asian Cooperation Dialogue

Bhutan became a member of the Asian Cooperation Dialogue (ACD) in April, 2005. The ACD is a continent-wide forum, the first of its kind in Asia, which was first inaugurated in June 2002. It aims to constitute the missing link in Asia by incorporating every Asian country and building an Asian community without duplicating other organizations or creating a bloc against others. A key princi-ple is to consolidate Asian strengths and fortify Asia's competitiveness by maximizing on the diversity and rich resources evident in Asia. Currently the ACD comprises 30 countries: Bahrain, Bangladesh, Brunei, Bhutan, Cambodia, China, India, Indonesia, Iran, Japan, Kazakhstan, Republic of Korea, Kuwait, Laos, Malaysia, Mongolia, Myanmar, Pakistan, Philippines, Oman, Qatar, Singapore, Sri Lanka, Thailand, United Arab Emirates and Vietnam, Russia, Saudi Arabia, Tajikistan and Uzbekistan.

The 10th Round Table Meeting, Thimphu 2008

BHUTAN AND DEVELOPMENT COOPERATION PARTNERS BASED IN THE KINGDOM

> *Bhutan differs from most of the aid-dependent countries as the country follows a policy of limiting the number of donor countries/institutions. Foreign aid used to represent half of the government budget during the 1980s but this proportion has declined over the years.*

AUSTRIA

Austrian Coordination Office for Development Cooperation (ACO)

Austrian
= Development Cooperation

The primary aims of the Austrian Development Cooperation (ADC) is to safeguard peace and human security, reduce global poverty and preserve the environment.

Austrian development assistance to Bhutan started with the provision of training for the tourism sector in the late 1970s. An Austrian Coordination Office for Development Cooperation (ACO) was set up in Thimphu in 1994 to supervise the various development aid programmes. ACO is affiliated to the Austrian Embassy, New Delhi and the Resident Coordinator in Bhutan has diplomatic status as Counsellor for Development Cooperation Affairs.

In the focus sector of energy, the ACO supported Rangjung and Basochhu hydropower plants. Technical assistance is being provided to Dagachhu and the rural electrification programme. In the tourism sector, the Sustainable Tourism Development Strategy (Master Plan) and the classification system of tourist accommodation were developed. The construction and curriculum development of the first institute in Bhutan for tourism and hospitality management is under implementation. In the area of governance, Austria supports capacity development for local governments and the judiciary as well as the establishment of Bhutan National Legal Institute and the construction of Dzongkhag Courts in Trongsa and Bumthang. Within the cultural cooperation between Austria and Bhutan until the year 2008 the renovation of Trongsa Dzong and the reconstruction of Ta Dzong as a state of art museum have been completed.

Facing the challenges of climate change adaption, ADC is currently co-financing the lowering of the Thorthormi glacial lake and the installation of an early warning system for Glacial Lake Outburst Floods (GLOF) in Bhutan.

BANGLADESH

Bhutan and Bangladesh share close ties of friendship. While diplomatic relations between the two countries was established in 1973, the Bangladesh resident mission in

Thimphu was established in 1980. The areas of cooperation include higher studies and training in medicine, engineering and agriculture. Bangladesh is also the second most important trading partner for Bhutan after India. Bhutan exports fruits, mineral, stones, boulders, cement, timber, cardamom and processed fruit products to Bangladesh and in 2008 earned Nu. 632.41 million. Imports from Bangladesh include jute bags, jute carpets, condensed milk, ready-made garments, pharmaceutical products, ceramic and melamine products.

DENMARK

Liaison Office of Denmark

 The over riding objective of the Danish development policy is to promote sustainable development through proper economic growth. The Danish development cooperation with Bhutan was initiated in 1978, and in 1989 Bhutan was chosen as a partner programme country. Danish assistance has focussed on areas of health and education, urban development, environment and good governance. A substantial part of the assistance is now being provided as sector budget support reflecting the strength of the partnership between Bhutan and Denmark.

The strong focus in Bhutan's domestic policies on poverty reduction and democratic change, and positive past experiences encourage the partnership. The overall objective of cooperation is poverty reduction through the promotion of sustainable economic development, strengthening of the private sector, democratization and good governance, gender equality and respect for human rights.

The Danish Government has committed about DKK 350 million (USD 70 million) to Bhutan for period 2008-2013, making Denmark the second largest bilateral development partner after India. During this period Denmark will continue its support towards the health and education sectors, environment and urban development as well as good governance. Under the good governance programme, Denmark will support the National Land Commission, the Judiciary, Local Governance and Civil Society. A 'Business to Business' programme between Danish and Bhutanese private companies is also a priority.

The first three Bhutanese Torch Bearers join the MDG3 Global Call to Action on economic empowerment of women. The MDG3 Global Call to Action campaign was initiated by the Government of Denmark on 7th March 2008 to make gender equality and women's empowerment a high priority on the international agenda in order to accelerate the achievement of all the Millennium Development Goals (MDGs).

INDIA

 Bhutan and India enjoy close ties of friendship and cooperation. The foundation for the friendship was laid by the 1949 India-Bhutan Friendship Treaty which was revised in 2007.

India is Bhutan's largest donor and provides approximately 50 percent of the Kingdom's development assistance. While formal diplomatic ties were established in May 1968, relations between Bhutan and India took a substantive form following the visit by Third Druk Gyalpo, His Majesty Jigme Dorji Wangchuck to India in 1953 and Indian Prime Minister, Pandit Jawaharlal Nehru to Bhutan in 1958. Since then, the trust and cooperation between the two countries has been growing and over the years has developed into a mutually beneficial relationship. This special relationship is further sustained by the tradition of regular visits and extensive exchange of views at the highest levels between the two countries.

A major step towards this long-standing cooperation was the 336MW Indo-Bhutan Friendship Project, commissioned at Chhukha, followed by the 1,020MW Tala Project. Some of the other major projects in Bhutan carried out with Indian support include 60 MW Kurichhu Hydroelectric Project, Penden Cement Plant, Paro Airport, Bhutan Broadcasting Station, Major Highways, Electricity Transmission and Distribution System, Indo-Bhutan Microwave Link and JDWNR Hospital in Thimphu. The two countries have also agreed to implement 10 mega hydropower projects in Bhutan with the aim to develop at least 10,000MW power by 2020. Other major ongoing bilateral projects are 1 million tonne capacity Dungsum Cement Plant at Nganglam, construction of the first ever rail link between India and Bhutan, connecting Hashimara to Phuentsholing, called the "Golden Jubilee Rail Line", the capacity building in ICT sector and the establishment of Bhutan Institute of Medical Sciences.

India-Bhutan economic cooperation today encompasses almost every area of bilateral interaction -hydropower, transport, communications, infrastructure, education, HRD, IT industry, environment, medicine and agriculture. Bhutan enjoys nearly 82 % of its trade with India. A free trade regime exists between India and Bhutan. The India-Bhutan Trade and Commerce Agreement which expired in March 2005, has been renewed for a period of 10 years.

JAPAN

JICA Bhutan Office

 The Japan International Cooperation Agency (JICA) is an implementing agency for technical cooperation of Japan's official development assistance. Its aim is to contribute to the socioeconomic development of the developing countries.

The Japanese Government has supported Bhutan since 1964, when Dasho Keiji Nishioka was assigned as an agriculture expert. Besides grant aid, Japan provides technical assistance through its technical cooperation projects, JICA volunteers, training programmes, in a variety of fields which include agriculture, infrastructure, governance, health and education. JICA currently supports agriculture and rural development, balanced infrastructure development, improvement of social services, and improvement of government functions.

NETHERLANDS

SNV - Netherlands Development Organization

SNV SNV is a Netherlands based international organization headquartered in The Hague with a presence in 34 countries world-wide. It is dedicated to a society where all people enjoy the freedom to pursue their own sustainable development and therefore contributes to this by strengthening the capacity of local organizations and groups allowing them to better contribute to the effective realization of poverty reduction and good governance.

Since 1988, SNV has supported Bhutan in achieving the goals and objectives of its development as laid out in subsequent Five Year Plans which includes support in areas such as irrigation, rural water supply schemes, integrated pest management, integrated area development, watershed management, private sector development, micro-finance, tourism, civil service reform, agriculture, road construction, forestry and civil society development.

SNV Bhutan works in four sectors, namely; water, sanitation and hy-

giene; smallholder cash crops; forest products and pro-poor sustainable tourism. SNV also provides expertise in governance and gender as cross-cutting themes across all its sectors activities. Currently SNV provides support to the government of Bhutan and other local organizations through the provision of 25 advisory staff, and numerous local capacity builders and short term consultancy services.

SWITZERLAND

Helvetas Coordination Office

◀ helvetas Bhutan ▶

Helvetas is a Swiss Association for international cooperation that was founded in 1955 in Zurich as the first private organization for development co-operation in Switzerland. It is a non-profit, politically independent association supported by 45,000 members, 50,000 regular sponsors, 15 Helvetas regional groups in Switzerland. However 75 percent of the total budget is financed by the Swiss Federal Government. As the first NGO to come to Bhutan, Helvetas is one of Bhutan's oldest development partner.

The start of Swiss assistance to Bhutan dates back to the late 1960s through the 'Swiss Foundation Pro Bhutan' of Mr. Fritz von Schulthess, a close friend of Third Druk Gyalpo. It included support for livestock and dairy development, agriculture, sustainable forestry utilization, food processing, craftsmanship, and medical services. Helvetas, took over these development activities on July 1, 1975. Since the opening of the Joint Coordination Office in 1983, Helvetas is mandated to execute development programmes of the Swiss Federal Government in the country and is guided by a Joint Bhutan Country Programme of Helvetas and SDC (Swiss Agency for Development and Cooperation) that prioritizes mainly four development sectors: RNR, rural infrastructure, education, youth and culture, civil society and the state.

With the overall goal, "to contribute to the reduction of poverty and socio-economic disparities through a sustainable social, economical, and environmental development that also balances regional needs," the Swiss assistance in Bhutan aims at the following: promotion of good governance, alleviation of poverty and social disparities, encouragement of sustainable economic development, sustainable natural resource management and conservation of the environment, advancement of decentralized participation and private initiatives.

During the period 2008 – 2013, Helvetas/SDC will be collaborating with the RGoB in promoting rural development initiatives (RDI) and rural development governance (RDG) with the view to contribute towards overall goals of poverty alleviation and democracy and good governance; ensuring environmental sustainability, gender equality, equity and inclusiveness; institution and human capacity building; and harnessing the use of ICT.

RESIDENT UN AGENCIES IN BHUTAN

 Relationship between the Royal Government of Bhutan (RGoB) and the United Nations (UN) has been intimate and fruitful. The UN system has been associated with almost every sphere of social, economic and human development efforts of Bhutan over the years. Of the United Nations organizations to which Bhutan is a member, six have offices in Bhutan namely: FAO, UNDP (which includes UNCDF and UNV), UNFPA, UNICEF, WFP and WHO. The Millennium Declaration and the associated Millennium Development Goals (MDGs) form the framework within which the UN Country Team operates in Bhutan.

Although Bhutan started late in its development plan, it is already ahead of many South Asian countries towards achieving most of the MDGs by 2015. Bhutan has already met 3 of the MDG indicators (halving the proportion of under-weight under-5 children; halving the proportion of people without sustainable access to safe drinking water and sanitation, and halving the proportion of people without access to improved sanitation by 2015), and is on track to meet other MDG targets.

With the objective to enhance development effectiveness of UN activities in Bhutan through improved UN coordination, effectiveness and efficiency in supporting national goals, 14 UN agencies working in Bhutan (resident and non-resident agencies) have signed a Common

Country Programme Action Plan for the next five years (2008-2012). The five priority areas that the UN System will be supporting Bhutan as per the common operational plan are: (i) increased opportunities for generation of income and employment in targeted poor areas; (ii) increased access to, and utilization of, quality health services, with emphasis on reproductive health, maternal and child health and nutrition, HIV/AIDS, tuberculosis, malaria and non-communicable diseases; (iii) improved access to quality education for all, with gender equality and special focus on the hard-to-reach population; (iv) strengthened institutional capacity and people's participation to ensure good governance; and (v) strengthened national capacity for environmental sustainability and disaster management.

Food and Agriculture Organization (FAO)

 FAO leads international efforts in defeating hunger. Bhutan and the FAO first commenced their long standing partnership in 1973, even before Bhutan obtained FAO membership in 1981. The present Office in Thimphu was opened in April 1985.

FAO's cooperation in the forestry sector, launched in 1973 through a UNDP-funded project has expanded through a series of projects that have progressively diversified into more extensive and specialized disciplines. FAO's past assistance includes, drafting new forest legislation, mushroom development, forest products pricing policy, and contribution on social forestry and wood energy for the master plan for forestry development, including the preparation of a forestry sector programme framework while recent involvement includes assistance in forest management, forestry extension, and institutional development.

United Nations Development Programme (UNDP)

 UNDP is the UN's global development network, advocating for change and connecting countries to knowledge, experience and resources to help people build a better life. With 42 years of development service, UNDP is on the ground in 166 countries. UNDP started its assistance programme in Bhutan in 1973, although its office was established only in 1979. In Bhutan, the foundation of UNDP's work is to ensure that progress is based on people - on their needs, efforts and rights. UNDP mobilizes and coordinates support from other partners and pilots new solutions that can be replicated. It also offers a global network which Bhutan can draw upon for ideas and resources.

UNDP's assistance in the country is focussed mainly in the areas of democratic governance which constitutes one of the thrusts of UNDP's support to Bhutan. The support falls within the areas of decentralization and local governance, support for parliamentary democracy, and e-governance and strengthening media. Poverty reduction and achievement of MDGs is the second area of support. The third area of assistance is sustainable energy, environment and disaster risk management. UNDP is also a key partner of Bhutan in helping promote gender equality and empowerment of women through various interventions and has supported series of activities aimed at enhancing capacity of its national counterparts in gender mainstreaming mainly partnering with the National Commission for Women and Children.

United Nations Population Fund (UNFPA)

 UNFPA is an International Development Agency that promotes the right of every woman, man and child to enjoy a life of health and equal opportunity. Since 1981, UNFPA's support in Bhutan is broadly divided into three main areas of work: to help ensure universal access to reproductive health, including family planning and making motherhood safer; support towards adolescent sexual reproductive health and prevention of HIV infection among adolescents and youth; to support population and development strategies that enable capacity-building in population programming and to promote awareness of population and development issues; and promoting gender equality.

One of the key determinants of UNFPA's success in Bhutan has been the tireless efforts of Her Majesty the Queen Ashi Sangay Choden Wangchuck, UNFPA Goodwill Ambassador since 1999. The advocacy efforts of Her Majesty placed reproductive health, including family planning, HIV/AIDS infection, population and development, and gender equality squarely and prominently at the center of the country's development dialogue.

United Nations Children's Fund (UNICEF)

With presence in 190 countries, UNICEF is the driving force that helps build a world where the rights of every child are realized. UNICEF's assistance in Bhutan began in 1974 with the water supply and sanitation programme. Since then, its has expanded its support to improve the lives of Bhutanese children and women.

Based on the core principles of the Convention on the Rights of the Child (CRC), UNICEF's programme focuses on four key areas which includes health, nutrition and sanitation programme that aims to strengthen quality and coverage of maternal and newborn care services, address micronutrient deficiencies and expanding water and sanitation services and health and hygiene promotion especially in primary schools and religious institutes; quality education which focuses on increasing retention and completion rates by improving the quality of primary education and ensuring equal access for all children. It also supports the increase of developmental readiness of young children for school and provides a second chance to education for out-of-school young people through non-formal education; enabling environment for child protection and planning, communication and participation through strengthening planning capacities of targeted ministries and departments and advocacy and promotion of behaviour change communication. HIV/AIDS prevention and care are cross-cutting elements of the programme.

World Food Programme (WFP)

 WFP is the UN's frontline agency in the fight against global hunger which started its assistance in Bhutan since 1976. The cornerstone of WFP activities in Bhutan has been and continues to be Food for Education Programme, through which thousands of children received school meals over the last three decades. Presently, there are 217 WFP assisted schools across the country with some 41,000 beneficiaries.

In the past WFP has also supported road and bridge construction, health, agricultural re-settlement, forestry, irrigation and dairy development projects and assisted with the establishment of a national emergency food buffer stock. WFP also aims to support Bhutan in improving access to education by providing nutritious meals for school children, particularly those from rural families and vulnerable to food insecurity. Particular attention is given to reducing gender disparity in education. The focus of WFP assistance during 2008–2012 will be on primary education and capacity-building of government counterparts.

World Health Organization (WHO)

 WHO is the directing and coordinating authority for health within the UN system and is responsible for providing leadership on global health matters. Although Bhutan officially joined WHO on 8 March 1982, its cooperation with Bhutan extends back further. Bhutan adopted the Declaration of Alma Ata as its core thrust in the development of modern health services in 1979. From the very beginning, cooperation between WHO and Bhutan has been based on mutual confidence and a close working relationship.

WHO's assistance in Bhutan is focused mainly in five areas which includes human resources development at all levels; strengthening of health system, reducing health risks to health, reducing the burden of diseases and promoting health environments for sustainable development.

RESIDENT WORLD BANK GROUP IN BHUTAN

 THE WORLD BANK

The World Bank is an international organization established in 1944 and currently owned by 184 countries. It is one of the world's largest sources of funding and knowledge to support governments of member countries in their efforts to invest in schools and health centers, provide water and electricity, fight disease and protect the environment.

Bhutan became a member of the World Bank in 1981. Through the International Development Association (IDA), the World Bank's concessionary lending affiliate that provides interest-free loans, the Bank began its assistance in the early 1980s. There are currently seven ongoing projects for a net commitment of USD 73 million. The current project is focusing on education, health, private sector, roads and rural development. In addition, a Development Policy Financing for Institutional Strengthening was disbursed in June 2009 in the amount of USD 20.2 million budget support.

The World Bank's support to Bhutan includes both financing and knowledge sharing. It provides support for analytical work and technical assistance in a number of areas, including climate change, environment, investment climate, public financial management and procurement, among other. A new Country Assistance Strategy is being jointly prepared with International Finance Corporation and will build on the RGoB's Tenth Five-Year Plan.

International Finance Corporation (IFC), a member of the World Bank Group, creates opportunity for people to escape poverty and improve their lives. It fosters sustainable economic growth in developing countries by supporting private sector development, mobilizing private capital, and providing advisory and risk mitigation services to businesses and governments. It helps companies and financial institutions in emerging markets create jobs, generate tax revenues, improve corporate governance and environmental performance, and contribute to their local communities to improve lives.

The creation of IFC in 1956 represented the first step by the global community to foster private sector investment in developing nations. Today, IFC has 182 member countries, which collectively determine its policies and approve investments. In fiscal 2009, IFC's new investments totalled USD 14.5 billion, helping channel capital into developing countries during the financial crisis.

After Bhutan joined IFC as a member country in 2003, IFC has made investments in high-end tourism infrastructure and global trade finance support to local banks. IFC continues to assess investment potential for IFC in education, telecom, hydropower, and financial markets. It also provided advisory services to improve the investment climate by simplifying regulation, strengthen the financial sector, and help promote the role of SMEs in private sector development.

INTERNATIONAL NGOS

Bhutan Foundation

Bhutan FOUNDATION The Bhutan Foundation (BF) is a non-profit organization which established its country office in Bhutan in January, 2007. The organization has a head office in Washington, DC and is working solely for the benefit of Bhutan and the Bhutanese people, and promoting a greater understanding between the two countries and beyond.

Guided by the principle of Gross National Happiness (GNH), the BF serves the people of Bhutan by supporting programmes that conserve the environment, promote sustainable development, contribute to good governance and preserve Bhutanese culture. It also seeks to increase awareness, knowledge, and understanding of Bhutan in the United States and around the world.

The primary objectives of the Bhutan Foundation includes fund-raising for Bhutanese not-for-profit organizations, promoting and enhancing friendship and understanding between individuals and organization in the United States and Bhutan and activity development support in finance, programme and human resources for Bhutanese not-for-profit organizations. In order to promote Bhutan, it also hosts several events to increase awareness, knowledge, and understanding in the United States.

The initiatives of the Foundation are carried out in partnership with other organizations and agencies within Bhutan.

Bhutan-Canada Foundation

The Bhutan Canada Foundation (BCF) is a charitable organization registered in Canada and managed by a Board of Directors with Sam Blyth as the Chair. The BCF was formally launched on 4 May 2009.

The current focus of BCF is the recruitment of Canadian teachers for the Ministry of Education, Royal Government of Bhutan. Under this programme, qualified Canadian teachers are posted at various schools depending on the needs.

The BCF also intends to enhance learning opportunities within classrooms with provision of educational supplies and aids. It also hopes to support various educational linkages between Bhutan and Canada for both secondary and post-secondary programmes.

The BCF is committed to improving education in Bhutan in partnership with the RGoB and continuing the Canadian association with Bhutan that started in the 1960s.

Save the Children

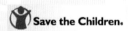

Save the Children is the member of Save the Children Alliance which is the world's largest non-religious, non-political independent movement for Children's Rights with a network of 27 national organizations working in 120 countries.

Save the Children started its first programme activities in Bhutan in 1982 in the remote community of

Edi in southern Zhemgang. Today, throughout 20 Dzongkhags, Save the Children is supporting programmes to provide access to quality education to needy children and in providing information, counselling and life skills education to thousands of adolescent and youth. It also supports improvement of teaching – learning process, capacity building and advocacy besides implementing adolescent development programs such as establishment of youth information centres, life skills education and career education and counselling, school-based parents education and awareness, and supporting research on adolescent and youth related issues.

More recently, Save the Children has been implementing street theatre and drama as a new medium of communication to convey to the youth on youth-related concerns. Besides cooperating with the government, Save the Children has also been partnering with local NGOs to support their initiatives to provide scholarships to the most disadvantaged children, to support youth development initiatives and to protect children, girls and women from violence.

Save the Children is also piloting early childhood care and develop-ment from 2010 onwards.

World Wildlife Fund (WWF)

 WWF-Bhutan began its conservation work as early as 1977 by providing training opportunities for the Bhutanese nationals. With the signing of MOU on 6th February 1992, between the Royal Government of Bhutan and the World Wildlife Fund, USA, the WWF Bhutan Programme became a full country programme.

Since then it has facilitated several conservation projects in Bhutan. The programme has focused on immediate conservation needs, such as establishing and managing a system of protected areas, direct species conservation, developing the nation's capacity to manage its natural resources by strengthening relevant institutions and promoting conservation education and public awareness.

Today, the Royal Government of Bhutan recognizes WWF as one of the closest international conservation partners in Bhutan

Agriculture plays a vital role in the Nation Economy and contributes about 64.2 percent to GDP

Robert Dompnier

Chapter 11

ECONOMY

Though the Bhutanese economy is one of the world's smallest, it has undergone significant changes since the inception of planned development from the 1960s. Within a short span of four decades, the country has been transformed from a predominantly subsistence agrarian economy to a modern trading economy with expanding regional and global economic ties. Bhutan's economy is based on agriculture, forestry, tourism and sale of hydroelectric power to India. In 2008, Bhutan's GDP per capita was USD 1,852 making it one of the fastest growing economies in South Asia.

Renewable Natural Resources

Renewable Natural Resources (RNR) which include agriculture, livestock and forestry play a vital role in the national economy. The contribution from the agriculture sector, including horticulture and livestock rearing to GDP was 18.9 percent in 2008 while its contribution towards employment activity was 64.2 percent in 2007. Exports of primary products from this sector accounted for around one-tenth of total exports in 2004 and contributes significantly in enhancing rural household food security, consumption and income.

The forestry sector contributes substantially to the national revenue through its wood and non-wood forest products. Forest wood is not only used for domestic consumption of fuel, fodder and timber but also for exports through various products such as furniture and handicraft items. Among the non-wood forest products such as medicinal plants, mushrooms, bamboos and spices, the products which fetch high value in the international market are cordyceps and masutake.

Forests have always played an important role in Bhutan's socio-economic development. Protection of watersheds and river catchments has contributed greatly to the development of hydropower. In addition, forests form an integral part of farming systems and is linked to agriculture and livestock development.

RNR will continue to be one of the largest contributors to national income and employment, particularly among the rural population.

Tourism

Since the opening of tourism in 1974, the country has witnessed significant expansion in the tourism industry. Today, it has become a major service industry that provides employment and generates valuable foreign exchange. In 2008, the total tourist arrivals touched 27,636 as compared to 287 visitors in 1974 and earned USD 38.8 million. The industry also figures consistently among the largest generators of convertible currency and is normally among the top three revenue earners. The tourism sector has also contributed towards growth of small and micro enterprises and strengthened Bhutan's image and identity around the world.

Tourism is projected to constitute 25 percent of the GDP by 2012 and it is anticipated that its revenues will have increased by 100 percent by 2012 and 150 percent by 2017. This means that the number of international arrivals will continue to grow. Despite the potential for higher foreign exchange earnings, Bhutan has followed a policy of regulating the number of tourists with its policy of 'high value low impact' tourism to avoid the possible adverse impacts of uncontrolled mass tourism on the country's fragile culture, heritage and environment.

Tourist in national costume with local Bhutanese

Geology and Mines

Bhutan is endowed with rich mineral resources that have allowed sustainable growth of a mineral based industry and export base. Mineral resource exploitation and value addition has helped generate employment and is contributing towards poverty alleviation. As of 2008 its contribution to GDP was 2.3 percent.

The mineral resources are one of the bases for private sector development, employment generation and generation of Rupee and hard currency reserve. The government gets benefit in terms of royalty of about Nu 150 million a year from these industries, apart from the 30 percent corporate income tax.

The minerals that are being currently exploited include limestone, dolomite, gypsum, coal, talc, chemical grade quartzite, marble and construction aggregates. A number of mineral based industries such as cement plants, ferro-silicon plants, gypsum based plants and a carbide plant are in operation and they depend on mining industry as the raw material. Many more mineral based industries are expected to be established in future.

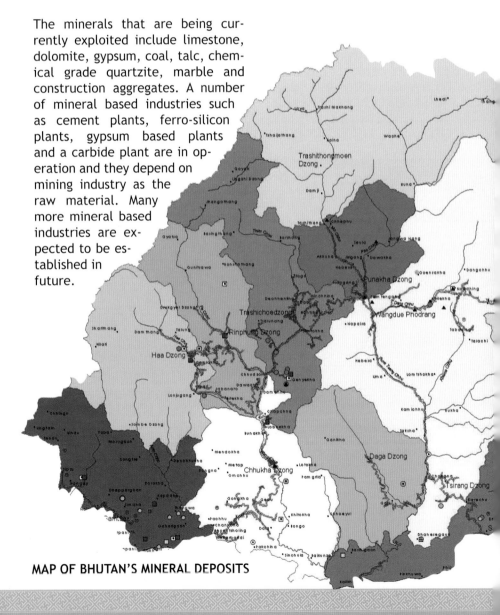

MAP OF BHUTAN'S MINERAL DEPOSITS

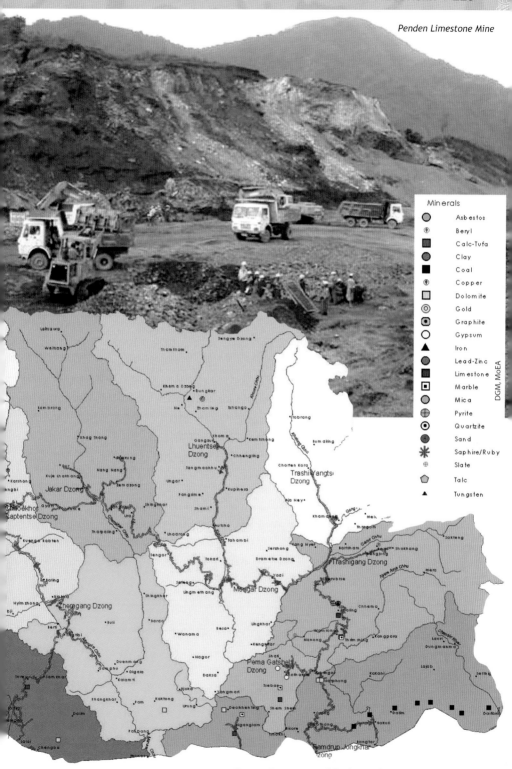

Penden Limestone Mine

Minerals

Asbestos
Beryl
Calc-Tufa
Clay
Coal
Copper
Dolomite
Gold
Graphite
Gypsum
Iron
Lead-Zinc
Limestone
Marble
Mica
Pyrite
Quartzite
Sand
Saphire/Ruby
Slate
Talc
Tungsten

DGM, MoEA

Source : Department of Geology and Mines, MoEA, RGoB, 2008

Energy

Bhutan is endowed with an enormous wealth of hydropower potential which is the backbone of the Bhutanese economy. The rapid altitudinal variations with swift flowing rivers has made Bhutan a natural haven for hydro power production with an estimated 30,000 MW hydropower potential out of which around 23,760 MW is techno-economically feasible. Currently, around 4.96 percent of this vast potential amounting to 1488.66 MW has been harnessed.

Hydropower energy production has been tapped effectively through a mutually beneficial and highly successful partnership with India. With the commissioning of the Chhukha Hydro Project in the 1980's, Bhutan substantially increased its electricity generation and became a significant exporter of electricity to India. The revenue earned from Chhukha (336MW), Tala (1020MW), Kurichhu (60MW) and Basochhu (64MW) has enabled the country to become economically more self-reliant. During the year 2008, the GDP contribution from the energy sector was 19.1 percent and the revenue contribution from the electricity sector alone was 42 percent of the national revenue. With further augmentation of the capacity by 2020, the energy sector is expected to dominate all other sectors in terms of its contribution to the GDP.

Bhutan also has a good potential for harnessing solar and other renewable energy resources besides hydropower. While electricity has provided the much needed revenue, the government has also prioritized network expansion in the country. It is expected that by 2013, the entire country will have access to electricity.

Kurichhu Hydro Power

Hon'ble Lyonchhen Jigmi Y. Thinley and Indian Prime Minister Dr. Manmohan Singh at the laying of the Foundation Stone of the Punatsangchhu-I Hydroelectric Project, 2008

Druk Green Power Corporation Limited

Druk Green Power Corporation Limited (Druk Green) was formed on 1 January 2008 with the merger of the Basochhu, Chhukha, and Kurichhu Hydro Power Corporations and placed under Druk Holding & Investments, the Holding Company on all government owned corporations. The formation of Druk Green placed the management of the most important resource of the Kingdom, generation of electricity from its rivers, under a single corporate entity. Prior to the formation of the Druk Green, these medium and large hydropower stations were operated and maintained as independent companies. Whereas the erstwhile Corporations were set up to operate and maintain the individual plants, one of the main objectives for amalgamating these plants and forming Druk Green was to draw on the synergies of the various plants and to enable better sharing of scarce resources. Apart from this, the driving force behind setting up of the Druk Green was for a single entity to represent the Royal Government of Bhutan's interests in the hydropower sector and to implement the RGoB's policy of accelerating hydropower development. In April 2009, Druk Green took over the Tala Hydropower Plant. Druk Green is also set to expand with its taking over of projects which are under construction and taking up of new projects on its own or through joint ventures with private and public partners.

Manufacturing and Industrial Sector

The manufacturing sector in Bhutan is mainly dependent on agro, forest and mineral based industries. The manufacturing sector which deals with mineral processing, agriculture and agro-processing, forestry and wood-based industries, livestock-based industries, transport, construction, light industries including power intensive industries contributed over 36 percent to GDP in 2006. The manufacturing sector received a boost to its growth after 1987/88. The sector witnessed a growth rate of 13 percent per annum during 2008 which is attributable largely to the increased output from some of the larger industries. The electricity sector is expected to grow in the next few years with the commissioning of more energy intensive industries, which are under various stages of construction.

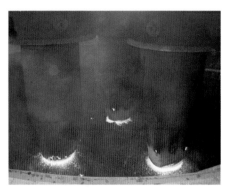

Mineral deposits that are commercially exploited include marble, dolomite, gypsum, limestone, ferro silicon, chemical grade quartzite, iron ore and slate. In addition, copper, gypsum, lead, tungsten, zinc, coal, beryl, mica, pyrites, tufa, and talc have been found, primarily through an exploration programme.

The industrial sector is in a nascent stage with predominantly small sized enterprises. A few large scale industries that have been established include cement, wood products, processed fruits, alcoholic beverages, calcium carbide, steel and ferro alloys.

Industrial establishment
(in numbers) December, 2009
Production & Manufacturing - 1,565
Services   - 17,907
Contracts   - 10,845
All sectors   - 30,317

Source: *Department of Industry, MoEA*

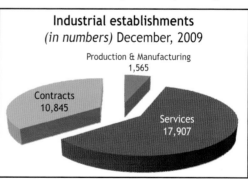

Industrial establishments
(in numbers) December, 2009

Production & Manufacturing
1,565

Contracts
10,845

Services
17,907

Trade

Bhutan has evolved from a closed economy to a trading nation. Today, business
houses employ over 20,000 people who
are directly or indirectly engaged in
retail or wholesale business. Bhutan's
strategic location between the two
most populous countries also offers im-
mense opportunity to become a more
vibrant trading nation.

Domestic Trade

The trade sector is currently limited to
trade in goods and is classified according to annual turnover. The service and
production/manufacturing are classified as the industrial sector.

Domestic trade in the country comprises a distribution system of wholesalers
and retailers. The wholesale and retail
regulations provide the enabling framework of the trading sector to grow under normal conditions of market competition.

The government has streamlined distribution of goods and ensured consumer
protection and fair competition. Since
April 2006, dramatic licensing reforms
were implemented to promote the
growth of trading enterprises. The micro trading category was de-licensed
to facilitate self employment. The distribution system in the country is being
developed under the international trading regimes.

Foreign Trade

Bhutan's volume of international trade
has increased significantly in recent
years. Trade is heavily concentrated
in the SAARC region and accounted for
86.62 percent of Bhutan's total trade in
the year 2008.

Gateway to Bhutan

At the bilateral level, Bhutan and India have enjoyed free trade since the two countries signed a Treaty of Friendship in 1949. A formal agreement on trade and commerce between the two countries was signed in 1972. In 2008, around 95.08 percent of Bhutan's total exports were to India, comprising electricity, cement, timber, wood products, minerals, cardamom, food products, potatoes, oranges, raw silk and alcohol. Over 73.80 percent of Bhutan's total imports are from India which includes petroleum products, rice, automobile and spares, machinery and fabrics.

Bhutan also has a Preferential Trading Arrangement (PTA) with Bangladesh and is pursuing further trade liberalization initiatives with Bangladesh through negotiations for deeper reductions in tariff, elimination of non-tariff barriers, and expansion of product coverage under the existing PTA. Bhutan also intends to negotiate PTAs at a bilateral level with Nepal and Thailand.

Bhutan is currently diversifying its trading base through the expansion of both bilateral and multilateral trading arrangements. Bhutan is currently a member of South Asian Free Trade Area Agreement (SAFTA) under SAARC and negotiations on BIMSTEC Free Trade Agreement and accession to WTO are at an advanced stage.

To support the growth of foreign trade, the government helps exporters with the distribution of information and organization of market research missions, trade missions and trade fairs. The government has undertaken market research for fruits and processed fruits in South East Asia, essential oils in Europe, handmade paper in Europe, traditional medicines in Europe and wood products in South East Asia.

Top Ten Exports
1. Electrical energy
2. Ferro-silicon
3. Of calcium
4. Other: Of refined copper wire
5. Manganese
6. Portland pozzolana cement
7. Vegetable fats & oils
8. Ordinary portland cement
9. Other of free cutting steel
10. Other (semi finished products of iron or non-alloys steel)

Top Ten Imports
1. Other light oils and preparations (HSD)
2. Motor and aviation spirit
3. Milled rice
4. Motor cars (> 2,500cc)
5. Ferrous products
6. Motor cars (≤ 1,500cc)
7. Manganese ores and concentrates
8. Coke and semi-coke of coal
9. Crude palmolein
10. Other (wood charcoal)

Other Export Potentials
According to a study conducted by the International Trade Center (ITC), there is a niche market for Bhutanese bottled water in Singapore, Japan, Taiwan and the United States. Among spices ginger, chillies, garlic and turmeric have a global market. There is also a large potential market for Bhutanese woven textiles which remain unexploited so far.

Bhutan and WTO
Bhutan joined as an observer to the World Trade Organization in April 1998 and formally applied for membership in October 1999. The memorandum of foreign trade regime was submitted in 2003 and initial offers on goods and services in 2005. Since then, Bhutan has maintained momentum on the accession process and held its fourth working party meeting on January 30, 2008. The country is in the last lap of the accession process.

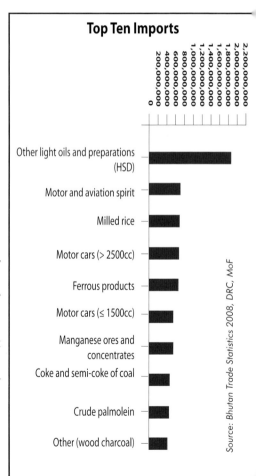

Top Ten Imports

Source: Bhutan Trade Statistics 2008, DRC, MoF

Trade Liberalization and Foreign Direct Investment Policy

Since the development of a formal private sector in 1987 the country has embarked on a programme to gradually liberalize trade, industries and financial policies to encourage and facilitate the development of the private sector. In 1996, it introduced customs tariff schedule, representing a significant reduction of customs duty on a range of imports from third countries. To support trade liberalization, the Foreign Exchange Regulations was introduced in 1997, removing several restrictions on foreign exchange transactions. An important element of the liberalization process has been the development of legislations and transparent rules and procedures.

Several legislations have been enacted and adopted to strengthen the legal framework. These, among others, include the Bankruptcy Act, 1999; Movable and Immovable Properties Act, 1999; Companies Act, 2000; Environmental Assessment Act, 2000; Sales Tax, Customs and Excise Act, 2000; Income Tax Act, 2001; Industrial Property Act, 2001; and the Copyright Act, 2001.

The RGoB approved the Foreign Direct Investment Policy (FDI) in 2002 and the FDI Rules and Regulation in 2005 but has been under revision since 2008. The policy adopts a positive list approach that encourages investment both in the services and manufacturing sectors. It is envisaged that with the opening of the economy to FDI, it will stimulate private sector investment and contribute to the growth of the economy.

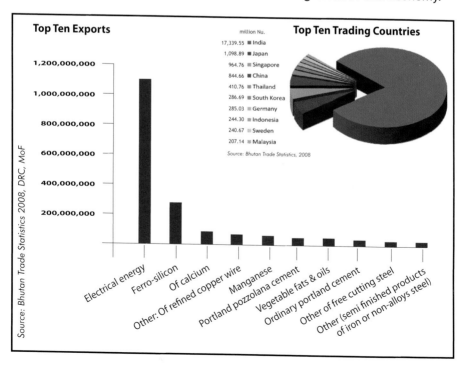

Top Ten Exports

Source: Bhutan Trade Statistics 2008, DRC, MoF

million Nu.

Top Ten Trading Countries

17,339.55	India
1,098.89	Japan
964.76	Singapore
844.66	China
410.76	Thailand
286.69	South Korea
285.03	Germany
244.30	Indonesia
240.67	Sweden
207.14	Malaysia

Source: Bhutan Trade Statistics, 2008

Electrical energy · Ferro-silicon · Other: Of calcium · Of refined copper wire · Manganese · Portland pozzolana cement · Vegetable fats & oils · Ordinary portland cement · Other of free cutting steel · Other (semi finished products of iron or non-alloys steel)

Druk Holding and Investments

Druk Holding and Investments (DHI) is a government owned Holding Company established by the Royal Government of Bhutan (RGoB) pursuant to the Royal Charter issued on 11 November 2007 in order to fully or partly own the shares of commercially oriented companies that used to be under the direct ownership of the Ministry of Finance. It is incorporated as per the Companies Act of the Kingdom of Bhutan 2000.

As the commercial arm of the Government, DHI's primary function is to hold and manage the existing and future commercial investments of the RGoB for the long-term benefit of the people of Bhutan and ensure a steady flow of dividends to the Ministry of Finance (MoF), RGoB. DHI is also required to lead, complement and spearhead the growth of a dynamic private sector.

Currently, DHI owns some of the largest corporations of Bhutan. DHI's portfolio includes six listed companies and eight unlisted companies in sectors such as hydropower generation, electricity transmission and distribution, banking, insurance, airline, telecom, trading, real estate, and minerals and natural resources. The total net worth (book value) of DHI Owned Companies (100% owned and BOB) is USD 1.246 billion and market capitalization of listed companies is USD 35.805 million.

DHI companies seeks to promote the competitiveness of Bhutan's economy by transforming into highly efficient and productive world class companies that strive for excellence, while safeguarding and enhancing the national wealth through prudent investments, and assisting in the creation of a strong dynamic economy.

Developments at DHI companies

Since its establishment, several initiatives have been undertaken by DHI to transform the functioning of the DHI companies into highly efficient and productive companies.

• Each year, Annual Compacts are signed with fully owned companies outlining the targets and deliverables of these companies for the year in terms of financial, operational, corporate governance, customer services and new initiatives. These Compacts are closely monitored and a Performance Based Variable Allowance is provided based on the achievements of the Compact targets.

• Over the last two years, DHI companies have provided increasing annual remittances to the MoF while at the same time DHI continues looking for new investment opportunities in areas such as mining and natural resources, IT Parks, real estate and domestic air service with many more under consideration. To fund its investments DHI is exploring new and innovative ways for raising capital at commercially competitive rates in both the domestic and international capital markets.

• DHI with two of its major companies namely, Druk Green Power Corporation (DGPC) and Bhutan Power Corporation (BPC) has adopted the SAP Enterprise Resource Planning (ERP) System Solution with scope for adoption by other DHI subsidiaries in the future.

• DHI has also in consultation with its companies issued Guideline on HR and compensation Rules for its companies to ensure that the rules are consistent with modern corporate practices.

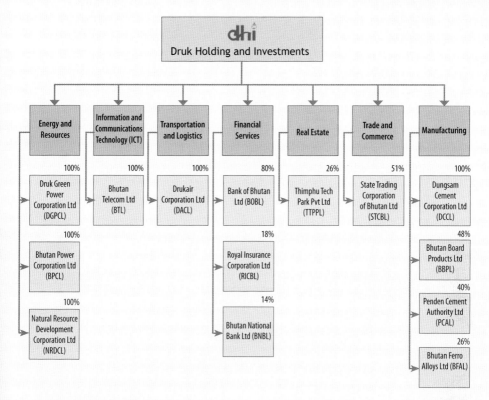

- BPC and DGPC have very significant roles to play in the energy sector. BPC is mandated with the goal of electricity for all by 2013 while DGPC is expected to play a significant role in achieving the 10,000 MW target of the government by 2020. Bhutan Telecom is expected to play a major role in extending telecommunication services to all the Gewogs and NRDC has to ensure that key construction materials like timber, sand and stones are provided at affordable rates and adequate quantities.

- DHI is also engaged in the implementation of major projects such as Dungsam Cement Project, Dagachhu Hydropower Project (first FDI in hydropower and a CDM project) and Thimphu Tech-Park (the first IT Park and SEZ Project in Bhutan).

- Recognizing the key role of private sector in the economic development of the country and in keeping with DHI's mandate to conscientiously lead and stimulate private sector development, DHI is finalizing a DHI/Private Sector Partnership Framework (DPP).

- To share best practices, experiences, ideas and exploit synergies amongst the DHI companies, a CEOs' Round Table Meeting is held quarterly.

- As the commercial arm of the Government, DHI is expected to be involved in the major projects to be initiated by the Government. At present, one mega project that the DHI is involved in is the development of the Education City where the Government has indicated that it will provide DHI with 1,000 acres of land as its equity.

Kana Tsho literally meaning "black and white lake" at Laya

Leki Dorji

Chapter 12

ENVIRONMENT

Bhutan belongs to the eastern Himalayas which forms part of the ten global bio-diversity 'hotspots' in the world and one of the 221 global endemic bird areas. Almost three fourths of the land area is covered by forests of alpine, temperate and sub-tropical species, that are a natural habitat for a diversity of flora and fauna. Its various ecosystems harbour some of the most exotic species of the eastern Himalayas.

Considering its size, Bhutan probably has the greatest biodiversity among Asian countries. The country has received international acclaim for its commitment to the maintenance of this biodiversity, reflected in its decision to maintain at least 60 percent of the land area under forest cover for all times to come and designate about half (51 percent) of its territory as protected areas (strict nature reserves, nature parks, wild life sanctuary, biological corridors and conservation areas)

Bhutan's long commitment to the maintenance of biological diversity and productivity is rooted in its understanding of the importance of forest systems to the survival strategies of remote and isolated communities, its beliefs and customs, and understanding of sustainable development. The country has placed environmental conservation at the core of its development strategy and is treated as a set of concerns that must be mainstreamed in its overall approach to development planning and must be strengthened by law.

The first 'modern' legislation enacted in 1969 was replaced by the 'Forest and Nature Conservation Act, 1995 which is specifically aimed at protecting the country's forests and wildlife. Since then many laws enacted are directly or indirectly related to the conservation of the environment.

Robert Dompnier

Rhododendron

Robert Dompnier

Rhododendron

Robert Dompnier

Robert Dompnier

Cherry Blossom

Robert Dompnier

Rhododendron

Robert Dompnier

Robert Dompnier

Rhuem Nobile

Gem Tshering, NCD, MoA

Flora

More than 60 percent of the common plant species of the eastern Himalayas can be found within Bhutan. The wealth of floral species include 5,400 vascular plants, 360 species of Orchids, 46 species of Rhododendrons, Junipers, Magnolia, Blue Poppies, Edelweiss, Gentians, Primulas, Artemisia, Daphne, Giant Rhubarb, carnivorous plants, high-altitude plants and over 500 species of medicinal plants. Botanists consider the entire country as one beautiful park.

Fauna

Bhutan is haven to a wide range of animals. Along its southern border, subtropical forests have Golden Langur, Pigmy Hog, Elephants, Tiger, Gaur, Wild Water Buffalo, Hog Deer, Clouded Leopard, Swamp Deer and other mammals and birds characteristic of Indo-Malayan species. The high Himalayan fauna include the Blue Sheep, Yaks, Takin, Snow Leopard, Wolf, Marmot and Musk Deer which are some of the species found in the high altitude. Temperate zone is home to Tiger, Leopard, Goral, Himalayan Black Bear, Red Panda, Sambar, Wild Pig, Barking Deer and the rare Golden Langur which is endemic to Bhutan, and other species characteristic of the pale arctic realm. The species of fauna are abundant because the great majority of Bhutanese, for religious reasons, neither hunt nor fish.

The rich forests of Bhutan harbours an estimated 770 species of birds which include the Himalayan Griffon, the unique high altitude Wader, the Ibisbill, the spectacular Hornbill, Barbets, Sunbirds, Fulvettas, Yuhinas, Cuckoos, and many more. Bhutan has about 464 resident bird species. These non resident birds are migratory, moving up and down the mountains depending upon the seasons and weather conditions. Around 50 species are known to be winter migrants. These include ducks, Waders, birds of prey, Thrushes, Finches and Buntings. About 40 species of summer visitors

Blue sheep in Jigme Dorji National Park

Rufous-necked Hornbill in Royal Manas National Park

or partial migrants to Bhutan include Cuckoos, Swifts, Bee-eaters, Warblers, Flycatchers and Drongos. The country has more than 28 species of internationally endangered birds. They are Pallas Fish Eagle, White-bellied Heron, Satyr Tragopan, Grey-bellied Tragopan, Ward's Trogaon, Blyth's Kingfisher, Yellow-rumped Honeyguide, Rufous throated Wren Babbler, Red-headed Parrotbill, Chestnut-breasted Partridge, Ward's Trogon, Wood Snipe, Dark Rumped Swift, Grey-crowned Prinia and the Beautiful Nuthatch all of which breed in Bhutan. The country also has a great variety of endangered species like the Satyr Pheasant, Peacock Pheasant, Raven and the Rufous-necked Hornbill. Greater spotted Eagle, Baer's Pochard, Imperial Eagle and Hodgson's Bush chat are also found. The country is also an important wintering ground for the vulnerable Black-necked Crane.

Nature Reserve and Biodiversity

As Bhutan is committed to the preservation and protection of its rich environment, various efforts of the government include afforestation and re-forestation programmes on barren, degraded and clear-felled areas; extension and education programmes to promote people's participation in the protection and management of forest resources; implementation of pilot schemes to promote social forestry in the form of community and private forests in several parts of the country.

Further, Bhutan has set aside approximately 51 percent of the country's total land area as national parks, nature reserves, wildlife sanctuaries and conservation areas constituting Bhutan's protected area system. This includes four national parks, four wildlife sanctuaries and one strict nature reserve, enriched with vascular plants, orchids, rhododendrons, medicinal plants and other rare and endemic species. Almost 9.53 percent of the country has been declared as biological corridors in which wildlife sanctuaries and a chain of nature reserves connect the protected areas to ensure that the wild animals and birds can move freely within a vast natural range The corridors form a "Gift to the Earth" from the people of Bhutan. Nine national parks and wildlife sanctuaries have some of the rarest animals in the world and form a haven for a number of the world's rare and endangered species.

Further, over 4,000 sq. km area in the northern frontier of the country was declared as the new national park in 2008. Each of these parks and sanctuaries has its own special character and are home to endangered animals, birds and plants.

> *Bhutan is one of very few developing countries where the natural resource base remains intact.*

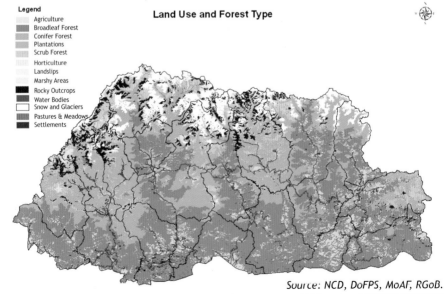

Legend
- Agriculture
- Broadleaf Forest
- Conifer Forest
- Plantations
- Scrub Forest
- Horticulture
- Landslips
- Marshy Areas
- Rocky Outcrops
- Water Bodies
- Snow and Glaciers
- Pastures & Meadows
- Settlements

Land Use and Forest Type

Source: NCD, DoFPS, MoAF, RGoB.

National Protected Areas and Biological Corridors of Bhutan

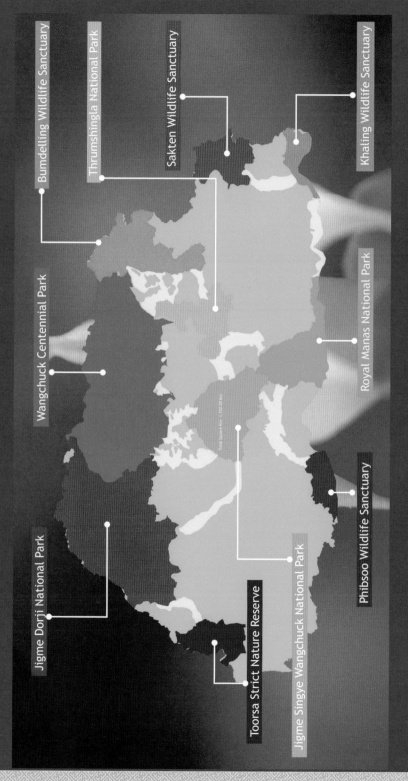

Jigme Dorji National Park

Wangchuck Centennial Park

Bumdelling Wildlife Sanctuary

Thrumshingla National Park

Sakten Wildlife Sanctuary

Khaling Wildlife Sanctuary

Royal Manas National Park

Phibsoo Wildlife Sanctuary

Jigme Singye Wangchuck National Park

Toorsa Strict Nature Reserve

Biological Corridors

Source: NCD, DoFPS, MoAF, RGoB.

Faunal Diversity in the

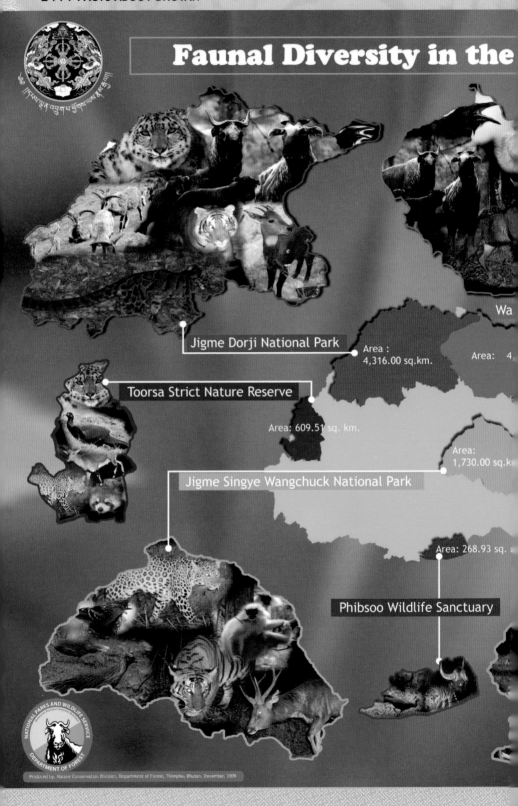

Jigme Dorji National Park
Area : 4,316.00 sq.km.

Wa

Area : 4,

Toorsa Strict Nature Reserve

Area: 609.51 sq. km.

Area: 1,730.00 sq.k

Jigme Singye Wangchuck National Park

Area: 268.93 sq.

Phibsoo Wildlife Sanctuary

Produced by: Nature Conservation Division, Department of Forest, Thimphu, Bhutan, December, 2009

otected Areas of Bhutan

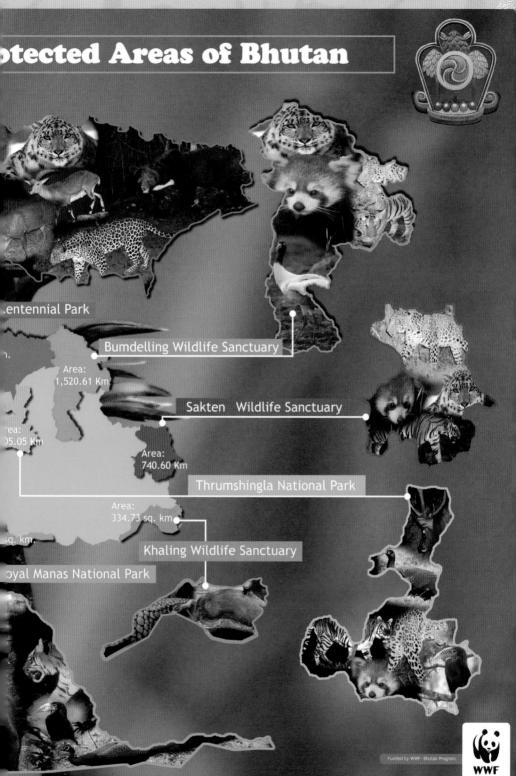

entennial Park

Bumdelling Wildlife Sanctuary

Area:
1,520.61 Km.

Sakten   Wildlife Sanctuary

ea:
5.05 Km

Area:
740.60 Km

Thrumshingla National Park

Area:
334.73 sq. km

Khaling Wildlife Sanctuary

oyal Manas National Park

Funded by WWF- Bhutan Program

WWF

Overview of the Protected System

Name of protected area	Area in square km	Dzongkhags (Districts)	Ecosystem representation
Bumdelling Wildlife Sanctuary	1,520.61	Trashiyangtse, Lhuentse, Mongar	Upland broad forests, winter roosting area of black-necked crane
Jigme Dorji National Park	4,316	Gasa, Thimphu, Paro, Punakha	Habitat for takin, snow leopard, blue sheep, rare alpine plant species
Jigme Singye Wangchuck National Park	1,730	Trongsa, Zhemgang, Wangduephodrang, Sarpang, Tsirang	Pristine upland broad leaf forests, habitat for clouded leopard, tiger
Khaling Wildlife Sanctuary	334.73	Samdrup Jongkhar	Temperature forests, only habitat of pigmy hog
Phipsoo Wildlife Sanctuary	268.93	Sarpang, Dagana	Natural sal forest, habitat for spotted deer
Royal Manas National Park	1,057	Zhemgang, Sarpang	Sub-tropical forest, habitat for tiger, elephants, leopard, golden langur
Sakten Wildlife Sanctuary	740.60	Trashigang, Samdrup Jongkhar	Pristine mixed coniferous forests, highest number of rhododendron plant species
Thrumsingla National Park	905.05	Bumthang, Mongar, Lhuentse, Zhemgang	Old growth fir forests with varieties of rhododendron, prime habitat for red panda, tragopan and monal pheasant
Toorsa Strict Nature Reserve	609.51	Haa, Samtse	Pristine temperature forests
Wangchuck Centennial Park	4,914	Gasa, Wangduephodrang, Bumthang, Trongsa and Lhuentse	Alpine and temperate forests, habitat of snow leopard, tiger, takin & Tibetan wolf

Source: NCD, DoFPS, MoAF, RGoB.

The National Environment Commission

The National Environment Commission (NEC) was first established as a Secretariat under the Planning Commission in October 1989 with the directives to incorporate environmental issues into the overall development planning process of the country. In 1992, it was de-linked from the Planning Commission with the objective to institutionalize environmental impact assessments for all development projects. Today, NEC is a high level multi-sectoral body and the highest decision making and coordinating body on all the matters relating to the protection, conservation and improvement of the natural environment.

With a mission to maintain a sustainable path of enlightened development through preservation of the environmental wealth of the Kingdom, the NEC is mandated to develop, review and revise environmental policies, plans and programmes; formulate, review and revise environment related Laws/Acts and monitor enforcement of the same; mainstream environment into the country's developmental policies, plans and programmes; promote environmental awareness amongst Bhutanese; adopt, review and revise environmental standards for the country; monitor ambient air and water quality and land-use changes promote and ensure an efficient system of gathering and sharing environmental information; promote and conduct environmental research; coordinate and facilitate the implementation of bilateral and multilateral environmental agreements, conventions, treaties or declarations; coordinate and monitor cross-sectoral issues related to water, forestry and mineral resources and waste management in the country.

Royal Society for Protection of Nature

Founded as a citizen based non-profit organization in 1987, the Royal Society for Protection of Nature (RSPN) is a primary Civil Society partner to the RGoB in the conservation and sustainable development of Bhutan. With the mission to inspire personal responsibility and active involvement of the people of Bhutan in the conservation of the Kingdom's environment through education, research and sustainable livelihood opportunities, RSPN programmes are based on its five year strategic plan and focuses primarily on the following thematic areas:

i. Environment Conservation and Sustainable Livelihoods programme that seeks to strengthen strong linkages between the environment and economic welfare of communities through environmentally friendly livelihood options. This programme has increased significance in the context of climate change and its impacts on communities.

ii. Education, communications and advocacy programme that aim to promote public education, awareness, and participation that instill personal responsibility and action for the environment.

iii. Research programme is aimed at enhancing RSPN's professional and scientific information base for backstopping its conservation and advocacy activities.

The organization invests in national and international networking and collaboration with partners, donors and stakeholders for realization of its goals and objectives. Institutional strengthening and capacity building remain priorities for the organization. Through its Environmental Resource Centre (ERC), RSPN seeks to be a major environmental resource for its members and general public.

Bhutan Trust Fund for Environmental Conservation is the developing world's first environmental trust fund. It was established in 1991 as a collaborative venture between the Royal Government of Bhutan, United Nations Development Program, and World Wildlife Fund. In May 1996, the Fund was legally incorporated in Bhutan under Royal Charter. The Fund is governed by the Royal Charter, and a Management Board that was fully Bhutanised in May 2001. The direct leadership of His Majesty King Jigme Khesar Namgyel Wangchuck, as Chairman of the Board, has ensured the Fund remains an effective, apolitical conservation grant making organization providing core, long-term funding to conserve Bhutan's natural heritage. In return, Bhutan has pledged to maintain 60 percent of its total area under forest cover

in perpetuity, a commitment since enshrined in the Constitution of Bhutan. The endowment was capitalized with USD20 million, through a USD10 million grant from the Global Environment Facility, and matching contributions from the governments of Bhutan, Denmark, Finland, the Netherlands, Norway, and Switzerland, and World Wildlife Fund. It has since grown to USD40 million, through prudent, pioneering investments in the international capital markets. To date, the Fund has spent USD9 million in several successful conservation interventions and general operations.

Jangsa Animal Saving Trust was established as a non-profit charitable trust which was initiated by a few citizens to cover the expenses relating to the establishment and maintenance of the Buddhist practice of *tsethar* (to save the lives of animals). Presently, the trust maintains about 600 bulls, 40 yaks, 137 pigs, 23 sheep, 2 goats and 9 ducks in the eastern and northern regions of the Kingdom of Bhutan. There are also 10 goats, 2 buffaloes and 2 pigs cared for in a village near Kalimpong in the hills of West Bengal, India. A further 58 bulls have found a home in Siliguri, India. Finally, at the monastery in Kalimpong, 4 bulls and a cow have also found refuge from being slaughtered.

Masagang 7194m
Teri Gang 7094m
Jaikangphu Gang 7194m
Gang 7094

Tsendagang 6994m
GASA

Gangchenta 6794m

Jichu Drake 6794m
Khang Bum 6494m

Jomolhari 7314m

Mo Chhu

495m

Rinchen zoe 5

PARO
PUNAKHA
WANGDI PHODRANG

Dochula 3116m
Punatsang Chhu
Dang Chhu
Pelela 3

Wang Chhu

THIMPHU

Cheleyla 3822m
Haa Chhu
Pachhu
Lawa

HAA

Amo Chhu

SAMTSE
Toorsa

Daga Chhu
DAGANA
TSIRANG
SAR

Wang Chhu
CHHUKHA

Shinchula 1600m
Sankosh Chhu

MAJOR RIVERS, GLACIER AND LAKES

Legend

— International boundary

— River

Glacier and Lakes

Tsorin, one of the many brilliant coloured lakes in Lunana

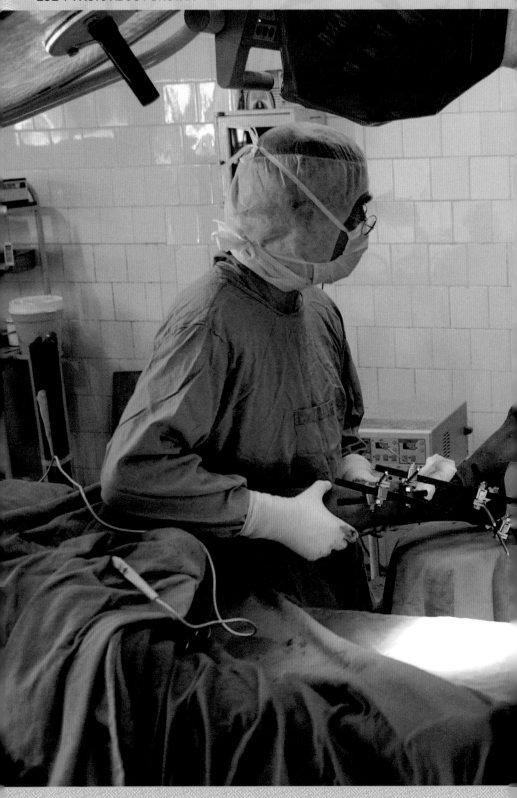

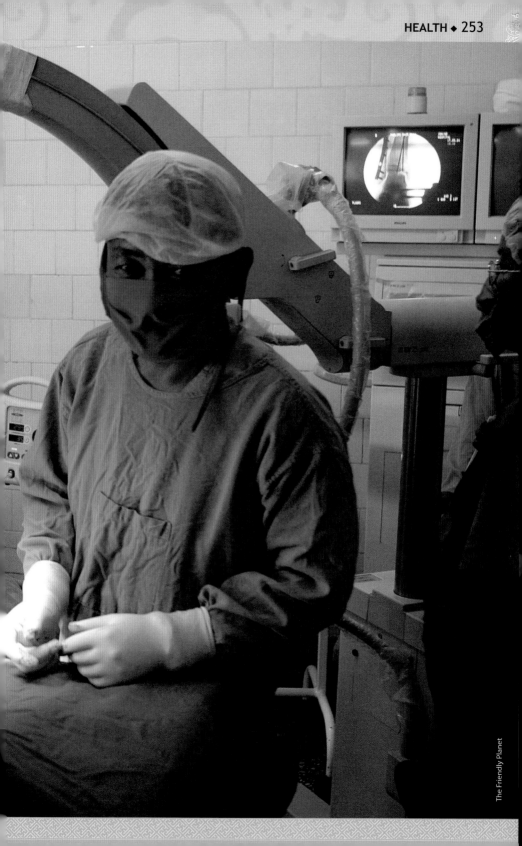

Chapter 13

HEALTH

Modern Health Care

Modern health care was introduced in Bhutan in 1961. Until then, the people relied on a rich indigenous medicinal system known was *So-Wa-Rigpa* (wisdom of health) for preventive and curative measures. Buddhist rituals and the village shaman played an important role in health. In the last three decades, the country saw great strides in the health sector. In 1961, there were only two hospitals (Thimphu and Samtse) and 11 dispensaries (Haa, Paro, Trongsa, Bumthang, Trashigang, Sipsoo, Tsirang, Samdrup Jongkhar, Kalikhola and Dagapela) and only two trained doctors in the whole country. Communicable diseases were widespread, and more than one-half of the children died at birth or within the first few years of their lives. Smallpox epidemic sometimes wiped out whole villages. In some parts of the country, malaria claimed hundreds of lives each year, while in others diseases such as leprosy deformed and ultimately killed many people. Water supplies were largely confined to springs and streams.

Physical infrastructure today consists of four-tiered network of National Referral Hospital, Regional Referral Hospital, District Hospital and Basic Health Units. Currently, the country has more than 31 hospitals, 178 Basic Health Units and 519 Outreach Clinics (ORCs). The national health care delivery system is characterized by the central level being responsible for administration, training and major referrals and the Dzongkhag managing the delivery of preventive and curative services to the population through a network of hospitals. Rural health care is provided through Basic Health Units staffed with a health assistant, nurse midwife and a basic health worker.

Since 1961, the health status of the population has remarkably improved with over 90 percent health coverage with basic services. Over 83.2 percent of the population have access to clean drinking water and there is 90.8 percent sanitation coverage. There has also been dramatic decrease in mortality and morbidity. As a result, the life expectancy of 33 years in 1960 has risen to 66 today. The population growth rate has decreased from 3.1 percent in 1994 to 1.8 percent in 2005. Around 66.3 percent of women in labour are attended by trained personnel.

Bhutan leads South Asia in the use of oral rehydration therapy for preventing deaths from diarrhoea and it was the first country in the region to iodize its entire salt supply, which has resulted in the virtual elimination of iodine deficiency. Bhutan has achieved universal child immunization and diseases such as polio, neonatal tetanus and diphtheria have been virtually eliminated, while malaria and leprosy are under control today.

These positive developments have in part been made possible by remarkable progress in the health sector.

Bhutan considers it's system of traditional medicine as an integral part of the health system. The indigenous system is integrated in to the present health care delivery system and patient have equal choice for traditional or modern medicine from any of the hospitals or BHUs in the country.

	(In numbers) 2009
Hospitals	- 30
BHUs	- 178
Traditional Medicine Hospital	- 1
Traditional Medicine Units	- 26
Doctors	- 171
Nurses	- 567
ORCs	- 519

Source: Ministry of Health, RGoB

Bhutan Health Trust Fund

As Bhutan's development philosophy lies the physical and spiritual well-being of its people within a safe and secure environment, investments in the social sector have always been accorded the highest priority. In the vital sector of health, the key concern of the Government of Bhutan is to enhance the accessibility and quality of primary health care services against rising costs and competing needs. To provide a dependable alternative for financing the priority needs of vaccines, essential drugs and needles and syringes, Bhutan Health Trust Fund (BHTF) was initiated in 1997 by former Health Minister, Lyonpo Sangay Ngedup. The BHTF was formally launched at WHO Headquarters in Geneva on 12 May 1998.

Lyonpo Sangay Ngedup and his team during the "Move for Health Walk", that covered over 500 kms within a period of 16 days that generated more than one million US Dollars for the Bhutan Health Trust Fund

Traditional Medicine Services

Bhutan's traditional medicine services is called *So-Wa-Rigpa* which incorporates ancient medical practices connected with magic and religion. Despite the introduction of modern medicine, *So-Wa-Rigpa*, has retained its role in providing health care. Ever since its introduction in the 17th century, *So-Wa-Rigpa* has played a significant role, along with spiritual remedies offered by religious institutions. It was recognized as the official medical tradition and integrated into the health system in 1967.

Access to traditional medicine in the country has greatly increased with 38 traditional *Drungtshos* (doctors) providing traditional medicinal services in all Dzongkhags of the country.

The rich tradition of indigenous medicine, based primarily on herbal treatment, is kept alive by the National Traditional Medicine Hospital, established in 1998 at Thimphu and 26 traditional medicine units scattered across Bhutan. Several forms of treatment are applied in traditional medicine, including indigenous surgical procedures such as *gtar* (blood letting), *bsregs* (cauterization), *gser khap* (acupressure by a golden

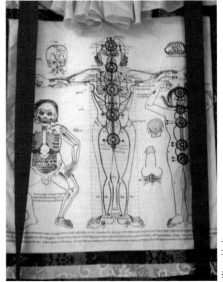

The inner mandala of subtle essence and energy currents used in tantric practice as the basis for spiritual transformation

Lily Wangchhuk

Acupressure by a golden needle is very effective in treating vertigo

Applying hot compression on pressure point to treat tinnitus

Herbal steam application

needle), *tshug* (cauterization with instruments of different herbal compounds), *dugs* (applying heat or cold to parts of the body), *byugspa* (medicated oil massage), *sman-chu* (stone-heated bath), *tsha-chu* (bath at hot spring) and *lum* (vapour treatment).

Diagnosis is made by the physician mainly through the reading of the pulse. Using the *So-Wa-Rigpa* method, it is possible for physicians to detect diseases of any organ by reading the pulse. The eyes, tongue and urine are also examined for signs which helps the diagnosis.

The components of traditional medicine include plants, minerals, animal parts, precious metals and gems which are all used in different combinations to make over three hundred medicines in the form of pills, tablets, powders, ointments and syrups. These traditional medicines are produced entirely for domestic consumption, though there is a plan to eventually export them in the future.

Various ingredients which includes plants, minerals, precious metals and gems are used for preparation of traditional herbal medicines.

>x cauterization treatment for ief from Lung disorders

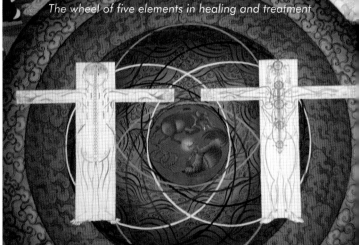

The wheel of five elements in healing and treatment

Morning Prayer at Laya Primary School

Chapter 14

EDUCATION

Until the late 1950s, only monastic education was available in the country. Those fortunate enough to live near Dzongs and monasteries could choose to send their sons for instruction by monks and *gomchens* (lay practitioners), who sought to enlighten their pupils not only by teaching reading and writing but also through instruction in poetry, ethics and morality. For the vast majority of people, education was either simply unavailable or a luxury that had no place in family survival strategies. Few Bhutanese were able to read and write, and most of those who could, were men. It was not until 1968 that the first 20 Bhutanese completed high school education within the country.

While monastic education continues to play an important role in Bhutan, modern education has been promoted and expanded since the first Five-Year Plan in 1961. The education structure today can be divided into general education, monastic education and non-formal education. However, general education is by far the biggest and is commonly seen as the only education structure. Students

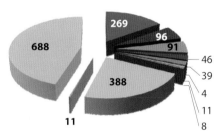

Summary of schools, institutes and centres

- 269 Community primary schools
- 96 Primary schools
- 91 Lower secondary schools
- 46 Middle secondary schools
- 39 Higher secondary schools
- 4 Special institutes
- 11 Tertiary education
- 8 Vocational institute
- 388 Monastic education institutes
- 11 Day care centre
- 688 Non formal centre

Source: Annual Education Statistics 2009, MoE, RGoB

Late Lopen Sangay Wangchhuck

The first batch of students of Paro Gaupay School, 1958 seen with their teachers, Lopen Sangay Wangchhuck and Lopen Sherub. Many of these students went on to become Government Ministers, Senior Government Officials and successful businessmen

enrol in monastic education at different stages in their life. For those who could not attend or complete general or monastic education, basic literacy courses are offered all over the country in non-formal education centres. For adults who wish to complete their basic education or class XII, the government has initiated a continuing education programme.

Since its introduction, the government has been able to expand the modern education system from primary to tertiary level. From just 11 schools with 400 students in 1961, the education system today includes 1,651 schools and institutes with 197,832 students/learners and 8,418 teachers, lecturers, instructors, trainers, *lopens* and care-givers. The literacy rate is 59.5 percent with 69 percent male and 49 percent female. The gross primary enrolment rate is also increasing annually at a rate of 4 percent. Among the factors

responsible for rising enrolment are increased awareness of the value of education among the parents and the government's policy of ensuring that all children enjoy access to basic education (Class X or 11 years of schooling) within their Dzongkhags.

In modern Bhutan, education is also accessible to everyone and every child has the opportunity to join school and graduate from class X, XII and college. All schools are co-educational and academic session is from February to December with long winter vacation. Students are provided with free tuition, textbooks, sports equipment, meals and boarding facilities where required. Students in rural schools are even provided with free stationery.

Over the years, moral science and value education have also been given special attention within the education programme with the introduction of school-based career education and counselling to help the youth cope with the multitude of issues that beset them. School-based scout's programmes assist youth in achieving their full physical, intellectual, social and spiritual potential.

General Education Structure

The formal educational structure in Bhutan consists of seven years of Primary Education (including Pre-Primary) and 6 years of Secondary Education, comprising two years each at the lower, middle and higher secondary levels. This is followed by a three-year and four-year Degree Programme at Sherubtse College, the Institute of Language and Cultural Studies and a four-year Degree Programme at the Royal Bhutan Institute of Technology and the two Colleges of Education at Paro and Samtse.

Basic education of 11 years, up to class X, is free and available to every citizen in the country. Promotion from one class to the next is based on a system of continuous assessment, maximum attendance and term examinations.

Schooling System

Primary Education

The minimum official entry age into the formal education system is six at the pre-primary (PP) level. Primary schooling (PP-VI) is provided in the community, primary, lower secondary and middle secondary schools.

Secondary School

Lower secondary schooling (classes VII and VIII) is provided in the lower, middle and some higher secondary schools while classes IX-X are provided in the middle and higher secondary schools. There are presently 16 higher secondary schools which offer classes XI and XII. Access to post-basic education (XI) is based on the students' performance in the national examinations at the end of class X. Those who do not qualify for higher secondary education repeat or seek admission in vocational training institutes. Others, who can afford the fees, go abroad to pursue their further studies or join the private higher secondary schools that offer class XI.

The Friendly Planet

Vocational and Higher Education

Sherubtse College, the Colleges of Education at Paro and Samtse, the Institute of Language and Culture Studies, the National Institute of Health Sciences, the College of Science and Technology, Royal Thimphu College, and the National Traditional Medicine Hospital offer higher education in Bhutan.

The government also offers scholarships for class XII passed Bhutanese students to pursue undergraduate programmes outside the country in the various fields of science, engineering, law, medicine, education and information technology, including the arts and humanity areas as prioritized by the government.

India and Bhutan have been closely associated on the educational front for decades. Many Bhutanese youth study in Indian schools and colleges under various scholarship schemes offered by the government of India.

Continuing Education

The government introduced the continuing education programme in 2006 to enable those individuals who dropped out of school to complete the education. Currently the programme allows qualifying individuals to attend classes IX-XII as part-time students in selected private schools at subsidized rates. There are plans to further expand this programme downwards to allow more individuals to avail of continuing education opportunities. This programme ensures life-long learning and enables individuals to upgrade their qualifications and improve their career prospects.

Adult Education

In 1992, an adult literacy programme was introduced for those individuals who were unable to attend formal school or had to drop out early from school. The number of non formal education centers has increased

The Friendly Planet

from 6 in 1992 with 300 learners to 688 centers with 13,160 learners in 2009.

Vocational and Skills Training

The government further provides vocational training, skill development programmes for students who do not qualify for higher education. The training programme is focussed on developing and improving skills for employment which includes certificate courses, apprenticeships, and short-duration training that offers good prospects for wage employment, or provide a base for self-employment. Some examples of vocational courses are traditional arts and crafts, plumbing, carpentry and construction.

The Kingdom stretches across all climatic zones; from the sub-tropical jungles in the south, to the moderate heights of 2000 – 2500m in the centre and up to the alpine world of the towering Himalayas and glaciers of the north.

ANNUAL PRECIPITATION

Legend
Precipitation (mm)

< 400
401 - 800
801 - 1600
1601 - 2500
2501 - 3500
> 3500

Thanza
Gasa
Lhedang
Thunkar
Yangothang
Lhuntshi
Trashiyangtse
Paro
Wangdi Phodrang
Tongsa
Bumthang
Thimphu
Chuzom
Mongar
Tashigang
Shemgang
Bangbay
Pemagatsel
Phuntsholing
Sarbhang
Deylegphug
Manas
Samdrup

Chapter 15

GEOGRAPHIC REGIONS

Dzongkhags in Western Bhutan:

Chhukha

Thimphu

Paro

Punakha

Wangduephodrang

Haa

Gasa

WESTERN BHUTAN

Seven Dzongkhags form the region — Chhukha at 2240m, Thimphu at 2,320m, Paro at 2,280m, Punakha at 220m, Wangduephodrang at 1,240m, Haa at 2,700m and Gasa at 2770m.

The Black Mountains at 4,200m have traditionally marked the boundary between western and central Bhutan.

CHHUKHA

Altitude 2240m

Chhukha Dzongkhag was established in April 1987. The Dzongkhag has one Thromde, one Dungkhag and 11 Gewogs which includes Chapcha, Bjacho, Bongo, Getena, Geling, Dungna, Metakha, Logchina, Darla, Sampheling/ Bhalujhora and Phuentsholing. The major town is Phuentsholing which is the main entry point for imports and is the commercial hub of the country. Chhukha is also the commercial and the financial capital of Bhutan with Chhukha Hydro Power Plant, Bhutan's oldest, completed in 1985 and the Tala Hydro Power Plant commissioned recently. They are the key sources of national income. This comparative advantage has fostered the rapid economic growth of the Dzongkhag.

Chhukha Dzongkhag has a total area of 1,875.65 sq. km with altitude ranging from 160m to 4480m. Only around nine percent of the total area of the Dzongkhag is cultivable due to terrain conditions. Therefore, the majority of the people depend on livestock and subsistence farming. Mandarin, potatoes and cardamom are the principal cash crops in Chhukha.

Gewogs : 11
Dungkhag : 1
Thromde : 1
Population :
79,942 (2009 est.)
Male : 45,415
Female : 34,528
Hospitals : 3
BHUs : 8
ORCs : 47
Traditional
Med. Units: 2
Schools : 40

BHUTAN
Chhukha

Chapcha

Metakha

Dungna

Bjacho

Geling

Chhukha

Logchina

Bongo

Getena

Phuentsholing

Sampheling

Darla

Legend
—— DZONGKHAG ROAD
---- FARM ROAD
—— FEEDER ROAD
—— HIGHWAY
—— INDUSTRIAL ROAD

PHUENTSHOLING

Altitude 300m

Phuentsholing, under Chhukha Dzongkhag is a thriving commercial centre on the northern edge of the Indian plains. Situated directly at the base of the Himalayan range and sharing the border with India, Phuentsholing blends in the fascinating mix of Indian and Bhutanese cultures. Being the frontier town Phuentsholing serves as the convenient entry/exit point for Bhutan and also the important link to visit the Indian state of West Bengal, Sikkim and Assam.

Places of interest in Phuentsholing, Chhukha

Kharbandi Goenpa, a beautiful monastery situated at an altitude of 380m amid a garden of tropical plants and flowers, was founded in 1967 by the Late Royal Grand Mother, Ashi Phuntsho Choden. The monastery contains paintings on the life of Buddha and statues of Zhabdrung Ngawang Namgyal and Guru Padmasambhava. From the monastery garden, there is a fascinating view of Phuentsholing town and the surrounding plains.

Zangto Pelri, in the centre of Phuentsholing town is a small temple modelled like Zangto Pelri, literally meaning 'copper-coloured mountain'. On the ground floor there are statues of the eight manifestations of Guru Padmasambhava and paintings on the life of the Buddha. The next floor contains eight Bodhisattavas

and statues of Avalokiteshvara and Zhabdrung Ngawang Namgyal. The main statue on the top floor is that of the Amitabha.

Tshamdrak Goenpa is located in Chapcha. It was founded in the 17th century by Lama Ngawang Drakpa, a descendent of the Drigung Chopa Rinpoche and brother of the 13th Chief Abbot Yonten Thaye. Besides many scriptures and statues, the main relics of the monastery are treasure stone slab offered by Ap Chhundu, the guardian deity of Haa and the treasure of 100 drums. According to local folklore, there are no other people who can play the drum like the people of Tshamdra since their place is graced by the discovery of 100 treasure drums.

Tshamdrak Goenpa

Zangto Pelri

Phuentsholing town

Thimphu

BHUTAN

Gewogs : 8
Dungkhag : 1
Thromde : 1
Population : 101,884
(2009 est.)
Male : 55,058
Female : 46,825
Hospitals : 4
BHUs : 7
ORCs : 19
Traditional Hospital: 1
Schools : 41

THIMPHU

Altitude 2,320m

Thimphu has been the capital of Bhutan since 1955. It is the seat of government, religion and commerce. The harmonious mix of modern development with ancient traditions makes it a unique town. Thimphu a home to the Royal Family, the monk

Tashichhodzong, Fortress of the Glorious Religion

to 7,160m. The Dzongkhag has one Dungkhag, one Thromde and eight Gewogs and has a relatively good road network, especially in the lower Gewogs which includes Chang, Dagala, Geney, Kawang and Mewang. These Gewogs fall directly under the Dzongkhag administration. The three Gewogs in the northern part of the Dzongkhag which includes Lingzhi, Naro and Soe under Lingzhi Dungkhag have a rugged and mountainous terrain with extreme cold climate. They are connected only by mule tracks making access and delivery of development services difficult and expensive.

Most of the lower Gewogs have easy access to the national referral hospital, national research centers, central ministries, agriculture related corporations and the financial institutions, extension services are available in all the Gewogs as well facilities for primary education and health care.

More than 60 percent of the households have electricity. Rice, which is the staple food, is grown extensively by a majority of the people in the lower Gewogs. People also cultivate wheat as a winter crop. The dry land owned by the people is used for orchard plantation and vegetable cultivation for commercial purposes. The other remote Gewogs in the northern part depend on livestock farming as the main economic activity.

body, civil servants and expatriates maintains a strong national character in its architectural style. Once a small rural settlement, it is home now to 101,884 people.

Thimphu is amongst the more developed Dzongkhag in the country. It has a total area of 1,792.79 sq. km with altitude ranging from 1,200m

In autumn, Thimphu attracts many international visitors and local families to Thimphu *Drubchen* (the rite of great accomplishment) and Tshechu which are held each year on the 5th to 9th day of the 8th month and 10th to 12th day of the 8th month respectively.

Places of interest in Thimphu

Tashichhodzong or the 'Fortress of the Glorious Religion', was built in 1641. The Dzong was later rebuilt by the Third King, His Majesty Jigme Dorji Wangchuck in 1965. Tashichhodzong is Bhutan's administrative and religious centre and houses the throne room of His Majesty the King, government ministries, the nation's largest monastery and headquarters of His Holiness the *Je Khenpo* and the monk body. The National Assembly Hall is located in a building across the river.

The National Textile Museum showcases a range of beautiful Bhutanese textiles. It was opened in 2001, under the patronage of Her Majesty the Queen Mother Ashi Sangay Choden Wangchuck. The museum has exhibits on six major themes: warp pattern weaves, weft pattern weaves, role of textiles in religion, achievements in textile arts, textiles from indigenous fibres and the royal collection. The museum introduces visitors to major weaving techniques, styles of local dress and the variety of textiles. The crowns and attire of Bhutan's Monarch and other accessories used by members of the Royal Family can be found in the museum.

The Folk Heritage Museum, also known as Phelchey Toenkhim, is a restored three-storied traditional building which dates back to mid 19th century. It was established at the initiative of Her Majesty the Queen Mother Ashi Dorji Wangmo Wangchuck. It provides a fascinating insight into the traditional Bhutanese farm house and rural past through exhibits and documentation of rural life. To present a typical Bhutanese rural setting, a traditional watermill (with mill stones that date back more than 150 years), traditional style kitchen garden with vegetables and the famous traditional hot stone bath complement the museum building and the exhibits within.

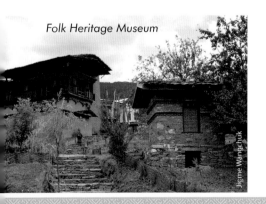

Folk Heritage Museum

Jicme Wangchuk

Thimphu by Night

TCB

production facility where pills, tablets, ointments and medicinal teas are manufactured. The small museum within the complex has an interesting variety of medicinal plants, minerals, animal parts, precious metals and gems.

Takin Preserve houses the rare national animal of Bhutan. The best time to see them is early mornings when they gather around the fence to feed. The Takin is listed by international conservation agencies as a vulnerable species and it is a rare animal found only in Bhutan, Nepal, Burma and China. This animal is chosen as the national animal of Bhutan for its uniqueness and its association with the country's religious history and mythology.

The National Library holds a vast collection of Buddhist texts and manuscripts, some dating back several hundred years, as well as modern academic books mainly on Himalayan culture and religion. The library also has modern academic books and the world's largest published book titled BHUTAN, measuring 5x7feet and weighing nearly 150 pounds. Its illustrated pages are turned one page each month.

The National Institute for Zorig Chusum or the School of Arts and Crafts is an Institute where students undertake a six-year course on the 13 traditional arts and crafts of Bhutan. The students follow a comprehensive course that starts with drawing and progresses through painting, wood carving, embroidery and statue-making. On a visit one can actually see students at work.

The National Traditional Medicine Hospital is where Bhutan's famous traditional medicine are compounded and dispensed, and traditional medical practitioners are trained. It is also a unit where traditional doctors diagnose patients and prescribe medication or treatments. The Institute operates a large laboratory and

World's biggest book

Lily Wangchhuk

National Memorial Choeten

Changangkha Lhakhang is an old fortress-like temple perched on a ridge above Thimphu. The temple was built in 12th century by Lama Phajo Drugom Shigpo's son Nyima. The central statue here is Avalokiteshvara in a manifestation with eleven heads. From the temple once can get a fascinating view of the Thimphu valley.

The National Memorial Choeten is a sacred shrine built in 1974 in memory of the 'Father of Modern Bhutan', Third Druk Gyalpo Jigme Dorji Wangchuck under the initiative of Royal Grand Mother Ashi Phuntsho Choden Wangchuck. It is dedicated to the world peace and prosperity. The numerous religious paintings and complex tantric statues housed inside the monument reflect both the peaceful and wrathful aspects of Buddhist deities.

Changangkha Lhakhang

Zangto Pelri Lhakhang, a private temple built in 1990s by Late Dasho Aku Tongmi, a musician who composed Bhutan's national anthem, is near the weekend market. It is said to be a replica of Guru Padmasambhava's celestial abode and houses many large statues of Guru Padmasambhava in different manifestations.

Semtokha Dzong which stands on a lofty ridge five miles from Thimphu town was built in 1627 by Zhabdrung Ngawang Namgyal. It is the oldest Dzong in the country and now houses the Institute of Language and Cultural Studies.

Dechenphodrang Monastic School

Dechenphodrang is a monastic school with more than 450 monks currently undergoing their studies. On a visit, one can see many little monks either at prayers or at play. The temple at the school houses 12th century paintings which have been restored.

Semtokha Dzong

Phajoding Goenpa is three hours walk from upper Thimphu. The monastery was built in the 15th century by Shagcha Rinchen who introduced the Drukpa Kagyu School in Bhutan in the 13th century. It was once one of the richest monasteries in the country.

Tango Goenpa is a half hour drive from Thimphu town and one hour leisurely walk to the monastery. It was founded by Lama Gyalwa Lhanangpa in the 12th century and the present structure was built in the 15th century by Lama Drukpa Kunley. The picturesque three-storied tower and several surrounding buildings were built in the 18th century by the eighth *Desi*, Druk Rabgye and Zhabdrung Jigme Chhogyel added the golden roof in the 19th century.

Cheri Goenpa is a half hour drive from Thimphu town and an hour walk to the monastery. The trail starts from a quaint bridge that spans the Thimphu Chhu, and then climbs steeply to the monastery. It

was built by Zhabdrung Ngawang Namgyal in 1620. A silver choeten inside the monastery holds the ashes of Zhabdrung's father.

Wangduetse Lhakhang is a leisurely half hour walk from Sangaygang. In 1567, a great Bhutanese Lama known as Lama Tenzin Dendup built a Dzong at the present place of the temple. Known as Dzong Gongma (upper Dzong), it housed the palace of the *Deb Raja* and was used for administrative purposes. For monastic purposes, Dechenphodrang was built as the *Dzong Wongma* (lower Dzong). In 1641 the Dzong was shifted to the present day Tashichhodzong. The Dzong was five storied high when it was first built but was renovated into a one storied temple by Thimphub Kuenzang Thinley.

Wangduetse Lhakhang has many sacred artefacts with the main relic being the statue of Jowo Sakyamuni (Buddha), said to have been made from ancient silk. A special feature of the temple is that it houses eight huge choetens made out of red cy-

Tango Goenpa

TCB

Druk Wangyel Lhakhang

prus known as *Desheg Choeten Gyed* (eight types of choetens built to celebrate different events in the life of Buddha). These choetens possess different names and all are unique from each other. Remnants of the *Neten Chudrug* (sixteen Arhats) and *Chenrizig* (Avalokiteshvara) adorn the walls of the temple.

The **Druk Wangyel** *Lhakhang* on top of the hillock overlooking the Druk Wangyel Choetens at Dochula is certainly worth the visit. It was built by Her Majesty the Queen Mother Ashi Dorji Wangmo Wangchuck as a tribute to His Majesty the Fourth Druk Gyalpo for his selfless sacrifices for the nation. Built with the finest

wood and stone work carefully hand crafted by the best artisans in the country, it is one of the most sacred man-built monuments ever constructed in recent times.

The main shrine in the lhakhang is adorned by the statues of Buddha in the centre, Guru Padmasambhava on the left and Zhabdrung Ngawang Namgyal on the right. Two wooden stairways on right and left sides of the statues lead a balcony/gallery which covers the three sides overlooking the main hall of the lhakhang. The walls of the balcony/gallery are painted with pictorial history of the Wangchuck Dynasty depicting the great achievements

Kang Bum
5198

Kangcheda Gang
6800

Gangchen Tag
6794

Masang Gang
7194

Tsenden Gang
6400

Tari Ga
709

A view from Druk Wangyel Lhakhang

Jigme Singye Wangchuck Range

of Their Majesties the Kings in the service of the people, protecting the sovereignty and development of the country.

In the room adjoining the main hall of the lhakhang, a powerful telescope is installed. Through this telescope peaks such as Kang Bum, Kangcheda Gang, Gangchen Tag, Masagang, Tsenden Gang, Tari Gang, Jaigangphu Gang, Gangchhen Singye and Gangkar Puensum from left to right which has now named as Jigme Singye Wangchuck Range in honour of the Fourth Druk Gyalpo can be sighted, along with the valleys of Gasa, Punakha and Wangdue. Talo and Nobgang villages the ancestral home of Their Majesties the Queens and Zhabdrung Jigme Dorji can also be seen very prominently from here.

The Royal Botanical Park at Lamperi is a leisurely 45 minutes drive from Thimphu towards Punakha. It is a great destination for nature lovers. Situated at an altitude range of 2100m to 3800m and covering an area of 47 sq. km, the park contains a rich biodiversity of high conservation value. The park features a variety of forest types: alpine, cool temperate broadleaf forest, old growth of broadleaf and conifer forests. Around 300 species of plants are found in the park including those species of plants and animals such as Himalayan yew (Taxus battaca), Panax pseudoginsend, Tetracentron sinensis, native Rhododendron, Royal Bengal Tiger, Red Panda, Musk Deer, Himalayan Monal and Blood pheasants. The park is also host to Tetracentron, an ancient relict angiosperm with no vessel in its trunk.

One of the main attractions of the park is the rhododendron garden. Of the total 46 species of rhododendron grown in Bhutan, 40 species are found in the rhododendron garden including 28 species already grown in the area. Different shades of rhododendrons start to bloom through mid-March until August changing the whole colour of the landscape. The park has 14.5 km of trails for eco trek which takes you through thick oak forest and mountain streams. It also offers secured eco-camp equipped with all the essentials for camping and a picnic spot with children's playground. The visitors are required to pay a reasonable entry fee.

Jaikangphu Gang
7194

Ganchhen Singye
7094

Gangkar Puensum
7564

Courtesy : Her Majesty the Queen Mother Ashi Dorji Wangmo Wangchuck

PARO

Altitude 2,280m

Situated in the north-western part of the country, Paro is a beautiful valley rich in culture, scenic beauty and abounds in myths and legends. The Dzongkhag is home to many of Bhutan's oldest temples and monasteries, the country's only airport and the National Museum. Paro has 176 *lhakhangs* and 427 *choetens*, the most famous being Taktsang Monastery (tiger's nest) and Kyichu Lhakhang. Most of the trade of Bhutan in olden times was conducted through Paro via Tremo La to Phari Dzong in Tibet.

Paro is one of the most developed Dzongkhags in the country with moderate climatic conditions, fertile land suitable for agriculture and horticulture, good road network and bridges connecting the villages, schools, institutes and organizations with the main town, and the existence of a number of important

Paro

Legend
— DZONGKHAG ROAD
— FARM ROAD
— FEEDER ROAD
— HIGHWAY

Tsento

Dotey

Dopshari
Lango   Hungrel
      Wangchang
Lungni   Shaba

Dogar

Naja

BHUTAN
Paro

Gewogs : 10
Population : 39,118
(2009 est.)
Male : 20,613
Female : 18,505
Hospitals : 1
Traditional Med. Unit: 1
BHUs : 3
ORCs : 27
Schools :23

Rinpung Dzong, Fortress on a Heap of Jewels

Jigme Wangchuk

government institutions and the country's only airport. It has a total area of 1,284.727 sq. km with altitude ranging from 1,960m to 5,680m. The Dzongkhag has 10 Gewogs which includes Dogar, Dopshari, Dotey, Hungrel, Lango, Lungni, Naja, Shaba, Tsento and Wangchang.

The valley is often known as the 'rice bowl' of the Kingdom as it produces a bulk of the red rice from its fertile terraced fields. Paro is also known for production of wheat, millet, potatoes, apple and seasonal vegetables, which are mostly grown on a commercial scale.

During spring, Paro attracts many international visitors and thousands of families to Paro Tshechu which are held each year from 11th to 15th day of 2nd month of the Bhutanese calendar.

Dungtse Lhakhang

Jigme Wangchuk

Places of interest in Paro

Rinpung Dzong, meaning "Fortress on a Heap of Jewels" was built in 1646 AD by Zhabdrung Ngawang Namgyal mainly for defence purpose against frequent incursions. Historically, it was an important administrative centre and the seat of many feudal lords and *Penlops*. Today, it houses the administrative offices which includes the legislative, executive, judicial and religious centre for the people of Paro. The approach to the Dzong is through a traditional covered bridge called the Nemi Zam. A walk through the bridge to the Dzong, over a stone inlaid path, offers a good view of the Dzong.

Ta Dzong built in 1951, was once the watch tower for the defence of Rinpung Dzong during inter-valley wars of the 17th century. It was reestablished as the National Museum in 1967 and has been rated among the best natural history museums in Asia. It holds a fascinating collection of art, relics, religious thangkha paintings, handicrafts, masks, costumes, armour and Bhutan's exquisite postage stamps. The museum's circular shape augments its varied collection displayed over several floors. The visit will provide an insight into the rich and unique cultural heritage and tradition of Bhutan.

Drugyal Dzong which means 'Victorious Fortress' was built in 1646 by Zhabdrung Ngawang Namgyal to commemorate his victory over Tibetan invaders, led by the Mongolian warlord. Strategically built over the only passage into Paro valley, the Bhutanese repelled several invading Tibetan armies during the 17th century from this location. The glory of Drukgyal Dzong remains even after it was gutted by fire in 1951. On a clear day, one can see the commanding view of Mount Jumolhari from the village below the Dzong.

Kyichu Lhakhang is one of the oldest and most sacred temple in the Kingdom, dating back to the 7th century. Composed of twin temples; the first temple was built by the Buddhist Tibetan King, Songtsen Gampo in the 7th century and the second temple was built in 1968, by Ashi Kesang Choeden Wangchuck, the Queen Grandmother of Bhutan.

Kila Goenpa is a serene home for Buddhist nuns who have dedicated their life to spiritual fulfillment and lead undisturbed lives of religious studies, prayer and meditation. The goenpa is nestled on the mountain side below the Chele La. From Chele La the goenpa is about one hour walk through magnificent woods.

Druk Choeding Lhakhang also known as Tshongdoe Naktsang, is the town temple. It was built in 1525 by Zhabdrung Chhogyel.

Ta Dzong, Paro

Drugyal Dzong

Dungtse Lhakhang was built in 1433 by the iron bridge builder Thangtong Gyalpo. It has three floors representing hell, earth and heaven with some remarkable paintings.

Chumphug Lhakhang is about five hours walk from Paro town but two hours of walk could be saved if one drives up the valley through unpaved road. According to the local folklore, it is named Chumphug which means 'cave of rice' because the huge cliff to the left of the temple is a hidden treasure of red and white rice. There are many several sacred sites one can visit around the monastery.

Dongkola Lhakhang founded by the speech incarnation of Terton Pema Lingpa stands on the highest peak between Paro and Thimphu. It is about a six-hour walk from the nearest road head from Thimphu and four hours walk from Shaba in Paro. One among many stories surrounding the Dongkola Lhakhang in Paro is that nothing can be stolen from the temple.

Tamchog Lhakhang located in Dokar Gewog was built in 14th century by Drubthob Thangtong Gyalpo. It is considered to be one of the most sacred temple in Bhutan.

Drakarpo Lhakhang located in Shaba is one of the most important hidden sacred places of Guru Padmasambhava. Besides the temple, there are many sacred sites surrounding the sacred place.

Hephu Thekchen Choling Goenpa is located 13 kms from Shaba, along unpaved road. It was founded in the 16th century by Yongzin Ngawang Drakpa. The ninth line of reincarnations of Hephu Tulku, Ngawang Shedrub Choki Nyima has renovated the monastery and established an elementary monastic school.

Hephu Thekchen Choling Goenpa

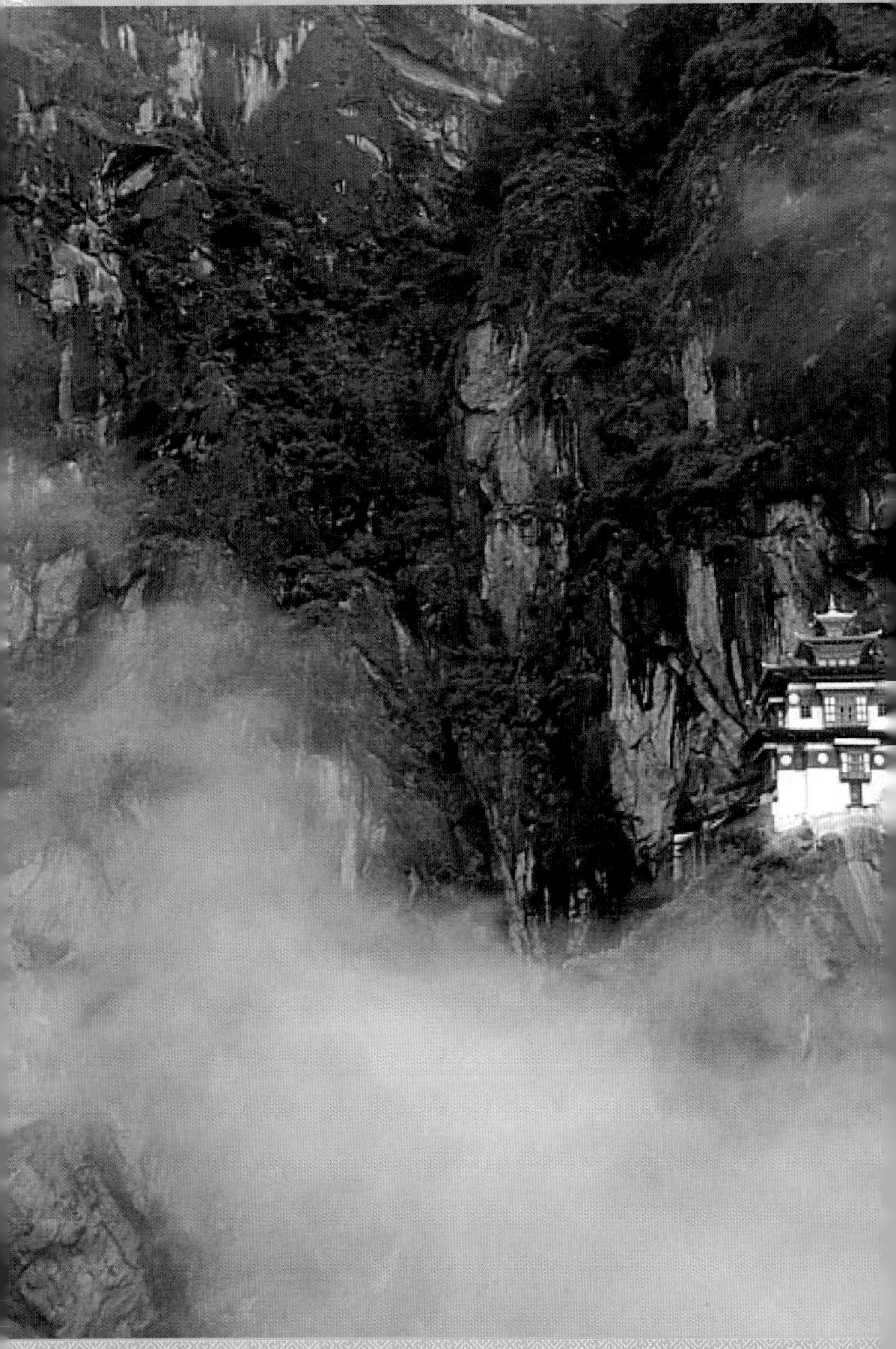

Taktsang Monastery popularly known as the Tiger's Nest, is Bhutan's most revered temple. It is perched on the side of a 900m cliff above the Paro valley. According to legend, Guru Padmasambhava is said to have flown here on the back of a tigress from Singye Dzong in Lhuentse, to meditate in a cave where Taktsang now stands. Hence the name 'Tigers Nest'. It was from there he propagated Vajrayana Buddhism that was prophesized by the Buddha at the time of attaining Nirvana. This site has been recognized as a sacred place and was visited by Zhabdrung Ngawang Namgyal in 1646. It is believed that a Bhutanese should visit the monastery at least once in their lifetime. In April 1998, a fire destroyed the main structure of the building and its religious contents but now this Bhutanese jewel has been restored to its original splendour. The hike to the monastery makes a splendid half-day excursion.

PUNAKHA

Altitude 1,220m

Punakha served as the capital of Bhutan until 1955. It continues to be the winter residence of the central monastic body. It has an area of 1,107.77 sq.km with altitude ranging from 1,200m to 5,050m. The Dzongkhag has 11 Gewogs consisting of Barp, Chubu, Dzomi, Goenshari, Guma, Kabisa Limbu, Shengana, Talo, Toeb and Toewang. Except for Talo and Guma Gewogs, most Gewogs are located along the banks of *Pho Chhu* (male river) and *Mo Chhu* (female river).

Blessed with a temperate climate and fed by the *Pho Chhu* and *Mo Chhu* rivers, Punakha is another fertile valley in the country with abundant crops from terraced rice fields, seasonal fruits and vegetables.

Places of interest in Punakha

Punakha Dzong also known as the 'Palace of Happiness', is a massive structure at the junction of the two rivers. Built in 1637 by Zhabdrung Ngawang Namgyal, it is 600 feet long and 240 feet wide, with a sprawling six-storeyed rectangular tower. Punakha Dzong is the most beautiful and well-known fortress connected with Bhutan's historical traditions and houses sacred artefacts.

The valley and Dzong of Punakha was the seat of power and politics in medieval Bhutan. The First Hereditary Monarch, Gongsar Ugyen Wangchuck, was enthroned here. Since then the Kings of Bhutan were enthroned after receiving the five colour scarf from the embalmed body of Zhabdrung Ngawang Namgyal kept in the Dzong.

Talo Sanga Choling Monastery is located at Talo valley. The site was founded by Chogtrul Jigme Singye the fourth reincarnation of Lama Thripa (Gyalsey Tenzin Rabgye) in 1767. Jigme Dakpa the third mind reincarnation of Zhabdrung Ngawang Namgyal, later renovated the area and built a monastery. He also installed statues that he had brought from Samye in Tibet. Thereafter, the monastery was renovated by several reincarnations of Zhabdrung Ngawang Namgyal including Zhabdrung Jigme Norbu, the fourth mind incarnation, Zhabdrung Jigme Chogyal, the fifth mind incarnation and Zhabdrung Jigme Dorji, the sixth mind incarnation. The monastery also served as their living quarters. Currently it accommodates the *Gonkhang* (inner chapel dedicated to guardian deity) and residence of the abbot. Talo Sanga Choling also houses many lhakhangs, in which *Neten Chudrug* (sixteen Arhats) Lhakhang is one of them.

Punakha

Gewogs : 11
Population : 25,205
(2009 est.)
Male : 12,793
Female : 12,411
Hospital : 1
BHUs : 5
ORCs : 7
Traditional Med. Un
Schools : 21

Punakha Dzong, Palace of Happiness

Khamsum Yulley Namgyel Choeten is an invigorating one hour hike from the road head. It was built to remove negative forces and promote peace, stability and harmony in the changing world. One can enjoy breathtaking views of the valley from the choeten which dominates the upper Punakha valley.

Chimi Lhakhang is a half hour walk across a local village and rice fields from the road head at Sopsokha. The temple was built in 1499 and is located on a hillock in the centre of the valley. It is dedicated to Lama Drukpa Kunley, who in the late 15th century used humour, songs and outrageous behaviour to dramatize his teachings and hence is was also known as the 'Divine Madman'. It is widely believed that childless couples who pray at this temple are usually blessed with children.

WANGDUEPHODRANG

Altitude 1,240m

Wangduephodrang is named after the Dzong in Wangdue. The name is said to have been given by Zhabdrung Ngawang Namgyal who was seeking a strategic location for a Dzong to prevent incursions from the south. At the chosen spot, he is said to have encountered a boy named Wangdue playing beside the river and thus named the Dzong, Wangduephodrang meaning 'Wangdue's Palace.' In the 17th century, Wangduephodrang played a critical role in unifying the western, central and southern Bhutanese Dzongkhags

Wangduephodrang has a total area of 4,028.68 sq.km with altitude ranging from 440m to 7,200 m. It is the second largest Dzongkhag in Bhutan and consists of 15 Gewogs which includes Athang, Bjena, Daga, Dangchu, Gangtey, Gasetshog Gom, Gasetshog Wom, Kazhi, Nahi, Nyisho, Phangyul, Phobjikha, Rubeisa, Sephu and Thedtsho. The summers are moderately hot with cool winters. The areas in the north remain under snow during the winter.

Wangduephodrang has about 65 per cent of its total land under forest cover, consisting of both broadleaf and conifers. Phobjikha Gewog is famed as the winter resting place of the Black-necked Cranes. The Jigme Dorji Wangchuck National Park extends into the northern part of the Dzongkhag and covers almost four Gewogs.

The higher altitude Gewogs of Phobji, Gangtey, Sephu and Dangchu provide rich pasture for livestock. *Chuzhing* (wetland) dominates agricultural land use in the Dzongkhag followed by *Kamzhing* (dryland), mixed farming and few patches of *Tseri* (slash and burn cultivation). Paddy is grown extensively, mostly along the Dang Chhu and Tsang Chhu in Nahi, Nyisho, Phangyul, Rubesa and Thedtsho Gewogs. Double cropping of rice is an important agricultural feature. Potato is an important cash crop, especially for the Phobji, Gangtey and Sephu Gewogs. The production

Wangduephodrang Dzong and its surroundings

Jigme Wangchuk

of citrus is increasing in Daga, Bjena, Phangyul and Rubisa Gewogs while ginger production is gaining popularity in Daga and Athang Gewogs as an important source of income.

Wangduephodrang is famous for its fine bamboo work, slate and stone carvings.

Wangduephodrang

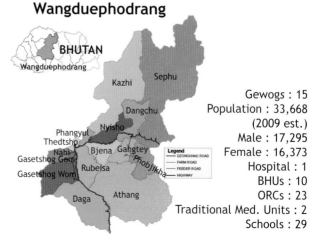

Gewogs : 15
Population : 33,668
(2009 est.)
Male : 17,295
Female : 16,373
Hospital : 1
BHUs : 10
ORCs : 23
Traditional Med. Units : 2
Schools : 29

Places of interest in Wangduephodrang

Nyinzergang Lhakhang

Wangduephodrang *Dzong* is located on top of a high ridge overlooking a river junction. It was founded by Zhabdrung Ngawang Namgyal in 1638 and was later enlarged by the fourth *Desi* Tenzin Rabgye who added another two storied *utse*. The seventh Wangduephodrang *Dzongpon*, Sonam Dhendup further added new structures to the Dzong.

The Dzong stands majestically on a spur and commands an impressive view over both the north-south and east-west roads.

Gangtey Sangacholing Goenpa is roughly two hours drive from Wangduephodrang town. It is situated on a ridge overlooking the beautiful Phobjikha valley. The monastery was founded in 1613 by Gyalse Pema Thinley the grandson of Terton Pema Lingpa. It was later expanded by second Gangtey Trulku Tenzin Legpau Dhendup.

Currently the ninth Gangtey Tulku manages the monastery and follows the Peling Nyingma School of Buddhism which is based on teachings of Pema Lingpa. It is the only Nyingma monastery in western Bhutan.

Nyinzergang Lhakhang is located in Nyinzergang village. The village was once said to have been afflicted by epilepsy caused by evil spirits but became free from it after Terton Wugpa Lingpa from Tibet arrived at Nyinzergang in the 13th century and subdued the evil spirits.

Nyinzergang Lhakhang was built by Terton Wugpa Lingpa. The main relic of the monastery is an object representing the *Za* (planetary deity). There is also a necklace with a bead of *Za* (rare and expensive knots of wood) which has the power to cure epilepsy. Many people with certain types of physical abnormalities visit this monastery to wear this necklace to get cured.

The *Kuenri* and *Tsow Ngaps Chaams* which are masked dances depicting the stage after death and before rebirth are performed only in Nyinzergang Lhakhang.

Gangtey Sangacholing Goenpa

Bey Langdra Nye

Bey Langdra Nye the holy site of pilgrimage is situated on a cliff in Kazhi. It is hour and half drive from town and another hour and half walk. This site is said to have been blessed by Guru Padmasambhava in the 8th century. There are many sacred sites along the way and around Bey Landgra Nye which includes the hidden cave with holy water drip-ping from the over head stalactites and stalagmites, the holy Cyprus tree and sacred cave where Guru Padmasambhava had meditated. The place remained in ruins for centuries, until it was revived and restored by the 14th Je Khenpo. Today it is the seat of Jatrul Rinpoche.

Statue of Guru Padmasambhava at the Bey Langdra Nye

Phobjikha Valley

A few kilometers past the Gangtey Goenpa, on the valley floor is the village of Phobjikha. This is the winter home of the rare Black-necked Crane, an endangered species that migrates from its northern habitats in Tibet and Siberia, each winter. There are about 450 to 500 cranes residing in Bhutan of which 250 to 300 live in this wide, beautiful alpine wetland valley. The elegant birds can be observed from early November to end March.

Phobjikha Valley

TCB

HAA

Altitude 2,700m

Haa is also known as "the Hidden-Land Rice Valley". Haa's major feature is its narrow north-south valley. Its new Dzong was built in 1915, near the older one which was destroyed by fire. Haa was the ancient centre of trade with Yatung in the Chumbi valley in Tibet. The valley has been the strong-hold of the Dorji family to which Her Majesty the Royal Grandmother, Ashi Kesang Choeden Wangchuck, belongs.

Haa Dzongkhag has a total area of 1,900 sq.km with altitude ranging from 800m to 5,600m. The Dzongkhag has six Gewogs which includes Bji, Esu, Gakiling, Katsho, Sama and Sombaykha. Haa is characterized by a rugged and mountainous terrain, which makes access and delivery of development services difficult as

Wangchuk Lo Dzong and its surroundings

well as expensive. It is constrained by short growing seasons and limited arable land as only about two percent of the land is cultivable. *Kamzhing* dominates agricultural activity, constituting an estimated 68 percent of the cultivated land. Most of the Gewogs consist of dryland areas and natural pastureland. The main crops grown in the valley are wheat, barley, millet and potato although some rice is grown in the lower reaches of the valley. Potatoes, chillies, apples and other cash crops are grown by farmers on the valley floor along terraced hillsides. Almost 78 percent of Haa is covered with forest, and forest products play an important

Haa

BHUTAN
Haa

Bji
Katsho
Esu
Sama
Sombaykha
Gakiling

Legend
— FEEDER ROAD
— HIGHWAY

Gewogs : 6
Population : 12,397
(2009 est.)
Male : 6,673
Female : 5,724
Hospital : 1
BHUs : 4
ORCs : 15
Traditional Med. Unit: 1
Schools : 11

part in local economy. Livestock rearing constitutes an important economic activity in Haa with many of the northern Gewogs depending on livestock as their major source of income. In 2002, the valley was opened to foreign tourism.

Places of interest in Haa

Chhundu Lhakhang is one several shrines dedicated to the valley's protecting deity, *Ap* Chundu. The temple houses statues of the blue-faced Chhundu and his red faced cousin Jowya.

Lhakhang Karpo or the white temple is located 3 kms south of Haa town in Dumchoe village. Built in the 7th century, it is the main seat of Haa's guardian deity - *Ap Chundu*. The temples conducts prayer ceremonies on various occasions. The annual Haa Tshechu is held for three days starting from the 8th till the 10th of the 8th month of the Bhutanese calendar.

Lhakhang Nagpo

Tenzin Namgay

Lhakhang Nagpo or the black temple is a few minutes drive from Haa town. Built in the 7th century, the temple is quite distinctive with its grayish black wall. Rituals are performed on special occasions co-inciding with *Zhabdrung Kuchoey* (death anniversary ritual) on the 10th day of the 3rd month of the Bhutanese calendar.

Lhakhang Karpo

Tenzin Namgay

Tagchu Goenpa is located nine kilometers away from Lhakhang Karpo in Lungse Kha village in Esu Gewog. It was founded by Dali Lam Sangay Jamtsho in the beginning of the 20th century. The monastery observes a lot of important occasions and performs various festivals. Further above the monastery is a rock that is said to resembles a tiger from where the water erupts. This is how the place was named as Tagchu (*Tag* - tiger, *chu* - water).

GASA

Gasa Dzong

Altitude 2,770m

Gasa lies in the extreme north-west of the country and spans the middle and high Himalayas.

Gasa is known for its *tshachus* (natural hot springs) found at several places with different medicinal values. The Dzongkhag also has a number of lhakhangs and choetens. The people of Gasa generally speak Dzongkha with a distinctive accent. Layaps and Lunaps who mostly lead a pastoral life rearing yaks and sheep have their own local dialect besides Dzongkha. Gasa has extremely cold winters with short and pleasant summer. Rainfall is scanty but there is heavy snowfall in the upper regions during winter.

Gasa has a total area of 3,130.53 sq.km with altitude ranging from 1,600m to 7,000m. The Dzongkhag has four Gewogs which includes Khamey, Khatoe, Laya and Lunana. Of the total area, about 35 percent are under scrub forest, 27 percent under fir forest, 15 percent under mix conifer and four percent under

Tenzin Namgay, Bhutan Times Ltd.

Jigme Wangchuk

Gasa

BHUTAN

Gasa

Gewogs : 4
Population : 3,346
(2009 est.)
Male : 1,750
Female : 1,596
BHUs : 4
ORCs :13
Traditional Med. Unit: 1
Schools : 5

Laya

Lunana

Khatoe

Khamey

Legend
FARM ROAD

broad leafed. Dryland covers an area of 19 percent under livestock rearing. The soil is sandy and supports dry cultivation.

The high altitude and scanty rainfall makes farming difficult so the people in Gasa earn their main source of cash income by being porters to local residents as well as tourists. Sale and bartering of livestock products is another source of income for Laya and Lunana Gewogs.

Laya women wear distinctive dresses with a hand woven hat embroidered with colorful beads.

The Friendly Planet

Late N. Wangchhuk

Yak herder's camp

Places of interest in Gasa

Gasa Dzong built on the slope facing east is the administrative head quarter of the Gasa Dzongkhag. It was built in 1646 by Zhabdrung Ngawang Namgyal.

Gasa Tshachu is most popular among all the hot springs. People from all over the country regularly visit these hot springs during winters, as they are claimed to offer many health benefits. There are also other hot springs located in Laya called Lungo *Tshachu* and Wachey *Tshachu* in Lunana.

Jigme Dorji National Park

Gasa has a forest cover of 33 percent and the entire Dzongkhag falls under the Jigme Dorji National Park. Gasa is rich in flora and fauna and boasts some rare species of birds and animals like the Takin, Musk Deer, Blue Sheep, Snow Leopard, Himalayan Black Bear, Tiger, Red Pandas, Raven, Wild Pheasants, Snow Pigeons, the Red Billed Cough, the Alpine Swift, the Snow Partridge, the Black-necked Crane and many others.

Lhuentse

Bumthang

Trongsa

Zhemgang

**Dzongkhags in
Central Bhutan:**
Trongsa
Bumthang
Lhuentse
Zhemgang

Central Bhutan is made up of Trongsa at 2000m, Bumthang (Jakar at 2700m; Ura 3120m), Lhuentse at 1460m and Zhemgang at 1900m. Central Bhutan is believed to be the first inhabited part of the country with evidence of prehistoric settlements in the Ura valley of Bumthang and the southern region of Khyeng in Zhemgang.

In addition to the high Himalayas which run east-west, mountain chains also run north-south at a height of 7200m-400m, traversing the country and forming veritable barriers between different regions. Each of the central valleys is thus a microcosm separated from the next valley by high passes ranging from 3,000m to 3,500m.

The Friendly Planet

TRONGSA

Altitude 2,000m

Trongsa is the central most Dzongkhag of Bhutan. It was from here that the present Royal Family emerged as the most powerful force in the beginning of the last century. Because of its highly strategic position as the only connecting route between east and west, the Trongsa Penlop was able to control the entire eastern region effectively from Trongsa.

Trongsa has a total area of 1,810.27 sq.km with altitude ranging from 600m to 5,040m. The Dzongkhag has five Gewogs which includes Drakten, Korphu, Langthel, Nubi and Tangsibji.

Jigme Singye Wangchuck National Park spread over two Gewogs (Langthel and Korphu) under Trongsa Dzongkhag preserves the wild life found within the area which includes the white Langur and Himalayan Bear and a variety of Deer.

People survive on farming. In some areas potato cultivation is the main source of cash income. Because of limited size of land holdings and lack of farm infrastructure, in particular farm roads, farm productivity is low.

Trongsa Dzong, Fortress on Tip of a Conch

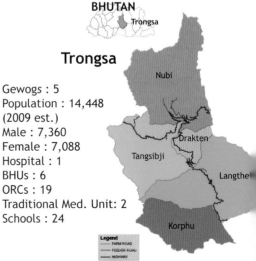

BHUTAN

Trongsa

Trongsa

Nubi

Drakten

Tangsibji

Langthel

Korphu

Gewogs : 5
Population : 14,448 (2009 est.)
Male : 7,360
Female : 7,088
Hospital : 1
BHUs : 6
ORCs : 19
Traditional Med. Unit: 2
Schools : 24

Legend
—— FARM ROAD
····· FEEDER ROAD
—— HIGHWAY

The Friendly Planet

Places of interest in Trongsa

Trongsa Dzong or 'Fortress on tip of a Conch' is the longest Dzong in the country. It is an impregnable fortress built on many levels into the side of a hill. The Dzong was originally built in 1648 by Zhabdrung Ngawang Namgyal, and was later extended by its powerful *Penlops*, and the 16th Desi Sonam Lhundub. The Dzong has 25 lhakhangs which houses sacred images and religious treasures.

Trongsa Dzong is the ancestral home of the Royal Family and both the First and Second Kings of Bhutan ruled the country from this ancient seat. The Crown Prince of Bhutan has always held the position of the Trongsa Penlop prior to ascending the throne.

Chendebji Choeten is situated at the confluence of two rivers on the way to Trongsa. This choeten is a replica of the Boudhanath temple in Kathmandu, Nepal with eyes painted at the four cardinal points. It was built in the 18th century by Lama Shida from Tibet to cover the remains of an evil spirit that was subdued at the spot.

Jigme Singye Wangchuck National Park covers an area of 1,730 sq. km and is a home for many globally endangered rare floras and fauna of the country, and it's a habitual place for one of the most globally endangered species Golden Langur. The Park was gazette in 2000 in order to protect large area of virtually untouched ecosystem ranging from mixed conifer in the north to chirpine / broadleaf forest in the south. The Monpa, who are believed to be the early inhabitants of the country, resides on the lower parts of the Jigme Singye Wangchuck National Park.

Chendebji Choeten

Taktsherla Choeje Lhakhang

Taktsherla Choeje Lhakhang located in Langthel is half an hour walk from a place called Womey. It was founded by Lam Gyalse Kuenga Gyeltshen in the 16th century. The temple has a mural of *Sangay Tong* (Thousand Buddhas) which is rarely found in any other temples and monasteries in the country.

Kuenga Rabten Palace constructed in 1928, was the winter residence of the Second King, His Majesty Jigme Wangchuck. Located at the slope overlooking the mighty Mangde Chhu, it is about one hour drive from Trongsa town. It offers a good insight into the early days of Bhutanese monarchy. Besides the palace, one can also enjoy the beautiful expanse of rice terraces in the lower Mangde Chhu valley and waterfalls.

Ta-Dzong Museum is situated strategically above the Trongsa Dzong. It was built by Choeje Minjur Tempa in 1652 and served as the watch tower for centuries.

The 300 year old monument was renovated and converted as state of the art museum in 2008. It highlights the history of the monarchy and showcase some of the rare and priceless artefacts of the Kingdom.

It contains must-see displays such as the Raven Crown of the First Druk Gyalpo, the spoken statues of Dorji Chang or Vajradhara, Gongsar Jigme Namgyel's extraordinarily long sword and a 500-year-old jacket and robe of Ngagi Wangchuk.

The museum has total of eleven galleries with one gallery fully dedicated to the history of Kings of the Wangchuck dynasty. There is also a gallery which showcases the history and the religious significance of Trongsa Chhoetse Dzong. It is equipped with state of the art technology including a media room where visitors can watch a documentary programme on the history of the monarchy.

Kuenga Rabten Palace

Ta-Dzong

Tenzin Namgay

Jakar Dzong, 'The Fortress of the White Bird' in Bumthang

Textiles made from yak and sheep wool

TCB

BUMTHANG

Altitude
Jakar 2,700m
Ura 3,120m

Bumthang is the spiritual heartland of Bhutan and home to its most ancient and precious Buddhist sites. The tales of Guru Padmasambhava and his reincarnates, known as *Lingpas*, linger in every nook and corner of this beautiful valley.

Bumthang has a total area of 2712.71 sq.km with altitude ranging from 1,800m to 7,000m. The Dzongkhag has four Gewogs which includes Chokhor, Chumey, Tang and Ura. It is one of the most prosperous Dzongkhag in the country with favourable terrain coupled with good road network and high number of tourists who visit the Dzongkhag. Income from potatoes, livestock farms and tourism are changing the economic landscape of the people in the Dzongkhags. Sale of cordyceps, masutake and medicinal plants have further enhanced the income of people from upper Chokhor and Ura Gewogs.

The language spoken in Bumthang is known as *Bumthangkha*, a Tibeto-Burman language closely related to *Khyengkha*. It is partially comprehensible to speakers of Dzong*kha*, which originated in the valleys to the west of Bumthang. Each of the four valleys of Bumthang has its own dialect, and the remnants of the Khyeng Kingdom to the south in Zhemgang speak *Khyengkha* which may be classified as a dialect of *Bumthangkha*.

Bumthang

BHUTAN

Bumthang

Gewogs : 4
Population : 17,256
(2009 est.)
Male : 9,315
Female : 7,942
Hospital : 1
BHUs : 4
ORCs : 14
Traditional Med.
Units : 2
Schools : 19

Chokhor

Tang

Ura

Chumey

Legend
—— FARM ROAD
—— FEEDER ROAD
—— HIGHWAY

Places of interest in Bumthang

Jakar Dzong, 'the Fortress of the White Bird' was initially built as a monastery in 1549. It was upgraded after the Zhabdrung had firmly established his power in 1646. The Dzong is now used as administrative centre for Bumthang valley and houses the regional monk body.

Jambay Lhakhang is a sacred monastery built in the 7th century by the Tibetan King, Songtsen Gampo. It is one of the 108 monasteries built by him to subdue evil spirits in the Himalayan region.

Kurjey Lhakhang is another sacred monastery which comprises three temples. The one on the right was built in 1652 on the rock face where Guru Padmasambhava meditated in the 8th century. The second temple is built on the site of a cave containing a rock with the imprint of the Guru Padmasambhava's body and is therefore considered the holiest. The third temple was built by the Queen Grand Mother Ashi Kesang Choeden Wangchuck. These three temples are surrounded by a wall with 108 *choetens*.

Tamshing Lhakhang located opposite Kurjey Lhakhang on the other side of the river was founded in 1501 by Terton Pema Lingpa. The lhakhang has ancient religious paintings such as the 1,000 Buddhas and 21 *taras* (female form of Bodhisattva). The temple was restored at the end of the 19th century.

Mebar Tsho or the burning lake is a sacred pilgrimage site, where sa-

Kurjey Lhakhang

cred scriptures hidden by Guru Padmasambhava in the 8th century was recovered by Terton Pema Lingpa in the 15th century. The extensive array of prayer flags and small clay offering called '*tsa tsa*' in rock niches bespeak the importance of this spot.

Tangbi Goenpa is a half hour walk north of Kurjey Lhakhang. It was founded in 1470 by Shamar Rinpoche of the *Kagyu* religious school. The temple has two sanctuaries and a temple of protective deities. The sanctuary on the ground floor contains statues of past, present

Ura Valley is about one and half hour drive from Jakar and is the highest of Bumthang's valleys. It is believed to be the earliest inhabited place in Bhutan. The road to Ura climbs to an amazingly open countryside, only occasionally running into forest. Large sheep pastures line the road up to 20km behind the southern tip of the Tang valley. The route crosses Ura La (3,600m) with a magnificent view of Mount Gangkar Puensum. Villages in Ura are made up of clustered houses, which is quite unusual in Bhutan. Above Ura village is a new temple dedicated to Guru Padmasambhava. The last 25 years have seen Ura transform from a marginal community to a prosperous valley.

Kencho Sum Lhakhang is in Chumey valley. While it was first built in the 7th century AD, the current structure dates from 15th century, when Terton Pema Lingpa restored it. It is believed to have been built on a large lake from where he had discovered several treasures.

and future Buddhas and three clay statues probably dating to the end of 15th century. The vestibule on the upper floor contains two remarkable paintings of the heavens of Guru Padmasambhava and Buddha Amitabha.

Ngang Lhakhang is few hours walk from Tangbi Goenpa. It was built in the 15th century by Lama Namkha Samdup, a contemporary of Pema Lingpa. A three-day festival with masked dances is held here each winter to honour the founder of the lhakhang.

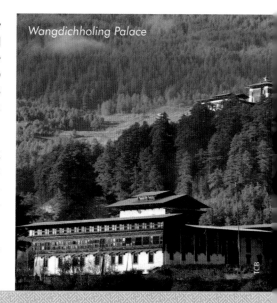

Wangdichholing Palace

LHUENTSE

Altitude 1,460m

Situated in the north-east of Bhutan, Lhuentse is one of the most isolated Dzongkhag. However, it enjoys historic importance as the Kurtoe region of Lhuentse is the ancestral home of the Wangchuck Dynasty, who descend from the noble family of Dungkhar Choeje. Lhuentse is also known for several renowned pilgrimage sites of Guru Padmasambhava which includes Singye Dzong, Baeyul Khenpajong and Phunying La.

Lhuentse has a total area of 2,853.54 sq.km with altitude ranging from 800m to 5,700m. The Dzongkhag consists of eight Gewogs which includes Gangzur, Jarey, Khoma, Kurtoe, Menbi, Minjey, Metsho and Tshenghar.

The people in the Dzongkhag mainly depend on agricultural activities for their livelihood, though farming remains largely subsistence since it is hindered by limited agricultural land and other farm infrastructure.

Places of interest

Lhuentse Dzong was built in 1654 and has two divisions, the Upper Dzong which belongs to the monk body and the Lower Dzong which houses the Dzongkhag administration.

Singye Dzong or the Legendary Lion Fortress in Kurtoe is located at an altitude of more than 3,000 m above sea level. It is a three-day uphill walk from Lhuentse town and is considered a very sacred place as Guru Padmasambhava meditated there during the mid-eighth century

after trying to suppress the demon King, Khikharathoed, who was exiled from Tibet. Singye Dzong gains further importance as the 19th century treasure discoverer Zilnon Namkha Dorji discovered a treasure at this site called *Tse-Drup-Chimi-Sogthig* – the religious scripture containing the means to prolong life.

Jangchubling Lhakhang located on a ridge in Gangzur is a four hour trek from the Lhuentse-Dungkar feeder road. It was founded by Choeje Pekar Jamtsho in the 18th century. In the 1940's HRH Late Ashi Wangmo daughter of Gongsar Ugyen Wangchuck supported the establishment of a bigger Shedra or a centre for Buddhist teachings at Jangchubling which could house about 150 monks. Jangchubling is considered one of the most significant Nyingma monasteries in the country.

The Khoma village in Lhuentse is notably famed for its weavers and special textiles and fabrics, generally considered to be the best in the country.

Sangay Lodro Nye

Tenzin Namgay

Lhuentse Dzong

Tenzin Namgay Bhutan Times Ltd.

BHUTAN
Lhuentse

Lhuentse

Gewogs : 8
Population : 16,301
(2009 est.)
Male : 8,156
Female : 8,145
Hospital : 1
BHUs : 11
ORCs : 33
Traditional Med. Unit : 1
Schools : 27

Kurtoe

Gangzur   Khoma

Menbi   Minjey
Metsho

Jarey   Tshenghar

Legend
——— DZONGKHAG ROAD
——— FARM ROAD
——— FEEDER ROAD
——— HIGHWAY

Dungkhar Naktshang

Dungkhar Naktshang is the ancient home of Dungkhar Choeje and the ancestral home of the Wangchuck dynasty. The visit to the three-storied Dungkhar Naktshang, said to have been built by Gongsar Ugyen Wangchuck, First Druk Gyalpo is a voyage into Bhutan's past.

Bhutan Times Ltd.

ZHEMGANG

Altitude 1,900m

Zhemgang is considered one of the most inaccessible Dzongkhag in the country with most of its Gewogs still situated far from road heads. *Khenrig Namsum* is the ancient name of Zhemgang Dzongkhag which literally means "the three divisions of Khyeng", Upper (Chikhor), Middle (Nangkor), and lower (Tamachok) Khyeng.

Zhemgang can be divided into three agro-ecological zones; Upper Khyeng which is characterized by high altitudes, remoteness and infertile soils on step slopes. The farming system is this region is, however well established.

Middle Khyeng, which is the most accessible part of the Dzongkhag, has good irrigation facilities and where people have begun to specialize in farm production aimed at generating cash income. Forest management and logging activities are concentrated in this region.

The Lower Khyeng is characterized by relatively fertile soils but has limited irrigation facilities. Farming system is therefore largely based on shifting or *Tseri* cultivation. However, with the opening of Panbang-Mathanguri road, cash crop production in the area has developed.

About 86 percent of total area of Zhemgang Dzongkhag is under forest cover due to which this Dzongkhag is very rich in bio-diversity, with the Manas National Park alone boasting

Zhemgang Dzong

Zhemgang

TCB

Gewogs : 8
Population : 19,797
(2009 est.)
Male : 10,012
Female : 9,786
Hospital : 1
BHUs : 14
ORCs : 38
Traditional Med. Unit : 1
Schools : 32

Zhemgang is known for its production of bamboo baskets and containers.

about 22 endangered animal species. The other protected areas are Jigme Singye Wangchuck and Thrumshingla National Park.

Agriculture and animal husbandry are the main sources of livelihood for about 90 percent of the population. They cultivate not only on wet and dry lands but *Tseri* is a dominant agricultural practice.

Zhemgang has a total area of 2,411 sq.km with altitude ranging from 100m to 4,520m. The Dzongkhag has eight Gewogs which includes Bardho, Bjoka, Goshing, Nangkor, Ngangla, Pangkhar, Shingkhar and Trong.

Places of interest in Zhemgang

Zhemgang Dzong is situated atop the peak of a triangular shaped ridge that rises sharply from the Mangde Chhu, facing the village of Trong and the town of Zhemgang. The Dzong was founded by Lam Zhang Dorjee Drakpa, a renowned scholar-sage of the Drukpa Kagyu school of Buddhism from Zhamling in Tibet. In his mission to spread Buddhism in Bhutan, he travelled as far as the present Zhemgang where he resided around 1163 A.D. at the site where the present Zhemgang Dzong is located.

In 1963 when Zhemgang created a separate Dzongkhag, the Dzong was renovated under the command of His Majesty the Third Druk Gyalpo and renamed as Dechen Yangtse or Druk Dechen Yangtse Dzong. The annual Tshechu of Zhemgang was introduced since the inception of *Rabdey* in 1966. It is held for five days from the 7th to the 11th of the 2nd Bhutanese month.

Tali Zangto Pelri Is a three-storied lhakhang in Nangkor which was constructed with financial contribution from His Majesty the Fourth Druk Gyalpo and His Holiness the 70th Je Khenpo, Trulku Jigme Chhoeda, who once headed the Zangtopelri.

Nabje Village is a two days walk from Zhemgang. It is an ideal place for visitors seeking a journey back into time. One can witness the Stone Pillar, which commemorates a peace treaty between King Sindaka (Sindu Raja) and King Naoche in the eighth century. This makes its one of the most ancient historical monument of Bhutan.

Buli Manmo Tsho (lake) is a leisurely half hour walk through paddy fields and a dense forest. According to local folklore, the lake can foretell the future. It is said, if the lake becomes very clear and exhibits extraordinary variations in colour and brightness, it foretells good fortune and luck but if it becomes dark and dull, it predicts misfortune. According to legend, Buli Manmo (deity of the lake) is said to have come from Bumthang who took shelter in a woman's house in a place called Buli Langbi. In the morning a big lake was formed below her house which gradually moved to its present location.

A local resident named Choney Zangmo is popularly known as the *Tsho gi Aum* (Lady of the Lake), because it

Tagma Lhakhang located at Tagma village, Trong is of vital significance for housing the remains of Terton Pema Lingpa, the great treasure discoverer for some time.

Bhutan Times Ltd.

is believed that the deity of the lake took shelter in her ancestral home before forming the lake. Even to this day, Choney Zangmo and her family perform rituals to the deity Manmo of the lake on every 15th day of the 5th and 10th month of the Bhutanese calendar.

Duenmang Tshachu is located on the right bank of Mangde Chhu on the steep foothill of Kamjong, and is widely known as Khyeng Tshachu as its lies in the heart of Khyeng region. The Tshachu is said to be beneficial for various human body ailments like joint pain, skin disease, ulcer, gastric and attracts number of people from al over the country.

The **Royal Manas National Park** is the first protected area in Bhutan with an area of 1,057 sq. km. The Park is designated to protect the habitat of Elephants, Tigers, Leopards and Golden Langur. In addition there are about 86 mammals, over 350 birds, and over 540 plant species. The park area is stretched over three Dzongkhag namely, Zhemgang, Sarpang and Pemagatshel.

Other places of interest
Other places of interest are Phumithang Lhakhang, Tharpa Choeling Lhakhang which is one of the oldest, in Tama Village built by Pema Lingpa to tame the tigers and the elephants, which posed dangers to villagers in Tama and adjacent areas. Also worth visiting is Tingkar Nye which is one of the most sacred place in the entire Khyeng Region and the Gomphu Lhakhang which was founded by Lam Sacha Yoezer. The Lhakhang has ancient scriptures and one thousand names of the Buddhas written in gold.

Eastern Bhutan

Eastern Bhutan made up of Monggar at 1,620m, Trashigang at 1,000 m, Trashiyangtse at 1,880m, Pemagatshel at 1,560m and Samdrup Jongkhar at 160m is the most densely populated region. In ancient times, eastern Bhutan was an important trade route between India and Tibet.

The *Tshanglas* or *Sharchops* are known to be humble and soft spoken and the women are famed for their matchless weaving skills. The language spoken in the east is *Tshanglakha* though there are many local dialects.

Eastern Bhutan is a region of deep V-shaped valleys dotted with several monasteries and stupas. Fields and dwellings cling to bare slopes. The climate is generally warmer and drier, the forests thinner and the altitudes lower than in the west. The main crop is maize, though rice and wheat are also grown.

Dzongkhags in Eastern Bhutan:

Monggar

Trashigang

Trashiyangtse

Pemagatshel

Samdrup Jongkhar.

Yeshey Dorji

MONGGAR

Altitude 1,620m

The journey from Bumthang to Monggar is one of the most beautiful in the Himalayas, crossing 3,800m high Thrumshing La. Monggar marks the beginning of eastern Bhutan and is the fastest developing Dzongkhag in eastern Bhutan and the second largest town in the east.

Monggar has an area of 1,939.75 sq.km with altitude ranging from 240m to 4,000m. The Dzongkhag has 17 Gewogs which includes Balam, Chali, Chaskar, Drepong, Drametse, Gongdue, Jurmey, Kengkhar, Monggar, Narang, Ngatshang, Saling, Shermung, Silambi, Thangrong, Tsamang and Tsakaling.

Of the total land area, about 1,119 acres are devoted to paddy and 7,806 acres to dryland farming. Potato and corn are the principal cash crops in the Dzongkhag. With only about 34km of feeder road, most settlements remain remote and scattered.

Gewogs : 17
Population :
39,922 (2009 est.)
Male : 19,996
Female : 19,926
Hospital : 1
BHUs : 24
ORCs : 57
Traditional Units: 4
Schools : 50

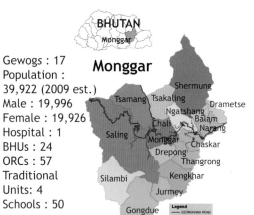

Places of interest in Monggar

Monggar Dzong is one of Bhutan's newest Dzong, built in the 1930s. It was built in keeping with the tradition of not using any drawings or nails. A visit to the Dzong provides the impression of how traditional Bhutanese architecture has continued to thrive through the centuries.

Yakgang Lhakhang is a privately owned monastery founded by Lam Sangdag, the sixth son of Terton Pema Lingpa and is located 20 minutes walk from Monggar town. It stands as one of the great cultural significance as it is a repository of

Monggar Dzong

a wide range of spiritual treasures and other sacred objects known to have been revealed by Terton Pema Lingpa.

Drametse Lhakhang is one of the largest and most important Nyingmapa monastery in eastern Bhutan. From the highway between Trashigang and Monggar, it is around 18km or one hour drive. Drametse Lhakhang was founded in 1511 by Ani Choeten Zangmo, the grand-daughter of the famous Bhutanese saint Pema Lingpa (1450-1521), who named the place as Dremetse, meaning no enmities place or peak. It is the home of Drametse Choeje family which has produced many eminent religious personali-ties including three Zhabdrung incarnations and the seventh Gangtey Tulku. The current spiritual head of Drametse is Sungtrul Rinpoche, who is believed to be the eleventh incarnation of Pema Lingpa.

The monastery is known for the origin of the Drametse Nga Cham (The Mask Dance of the Drums of Drametse). The monastery contains many ancient manuscripts or text books.

Zhongar Dzong is Monggar's original Dzong which has remained in ruins for centuries. It is half an hour drive from Monggar town and about half-hour walk from the nearest road point.

Drametse Lhakhang

Tagchu Goenpa is a privately owned lhakhang built in 1825 by one of the disciples of Togden Shakya Shri, a renowned lama from eastern Tibet. It is two hours walk from Themnangbi Lhakhang and four hours walk from Monggar via Gangula ancient mule trek.

Aja Ney is located at an altitude of more than 3,500m above sea level and is a three-day walk from Monggar Dzong. Guru Padmasambhava visited Bhutan in the 8th century to subdue the demons and to spread the Buddha Dharma. Three sacred places which was blessed by Guru Padmasambhava are Ombha in Trashiyangtse, Aja in Monggar and Hungrel in Paro. These places became sacred and important religious sites as the three sacred letters; *Om Aa Hung* were found imprinted onto rock surface there.

The history of Aja Nye dates back to 850 AD when according to legend, the last letter "*Aa*" in the Chokoey alphabet was miraculously imprinted in white on the reddish-brown rock in the cave after Guru Padmasambhava completed his three month meditation. Thus the sacred cave derived its name *Aja* from the 100 Aa printed on the inner wall of the cave. It is believed that the more one sees the sacred letters, the more merit one will gain and those without sin usually find the most.

Aja Nye holds a host of religious sites and symbols including Guru's foot prints, body prints, the print of his seat, prints indicating the subjugation of evil, Khandro Dowa Zangmo's foot prints, 108 retreat caves of Guru Padmasambhava, and the foot prints of Lam Karma Jamyang who discovered the hidden sacred sites. They are located in mountains, bamboo groves, meadows, gorges, and dense forests and takes a minimum of three days to complete visits to all these *Nyes*.

Drametse Nga Cham or the Mask Dance of the Drums from Drametse is a sacred dance performed during the Drametse festival. In 2008 it was classified by UNESCO masterpiece of oral and as an intangible world cultural heritage.

The dance features sixteen masked male dancers wearing colourful costumes and ten other men making up the orchestra. The dance has a calm and contemplative part that represents the peaceful deities and a rapid and athletic part where the dancers embody wrathful deities.

Dancers dressed in colourful robes and wearing wooden masks with features of real and mythical animals perform a prayer dance in the soeldep cham, the main shrine, before appearing one by one in the main courtyard. The orchestra consists of cymbals, trumpets and drums, including the *bang nga*, a large cylindrical drum, the *lag nga*, a small hand-held circular flat drum and the *nga chen*, a drum beaten with a bent drumstick.

The Drametse Nga Cham was introduced by Kuenga Wangpo, the fourth son of Terton Pema Lingpa. It was first performed in 1511 at the consecration of the Drubchu Goenpa in Drametse in Monggar. According to legend, Kuenga Wangpo was transported while in his dream to the celestial palace of Guru Padmasambhava where he witnessed the mask dance being performed.

Thus, its form has both religious and cultural significance, because it is believed to have originally been performed by the celestial beings. In the 19th century, versions of the Drametse Nga Cham were introduced in other parts of Bhutan and is now performed during festivals in most parts of the country. Today, the dance has evolved from a local event centred on a particular community into an art form, representing the identity of the Bhutanese nation as a whole.

Drametse Nga Cham being performed

Tenzin Namgay

TRASHIGANG

Altitude 1,620m

Trashigang is one of the largest and most densely populated Dzongkhag in the country after Thimphu. It is the heart of eastern Bhutan and was once the centre of important trade with Tibet. Trashigang town is the main market for those living in Merak and Sakten. It has warm and equitable climate and is rich in tropical crops and fruits.

Trashigang has a total area of 2,198.02 sq.km with altitude ranging from 520m to 4,500m. The Dzongkhag has three Dungkhags, Sakten, Thrimshing and Wamrong and 15 Gewogs which includes Bartsham, Bidung, Kanglung, Kangpara, Khaling, Lumang, Merak, Phongmey, Radhi, Sakten, Samkhar, Shongphu, Thrimshing, Uzorong and Yangneer. Though the Dzongkhag has over 93km of internal feeder roads, most settlements are still inaccessible by motorable roads.

The people in the Dzongkhag mainly depend on agricultural activities for their livelihood. While wheat, paddy, mustard and barley are the main cereals grown, maize is the dominant food grain besides rice. Potatoes, vegetables, essential oils and woven local textiles are the main source of cash income.

Trashigang is famed for its weavers and special textiles and fabrics, woven by mostly women.

'Bura Aikapur' is one the weaving specialities of this region

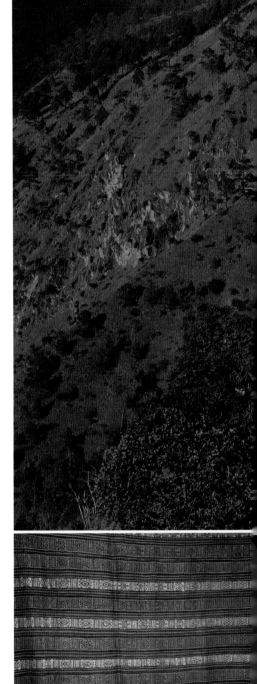

Bura Aikapur Kira

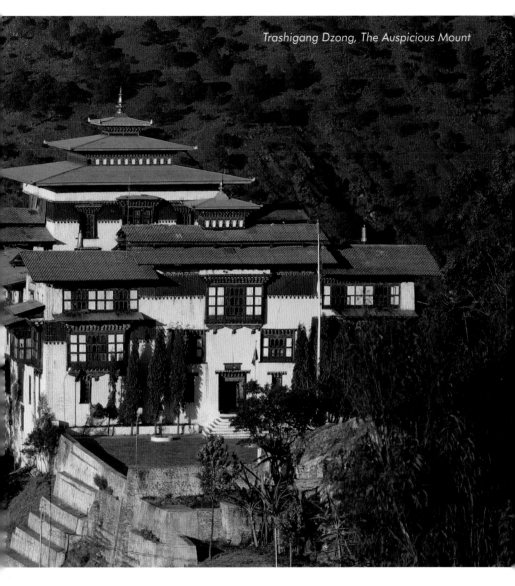

Trashigang Dzong, The Auspicious Mount

BHUTAN
Trashigang

Trashigang

Bartsham
Phongmey
Bidung
Yangneer
Sakten
Radhi
Kanglung
Samkhar
Shongphu
Uzorong
Merak
Khaling
Kangpara
Lumang
Thrimshing

Legend
FARM ROAD
FEEDER ROAD
HIGHWAY

Gewogs : 15
Dungkhag : 3
Population : 51,781
(2009 est.)
Male : 26,243
Female : 25,538
Hospitals : 3
BHUs : 19
ORCs : 57
Traditional Units : 4
Schools : 66

Places of interest in Trashigang

Trashigang Dzong meaning the 'Fortress of Auspicious Mount', is situated on a very steep hill overlooking the river, Drangme Chhu. It was built by Kudung Pekar Chopel in 1659 on the site originally planned by Chhoegyal Minjure Tempa, the third temporal ruler of Bhutan. Its *Dzongpons* dominated eastern Bhutan in the political history of the country. Today, the Dzong serves as the administrative seat for the Dzongkhag as well as the home of the monk body.

Trashigang Dzong has eight different lhakhangs which includes Lam Lhakhang in the central tower dedicated to Zhabdrung Ngawang Namgyal, the Tshechu Lhakhang with Guru Tshengye, the Goenkhang dedicated to deities Mahakala and Mahakali, the Dupthob Lhakhang for Dupthob Thangthong Gyalpo and other great Buddhist saints, the Kuenray Lhakhang, the Tshokshing Lhakhang which has the lineage of Drukpa, Karamapa, Nyingmapa and Zogchen displayed and the Dema Lhakhang with 21 kinds of Taras.

Chador Lhakhang earlier known as Goenpa Ringbu, is the most important temple in terms of its establishment and relic it holds in Bartsham. It is situated in Bartsham and is a two-hour drive from Trashigang town. Most of the religious festivals in Bartsham take place at Chador Lhakhang with the most important being Soldeb Tshechu or festival of mask dances lasting for three days on the 10th month of Bhutanese calender.

Ranjung Woesel Chholing monastery is more than half an hour drive from Trashigang town. It is a Nyingmapa

Robert Dompnier

monastery founded by Garab Rinpoche in 1990. One can get a good view of the valley from the monastery.

Yonphu Lhakhang located in Kanglung is said to have been founded by a Tibetan Lama from Kham. In the 16th century the place was visited by Sangdag, son of Terton Pema Lingpa who also built a lhakhang. The two lhakhangs were merged into one later. The lhakhang has many sacred *nangtens* (relics) which includes statue of Garab Dorji, Tshepamed, Dorji Sempa, Dolma and Guru Padmasambhava. All of these are believed to have been brought along by Sangdag and are considered *Termas* (religious treasures).

Unlike other places where Tshechus are conducted once in a year, it is conducted thrice in a year, here. The first Tshechu known as the Tenda Tshechu (birth anniversary ritual) is conducted from 8th to the 10th of the 5th month of Bhutanese calendar. The second one is conducted for a day in the 8th month and is known as *Tercham* (treasure dance) Tshechu. The last Tshechu is conducted from 14th to 16th in the 10th month of Bhutanese Calendar and

Ranjung Woesel Chholing

Jigme Wangchuk

Tercham, locally known as Homcham

on the 17th the important *nangtens* (relics) are brought out for public display. The mask dances of this temple are unique and different from the ones staged in other parts of the country.

Namdru Choling Lhakhang is located in Radhi, Trashigang. It was built in the early 20th century by Trongsa Droenyer Ugyen Dorji after his retirement, as a pledge to atone for the lives he had taken as a warrior. Droenyer Ugyen Dorji had played an important part in shaping Bhutan's history as he had served his masters Jigme Namgyal and Ugyen Wangchuck, First Druk Gyalpo for 58 long years as a gallant warrior and a swordsman extraordinaire during the most turbulent years in Bhutanese history.

The Lhakhang has numerous relics which includes of a set of *Kanjur* and *Tenjur*, a small horn from a rhinoceros, a Terma statue of Lord Buddha, sacred *Thangkhas*, cymbals and masks. The highlight of the temple's festivals is the annual masked dance which is said to have been introduced by Droenyer Ugyen Dorji.

Bhutan Times 140

Namdru Choling Lhakhang

TRASHIYANGTSE

Altitude 1,830m

Trashiyangtse is the newest Dzong-khag created in 1992 by separating the erstwhile Trashiyangtse Dung-khag from Trashigang Dzongkhag. It was once the gateway between Tibet and the neighbouring Indian states, via Arunachal Pradesh. Blessed by Guru Padmasambhava, Trashiyangtse has several pilgrimage sites. It is also endowed with a lot of natural beauty and biological diversity.

Trashiyangtse has a total area of 1445.95 sq.km with altitude ranging from 760m to 5,900m. The Dzongkhag has eight Gewogs which includes Bumdelling, Jamkhar, Khamdang, Ramjar, Toetsho, Tongshang, Yalang and Yangtse.

Of the total land area, only eight percent is under cultivation. Trashi-yangtse is also known for its Wildlife Sanctuary at Bumdelling.

*Trashiyangtse Dzong,
Fortress of Auspicious Fortune*

Gewogs : 8
Population : 18,994
(2009 est.)
Male : 9,431
Female : 9,564
Hospital : 1
BHUs : 7
ORCs : 23
Traditional Unit: 1
Schools : 30

*The Dzongkhag
is renowned
for finely made
wooden cups,
bowls and con-
tainers made
from avocado
and maple wood
using water-driv-
en and treadle
lathes.*

Trashiyangtse

Tenzin Namgay, Bhutan Times Ltd.

Places of interest in Trashiyangtse

Trashiyangtse has very important historical and religious sites. The best known among them are the Gomphu Kora located near Doksum in Tongzhang, the Rigsum Goenpa located in Bumdelling, Dechen Phodrang Lhakhang, Ombha Nye and Choeten Kora.

Trashiyangtse Dzong, meaning 'Fortress of Auspicious Fortune', was re-built in 1656 by Terton Pema Lingpa from the ruins of Dongdi Dzong of 9th century. It was further renovated and sanctified by a sacred consecration ceremony in 2005.

Choeten Kora which is patterned on the stupa of Boudhanath in Kathmandu, Nepal was built in 1740 by Lama Ngawang Loday to subdue a demon dwelling at the site where the choeten stands today along the river bank. After the construction, the

Choeten Kora

Robert Dompnier

demon that harmed the people was subdued and banished. Thereafter, it is said that the people in the valley continued to live in peace and harmony. It is a very sacred destination for the people of Tawang from adjoining Arunachal Pradesh in India.

During the second month of the Bhutanese calendar, one of the most ancient festivals in Bhutan is held here, popularly known as Choeten Kora Tshechu. Many people from the neighbouring Indian state of Arunachal Pradesh visit the festival every year as well as devotees from Merak and Sakten Gewogs.

Bumdelling Wildlife Sanctuary is a pleasant three hour walk from town. It is the winter roosting place for the Black-necked Crane which fly over from nearby Tibet to enjoy the winter months in a warmer climate. It is also home to Snow Leopards, Tigers and Red Pandas.

Ombha Nye meaning the sacred place of hidden Om is 33km from Trashiyangtse town and another four hour leisurely walk. It is one of the three sacred places blessed by Guru Padmasambhava which bears sacred letters; *Om Aa Hung* imprinted onto rock surface there. The letter *Om* is visible on the rock surface if one watches carefully from a distance of about seven yards.

Ombha was first revealed as a sacred *Nye* by some descendents of Guru Choewang. It was blessed by Terton Pema Lingpa and Ani Choeten Zangmo who spent sometime in meditation here. Guru Padmasambhava blessed the place while he was in pursuit of Yonglha alias Geygnen Choephel guardian deity of Gomphu Kora. About three hours walk down from here is another famous Nye called Gongza. It is believed that visiting such sacred places will purify one's minds and cleanse the sins committed. Thus, these scared places attracts pilgrims from all over the country.

Rigsum Goenpa is a seven-hour walk along a mountain trail from Choeten Kora. It is more than 300-years old and is regarded as one of the most sacred monuments in eastern Bhutan. It was founded in the 18th century by Lama Tshering Gyamtsho, a close disciple of the 9th Je Khenpo Shacha Rinchen. After his death, his nephew and spiritual heir Lama Jangchhub Gyeltshen renovated and extended the present-day lower lhakhang with the unique mural paintings of the Life History of Lord Buddha, which is a rare artefact not seen anywhere. Lama Jangchhub Gyeltshen's spiritual heir Lama Ngawang Loday further constructed the bigger lhakhang and installed valuable *Ku Sung Thukten* (sacred artefacts representing the body, mind and speech of the Buddha) including the statue of Jowo Shacha Muni, hundred volumes of *Kanjur* and *Desheg Chhorten Gyed* (the eight enlightening stupas of Lord Buddha) for the well being of the Bhutanese people.

Rigsum Goenpa

Bhutan Times Ltd.

Gomphu Kora Lhakhang is located about 12 km from Chazam in Trashigang towards Trashiyangtse. It is a sacred site where around 850 AD, Guru Padmasambhava subdued an evil spirit he chased all the way from Lhasa Samye, Tibet. There are several sacred places around the Gomphu Kora.

The annual festival at Gomphu Kora was initiated 400 years ago after the temple was built by Ngagi Wangchuck and consecrated by Terton Pema Lingpa. It is one of the biggest festivals in eastern Bhutan providing a welcome break for the locals to trade, socialize, and celebrate before the start of the farming season. Traditionally, the festival was an occasion for the people of eastern Bhutan, to choose their spouses. Unlike other festivities in the country the Gomphu Kora is known for its culture of nightlife, which has evolved around the festival.

PEMAGATSHEL

Altitude 1,560m

Pemagatshel meaning 'Blissful Land of the Lotus', is located in the south-eastern part of the country. The Dzongkhag is characterized by highly dissected mountain ranges, steep slopes and narrow valleys with little flat land. It has rugged terrain and scattered settlements.

Pemagatshel has a total area of 1019.46 sq.km with altitude ranging from 80m to 2,640m. The Dzongkhag has 11 Gewogs which includes Chimong, Chokhorling, Chongshing Borang, Dechenling, Dungmin, Khar, Nanong, Norbugang, Shumar, Yurung and Zobel.

About 53 percent of the total area is under forest cover, comprising mainly coniferous and broadleaf species. With about 45 percent of the total land area under cultivation, the Dzongkhag has a good percentage of arable land. Land holdings are, however, dominated by *Tseri* cultivation with only negligible wetland farming. Dry land cultivation is also a dominant agricultural practice with maize grown as the main crop.

Gewogs : 11
Population : 23,478
(2009 est.)
Male : 11,647
Female : 11,831
Hospital : 1
BHUs : 12
ORCs : 33
Traditional Med.
Units : 2
Schools : 37

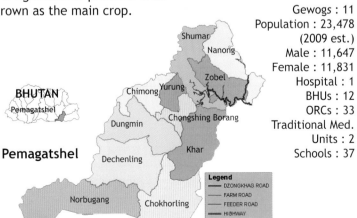

Pemagatshel

BHUTAN
Pemagatshel

Shumar
Nanong
Zobel
Chimong
Yurung
Chongshing Borang
Dungmin
Khar
Dechenling
Norbugang
Chokhorling

Legend
—— DZONGKHAG ROAD
—— FARM ROAD
—— FEEDER ROAD
—— HIGHWAY

Pemagatshel Dzong

Tenzin Namgay, Bhutan Times Ltd.

Pemagatshel is known for its production of cultural and religious items such as gyalings (similar to reed), dhungs (long horns) thonphu poe (incense), ngazhing jurmo (tea leaves) and yurung bura (made from raw silk).

Robert Dompnier

Places of Interest in Pemagatshel

Yongla Pelri Goenpa

Yongla Pelri Goenpa which was founded in the 18th century by Kheydrup Jigme Kuendrel, is one of the holiest shrine in eastern Bhutan. During the Duar War with the British in 1865, the monastery was used as a base fir religious ceremonies by Trongsa Penlop Jigme Namgyal. The monastery which houses around 100 monks observes number of festivals around the year.

Yongla Pelri Goenpa

Kheri Goenpa was founded in the late 15th century by Kheydrup Kuenga Wangpo, one of the five sons of the great treasure revealer Terton Pema Lingpa. It is said to have been built directly over a lake which is still believed to exist below it. The main relic of the monastery is Buddha Sakya Muni. Local community religious dance festival is held here on the 10th Day of the 4th Bhutanese calender.

Tenzin Namgay

SAMDRUP JONGKHAR

Altitude 160m

Samdrup Jongkhar lies in the south-eastern part of Bhutan bordering the Indian states of Assam and Arunachal Pradesh. The road from Trashigang to Samdrup Jongkhar was completed in 1960s and enables the eastern half of the country to access and benefit from trade with the south as well as from across the Indian border.

Samdrup Jongkhar has a total area of 1,871.56 sq.km with major portions of the Dzongkhag falling within the subtropical belt and altitude ranging from 80m to 2,640m. The Dzongkhag comprises of three Dungkhags - Bhangtar, Daifam and Nganglam and 11 Gewogs which includes Dewathang, Gomdar, Langhchenphu, Lauri, Martshala, Orong, Pemathang, Phuntshothang, Samrang, Serthi and Wangphu.

Place of Interest in Samdrup Jongkhar

Zangtho Pelri Lhakhang is a new monastery located across from the entrance to the Dzong which is worth a visit.

Samdrup Jongkhar Dzong

Samdrup Jongkhar

Gewogs : 11
Dungkhag : 3
Population : 36,608
(2009 est.)
Male : 18,782
Female : 17,826
Hospitals : 2
BHUs : 8
ORCs : 36
Traditional Unit : 2
Schools : 28

Tenzin Namgay, Bhutan Times Ltd.

Samdrup Jongkhar is the commercial hub for five eastern Dzongkhags.

Southern Bhutan: The Foothills

Southern Bhutan is made up of Dagana at 1,520m, Samtse at 420m, Sarpang at 325m, Tsirang, at 1,560m. The people from south are known as *Lhotsampas* who follow the Hindu religion and speak Nepali.

The proximity to markets in India have contributed to the development of these areas which has encouraged small trading towns to come into existence. There are also a number of manufacturing industries such as liquor, bricks, processed fruit juices and cement plants. Apart from rice grown for local consumption, other crops, including oranges and cardamom are grown for export.

Dzongkhags in Southern Bhutan

Dagana
Samtse
Sarpang
Tsirang

Samtse
Dagana
Tsirang
Sarpang

DAGANA

Altitude 1,520m

Dagana is one of the remotest Dzong-khags in the country. It falls within the temperate zone in the north and sub-tropical in the south and has hot and wet summers and cool and dry winters. About 79 percent of the total area in the Dzongkhag are under forest cover with trees like Champ, Arguray, Chirpine and Sal.

Dagana has a total area of 1,7119.13 sqkm with altitude ranging from 200m to 4,720m. The Dzongkhag has 14 Gewogs which includes Deorali, Dorona, Drujeygang, Gesarling, Goshi, Kana, Khibisa, Laja, Lhamoi Zingkha, Nichula, Tashiding, Tsendagang, Tseza and Tshangkha.

People in Dagana are simple and derive their daily sustenance from farming. Settlements in the Dzong-khag are fairly dispersed and remote.

Daga Trashi Yangtse Dzong

Places of interest in Dagana

Daga Trashi Yangtse Dzong was traditionally the stronghold of the powerful Daga Penlop. Today, it houses the district monastic body and the headquarters of the district administration of Dagana. Situated on a ridge overlooking an expansive valley, it was built in the 16th century by Zhabdrung Ngawang Namgyal and renovated in 1897.

The Dzong is unique in its shape and size and houses many sacred lhakhangs.

Zhabdrung Cholay Namgyal Lhakhang located in Nyindukha village, was the residence of the last Daga Dzongpon Rinzin Dorji, one of the six powerful regional governors in the early twentieth century. It is also the birthplace of Zhabdrung Sungtrul Cholay Namgyal (1708-1736) and till date *Zhabdrung Kuchoey* or the death anniversary ritual of Zhabdrung is observed on the 10th day of the 4th month of the Bhutanese calender. The day is marked with religious Buddhist ceremonies and funeral ceremonies for Zhabdrung.

Zhabdrung Cholay Namgyal Lhakhang and the house of late Daga Dzongpon, Rinzin Dorji

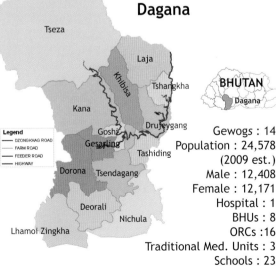

Dagana

Tseza
Laja
Khibisa
Tshangkha
Kana
Drujeygang
Goshi
Gesarling
Tashiding
Dorona   Tsendagang
Deorali
Nichula
Lhamoi Zingkha

Legend
— DZONGKHAG ROAD
— FARM ROAD
— FEEDER ROAD
— HIGHWAY

BHUTAN
Dagana

Gewogs : 14
Population : 24,578
(2009 est.)
Male : 12,408
Female : 12,171
Hospital : 1
BHUs : 8
ORCs :16
Traditional Med. Units : 3
Schools : 23

SAMTSE

Altitude 420m

Historically, Samtse was sparsely populated as the mountain-dwelling Bhutanese considered the low-lying Dzongkhag to be prone to tropical diseases. Samtse has a total area of 1,301.79 with altitude ranging from 180m to 4,200m. The Dzongkhag has two Dungkhags and 15 Gewogs which includes Bara, Biru, Chargarey, Chengmari, Denchukha, Dorokha, Dungtoe, Yoeseltse, Lehereni, Ugyentse, Pugli, Samtse, Sipsu, Tading and Tendu.

Majority of the Gewogs are located at the foothills bordering the Indian states of West Bengal and Sikkim. Proximity to markets in India offer excellent opportunity for horticultural development on a commercial scale. Mandarin, cardamom, ginger and areca nut are grown widely for cash income. Favourable terrain and fertile agricultural land makes significant contribution to farm productivity. Samtse also has abundant natural deposits of talc, dolomite and other resources which are exported on a regular basis. There are several major mining and mineral based industries in the Dzongkhag.

Samtse Dzong

Tenzin Namgay, Bhutan Times Ltd.

Samtse

BHUTAN
Samtse

Bara
Tendu
Biru Lehereni
Dungtoe
Chargarey Chengmari Denchukha
Sipsu Ugyentse Dorokha
Yoeseltse
Samtse Tading
Pugli

Legend
—— DZONGKHAG ROAD
—— FARM ROAD
—— FEEDER ROAD
—— HIGHWAY

Gewogs : 15
Dungkhag : 2
Population : 64,314
(2009 est.)
Male : 33,283
Female : 31,030
Hospitals : 3
BHUs : 9
ORCs : 18
Traditional Units : 2
Schools : 31

SARPANG

Altitude 325m

Sarpang Dzongkhag is situated in the central southern foothills bordering India. The area of the Dzongkhag stretches from Lhamoizhingkha in the west to Manas National Park in the east. It is one of the oldest towns in the country with access to motorable roads as early 1950s. Due to its close proximity to the Indian markets, Sarpang has been the commercial center for the central Dzongkhags.

Sarpang has a total area of 1,651.71 sq. km with an altitude ranging from 160m to 4,200m. The Dzongkhag is administratively divided into two Dungkhags which comprise Gelephu, the commercial hub for southern Dzongkhags and Lhamoizhingkha. It has 12 Gewogs which includes Bhur, Chuzargang, Dekiling, Dovan, Gelephu, Hilley, Jigmecholing, Sompangkha, Sershong, Singhi, Tarathang and Umling.

About 12 percent of the total area is under agriculture. Paddy, maize, wheat and millet are some of the major crops. Cash crops such as orange, areca nut, cardamom, ginger, guava, lemon, banana and mango are grown extensively.

Favourable terrain and climatic conditions combined with fertile agriculture land offer tremendous opportunity for farm mechanization and commercial horticultural development.

Lily Wangchhuk

Place of interest in Sarpang

Gelephu Tshachu is about 15km from Gelephu town. The hot spring is known for curing all types of aliments and attracts people from all parts of the country during winter.

Gewogs : 12
Dungkhag : 2
Population : 40,436
(2009 est.)
Male : 20,974
Female : 19,462
Hospitals : 2
BHUs : 10
ORCs : 11
Traditional
Med. Unit : 1
Schools : 22

TSIRANG

Altitude 1,560m

Located in the south-central part of the country, Tsirang is noted for its gentle slopes, mild climates and rich biodiversity. Favourable as well as diverse agro-ecological features provides the Dzongkhag with a high potential for the cultivation of different types of cereal grains as well as horticultural crops. Most of the Gewogs in the Dzongkhag have good transportation links and benefits from market access to major towns like Gelephu and Thimphu.

Tsirang has a total area of 636.47 sq.km with elevation ranging from 240m to 4,190m. The Dzongkhag has 12 Gewogs which includes Barshong, Patsharling, Dunglagang, Goseling, Kikhorthang, Mendrelgang,

Gewogs : 12
Population : 19,933 (2009 est.)
Male : 10,107
Female : 9,825
Hospital : 1
BHUs : 4
ORCs : 13
Traditional Med. Unit : 1
Schools : 14

Sergithang, Phuntenchu, Rang-thangling, Semjong, Tsholingkhar, Tsirangtoe. Damphu, located in Kikhorthang Gewog, is the main town and the administration center.

Approximately 58 percent of the land area is under forest cover comprising mainly broadleaf and chirpine forests while 42 percent is under agricultural cultivation. Paddy, maize and millet are the major cereals grown while orange, cardamom and vegetables are the principal cash crops. The sale of mandarin and cardamom constitute an important source of income for most of the farmers. Livestock rearing is also an important economic activity contributing to both subsistence consumption and to the income of farm households.

Places of interest in Tsirang

Namgay Choling Dratshang which spans over an area of 9.37 acres, was established in 1984. It houses three lhakhangs and sacred religious treasures.

Tashichhodzong and its surroundings covered in snow

Two monks dressed as terrifying deities are ready to enter a festival dance

Chapter 16

TOURISM

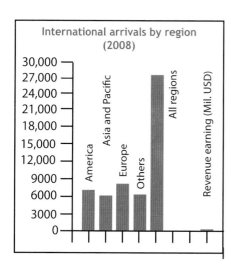

International arrivals by region (2008)

International arrivals by region (2008)	
America	6,941
Asia and Pacific	6,005
Europe	8,346
Others	6,344
All regions	27,636
Revenue earning (Mil. USD)	38.8

Source: Tourism Council of Bhutan, 2008

Tourism Policy

Tourism was first introduced in the country in 1974 with 287 arrivals. It was privatized by the government in 1991. Today it is a vibrant business with around 600 tour operators. Even though the potential for tourism development is enormous, Bhutan has taken a very cautious approach, recognizing the problems associated with mass tourism. As a control-free policy can have irreversible impact on the environment, culture and identity of the people, the tourism industry in Bhutan is based on the principle of sustainability, indicating that tourism must be environmentally and ecologically friendly, socially and culturally acceptable and economically viable. It therefore strongly adheres to the policy of 'high value low impact' tourism with the number of tourists visiting Bhutan regulated to manageable levels through a policy of government regulated tourist tariff.

Minimum Tariff

The policy of high value tourism is best supported by a system of daily minimum tariff of USD 200 per person per night fixed by the government of Bhutan. The rates can be higher, depending upon the nature of services desired beyond the entitlement for the minimum tariff. The minimum daily tariff with effect from 2011 is USD 250 per person per night halt.

The above tariff covers:
Government royalty/tourists/night
High Season   USD 65
Low Season   USD 55

2 percent government tax
High Season   USD 2.30
Low Season   USD 1.87

Contribution to Tourism Development Fund
USD 10 per tourist (whole duration)

The balance amount after all the above deductions covers:
- Accommodation
- Food and non-alcoholic beverages.
- Internal transport
- Guide
- Overheads
- Entrance fees for museums
- Trekking equipment
- Porter and pony charges
- Domestic operator's return

The minimum price applies to groups of three or more. For independent travelers daily surcharges in addition to minimum price apply at USD 40 each for a single traveller and USD 30 for two persons. Children less than five years can travel free.

The daily minimum price is most often misinterpreted to be extremely high. The fee in fact covers a package that include all internal taxes and charges including royalty, accommodation, all meals, services of licensed guides, internal transport and camping equipments and haulage for trekking tours.

The royalty portion goes to the government exchequer, which in turn mainly supports free medical care, free education and other welfare schemes. All visitors in a way therefore make valuable contribution to the welfare system of the country.

Filming in Bhutan

Foreign companies and foreign film-makers interested in any activities related to films, documentaries and advertisements in Bhutan are required to obtain filming permits from the Bhutan InfoComm and Media Authority (BICMA) and abide by the Bhutan Filming Regulation, 2007 which is available on www.bicma. gov.bt. Applications for a filming permit have to be submitted to BICMA at least 30 days in advance. The application will need to be accompanied by:

- Synopsis of the film-theme/ background/objective/purpose

- Specific locations/objectives/ activities

- Duration of filming activity in the country

- Composition of the team and list of equipment, accessories/ consumables

- Letter of recommendation from the sponsoring agency, company profile and resume.

- Any other additional information, as the Authority may require.

Filming Royalty

The filming royalty varies depending on the category as follows:

Documentary	Nu 150,000
Films	Nu 500,000
Advertisement	Nu 250,000
Music Video	Nu 150,000
TV Series (per episode)	Nu 150,000
News coverage	No royalty levied

In addition to the above, a security deposit of Nu 100,000 will need to be deposited with BICMA which is refundable upon submission of a copy of the final edited version of the film and after being reviewed by the Authority.

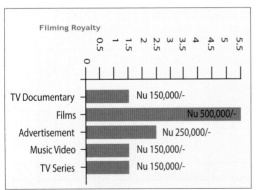

Filming Royalty

TV Documentary	Nu 150,000/-
Films	Nu 500,000/-
Advertisement	Nu 250,000/-
Music Video	Nu 150,000/-
TV Series	Nu 150,000/-

General information on visiting Bhutan

With the exception of travellers from India, Bangladesh and Maldives, all visitors to Bhutan require a visa. Visas can only be obtained through a Bhutanese tour operator after full payment has been made. Air tickets to Bhutan can only be issued after the visa is issued. Bhutanese Embassies and Missions abroad do not issue visa for private visitors to Bhutan.

Best Times to Travel

Winter (November – January) is the best time of the year for bird watching, trekking in the lower altitudes or a bicycle trip along the mountain roads. The trekking routes in the high mountains are covered in deep snow and are impassable at this time of year. The endangered Black-necked Crane spends the winter in the high valley of Bumdelling (in eastern Bhutan) and Phobjikha (in western Bhutan).

Spring (February - April) is a perfect time for kayaking, rafting and trekking in moderate altitudes. The most popular religious dance festival - Paro Tshechu takes place in Spring.

Summer (May - August) brings with it the monsoon, but this should not dissuade travellers. Rain falls for short periods daily but is manageable with adequate planning and equipment. Pleasant summer temperatures without heat or humidity can be found in central and western Bhutan. Treks in high mountain areas are characterized by mild temperatures and vibrant flora.

Autumn (September – October) is the traditional high season in Bhutan. September and October have the highest number of *Tshechus*. Trekkers particularly enjoy the clear view of the mountains in October and the low rainfall. Rice harvest means a picturesque landscape remarkable terraces and changing colour.

To reach Bhutan by air

The most convenient way of entering Bhutan is by Druk Air, the national carrier which operates daily flights from Bangkok (Thailand), three times a week from Delhi, three times a week from Kolkata, once a week from Bodh Gaya (India), three times a week from Kathmandu (Nepal), twice a week from Dhaka (Bangladesh) and twice a week from Bagdogra (India) to Paro (Bhutan). The flight timings and frequency vary according to season. The flight offers spectacular views of the Himalayan ranges including the Mount Everest region which is seen at its best during the winter months, when skies are generally very clear. The airport is about an hour drive from the capital, Thimphu.

To reach Bhutan by land

The southern border town of Phuentsholing has the road access open for tourists. It lies approximately 170km from the Indian domestic airport at Bagdogra, West Bengal (India). The travel time for the 176km stretch from Phuentsholing to Thimphu can be more than six hours.

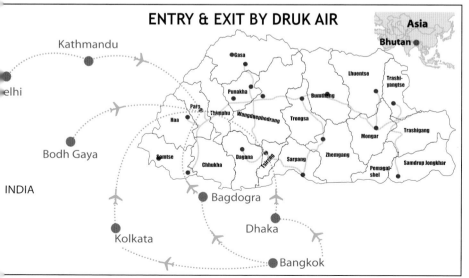

Customs

All arriving passengers and visitors are required to fill in the required details and submit the customs declaration form upon arrival at the Paro Airport.

Tourists

Visitors are allowed to import temporarily free of customs duty her/his personal and articles of high value such as sound recording equipment, film projectors, slides and film for demonstration, professional equipment, instrument and appliances like video recorders, provided that the visitors on arrival declare all dutiable goods in the passenger declaration form and produce the same form at the time of departure If these items are disposed off in Bhutan by sale or gift they become liable for customs duty.

Visitors are advised to be cautious while purchasing old and used items, especially of religious or cultural significance as customs authorities will not allow any old/used items to be taken out of the country unless certified as non-antique.

Tourists allowance

• Spirits: One bottle not larger than one litre

• Cigarettes: One carton (containing 200 pieces) subject to 100 percent customs duty and 100 percent sales tax

Free baggage allowance

Bhutanese nationals, other national working as a regular employee in Bhutan and resident in the country are permitted to bring in personal items up to the assessed value of USD 1000 without payment of duties and taxes, subject to the ceiling prescribed below:

• Spirits: Two bottles, not larger than one litre
• Perfume: One bottle, not larger than two ounces
• Gold: 50 grams
• Silver: One kilogram
• Clothing: Maximum of 10 pieces of each type
• Other household or personal goods including electronics and bedding are limited to one piece each
• Cigarettes: One carton (containing 200 pieces) subject to 100 percent customs duty and 100 percent sales tax

Restricted Goods

The following are some of the goods that require an import license or permits from relevant authorities:

ITEM	AUTHORITY
Fire arms, ammunition explosives and explosive devices	Royal Bhutan Police and Ministry of Home and Culture
Live animals and their products	Ministry of Agriculture and Bhutan Agriculture and Food Regulatory Authority
Plant and plant materials	Ministry of Agriculture and Bhutan Agriculture and Food Regulatory Authority
Industrial, toxic wastes and residues and ozone depleating substances	National Environment Commission and Ministry of Economic Affairs
Wireless, remote sensing and broadcasting equipments	Bhutan InfoCom and Media Authority
Scraps	National Environment Commission and Ministry of Economic Affairs
Drugs and pharmaceutical products	Drug Regulatory Authority and Bhutan Narcotic Control Agency
Chemical and fertilizers	Ministry of Agriculture
Plastics packing materials	Ministry of Economic Affairs
Gold, silver and currency in excess of free baggage allowance	Royal Monetary Authority

Source: DRC, MoF, RGoB

PROHIBITED GOODS

• Narcotics and psychotropic drugs and substances
• Pornographic materials
• Any other goods which are prohibited by laws or International Conventions or Treaties to which Bhutan is a signatory

The Kingdom of Bhutan Prohibits the Import and Export of:

♦ Plants / Plants Products
♦ Animals / Animals Products
♦ Insects / Insects Products
♦ Endangered Species

Without Prior Approval

DISTANCE MAP

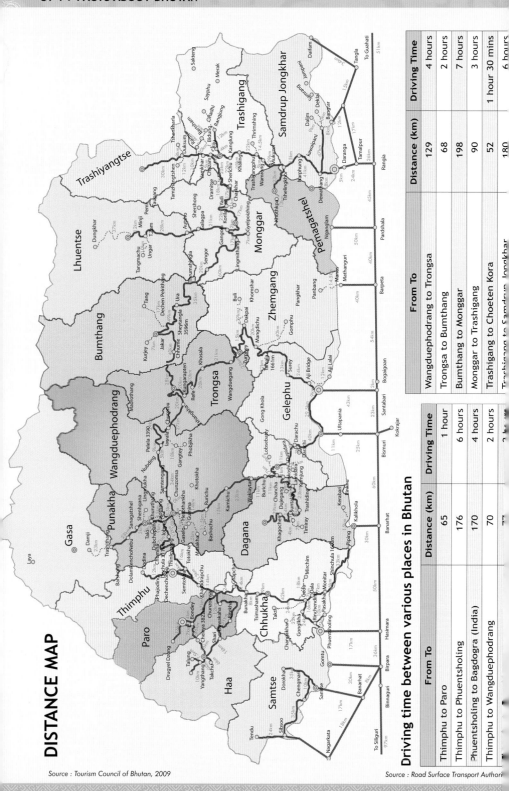

Source : Tourism Council of Bhutan, 2009

Driving time between various places in Bhutan

From To	Distance (km)	Driving Time
Thimphu to Paro	65	1 hour
Thimphu to Phuentsholing	176	6 hours
Phuentsholing to Bagdogra (India)	170	4 hours
Thimphu to Wangduephodrang	70	2 hours

From To	Distance (km)	Driving Time
Wangduephodrang to Trongsa	129	4 hours
Trongsa to Bumthang	68	2 hours
Bumthang to Monggar	198	7 hours
Monggar to Trashigang	90	3 hours
Trashigang to Choeten Kora	52	1 hour 30 mins
Trashigang to Samdrup Jongkhar	180	6 hours

Source : Road Surface Transport Authori

MONTHLY AVERAGE TEMPERATURE

Places	Jan		Feb		Mar		April		May		Jun		Jul		Aug		Sep		Oct		Nov		Dec	
	Max	Min	Max	Min	Max	Min	Max	Min	Max	Min	Max	Min	Max	Min	Max	Min	Max	Min	Max	Min	Max	Min	Max	Min
Paro	12.8	1.4	14.9	3.3	17.6	5.7	20.1	9.1	22.5	12.6	24.5	15.7	25.4	17.9	25.2	17.4	23.5	15.4	20.4	11.0	15.8	6.3	14.0	2.6
Thimphu	14.6	-3.3	15.8	-0.7	18.2	3.0	20.7	6.7	22.8	10.9	24.4	14.6	24.8	15.9	25.1	15.4	23.8	13.6	21.2	8.0	18.3	2.2	16.0	-2.1
Punakha	17.5	5.8	19.3	8.1	22.2	11.2	24.9	13.8	27.3	17.2	29.2	19.3	29.1	20.1	28.9	19.0	27.9	18.1	25.6	15.6	22.1	12.1	18.9	7.5
Wangdue	17.8	5.5	19.4	8.1	22.7	10.8	25.5	14.4	27.3	17.8	28.2	20.3	27.6	20.9	27.9	20.6	27.1	19.5	25.6	15.1	22.4	10.5	19.5	6.0
Trongsa	17.5	5.6	19.3	6.2	22.3	10.4	23.9	13.5	23.6	14.5	24.7	17.2	25.9	18.2	26.6	18.1	25.0	17.1	22.3	13.4	19.3	9.7	18.0	7.2
Bumthang	11.0	-4.2	12.5	-1.3	14.8	1.9	17.1	5.7	19.4	9.4	21.7	12.9	22.5	14.3	22.4	14.3	21.1	12.3	18.0	6.6	15.1	1.6	12.6	-3.6
Mongar	16.1	6.0	18.6	7.9	21.5	11.2	24.0	13.6	25.7	15.8	26.6	18.0	26.8	18.5	27.8	18.3	26.8	17.1	24.4	13.7	20.7	10.0	17.7	7.2
Kanglung	13.6	2.5	15.6	4.6	18.8	7.3	21.1	10.4	22.7	13.3	23.7	16.2	24.3	17.0	24.8	16.8	23.9	15.5	21.7	11.2	18.2	7.2	15.4	3.9
Deothang	21.0	9.5	22.9	11.5	25.3	14.3	26.2	16.3	27.6	18.6	28.5	20.6	28.8	21.1	29.4	21.2	28.6	20.1	28.1	15.9	25.9	14.1	23.0	11.1
Trashi-yangtse	12.3	3.6	14.8	6.2	16.7	8.2	19.8	11.1	22.2	14.2	23.2	17.0	23.7	18.5	23.6	17.9	22.4	16.5	19.9	12.3	16.5	8.1	13.2	4.1
Zhemgang	12.5	4.8	13.9	6.7	16.6	10.1	18.9	13.2	20.7	15.6	22.3	17.7	22.8	18.2	22.8	18.2	21.9	16.9	19.9	13.5	16.9	9.8	13.9	6.3
Phuentsh-oling	23.9	16.2	6.5	5.1	29.5	18.2	1.1	6.3	2.4	0.9	2.6	0.1	31.9	3.1	32.6	1.9	1.6	4.8	1.2	15.6	8.3	6.0	4.9	7.2
Samtse Sipsoo	20.5	13.3	22.7	16.1	25.7	19.0	27.3	21.0	28.0	22.6	28.3	23.9	27.8	24.3	28.5	24.5	28.4	23.6	27.7	21.1	25.1	18.2	22.7	15.2
Tsirang Damphu	14.1	4.6	15.7	6.5	18.7	9.5	20.7	12.9	22.1	15.7	23.1	18.0	23.5	18.6	24.0	18.3	23.4	17.2	21.8	13.4	19.2	9.4	16.3	5.8
Dagana	11.0	6.1	12.3	7.2	16.1	10.9	19.7	13.7	21.9	15.7	23.2	17.6	23.1	18.1	23.0	17.8	22.4	17.1	20.0	15.3	15.8	11.0	13.0	8.2
Gelephu Bhur	22.9	13.4	24.7	16.2	26.6	18.3	28.3	21.0	29.4	22.7	29.7	24.0	30.2	24.3	30.9	24.7	30.4	24.1	28.9	21.2	26.7	17.8	24.1	14.7
Haa Nam-jayling	10.0	-4.2	10.8	-2.0	13.0	1.5	15.3	5.1	17.8	9.4	19.4	12.8	20.3	14.2	20.3	13.9	18.8	12.2	16.4	6.4	13.8	0.8	11.5	-3.1
Pemagat-shel	16.6	5.6	18.1	7.3	20.6	10.1	23.0	12.7	25.0	15.2	25.9	16.9	26.8	17.6	26.4	17.2	25.8	16.2	24.3	12.9	21.2	9.7	18.8	7.0
Khomachu	17.7	6.7	20.3	8.5	23.9	11.8	26.3	14.5	27.2	16.7	28.5	19.3	28.9	19.6	29.3	19.7	28.2	18.7	25.6	14.8	22.7	11.4	18.4	7.9
Simtokha	14.6	-1.0	16.1	1.0	19.1	4.4	21.9	8.1	24.4	12.0	26.1	15.3	26.8	16.5	26.7	16.5	25.5	14.8	23.1	9.3	19.2	4.1	15.8	-0.0

Source: Meteorology Section, Hydromet Services Division, Department of Energy, MoEA, RGoB.

Recreational Activities for Visitors

Cultural Tours

The cultural tours will provide visitors with a first hand experience of many aspects of Bhutanese life and culture. These tours introduce visitors to unique aspects of Bhutanese history and preserved culture with visits to 17th century Dzongs, religious dance festivals, pilgrimage sites, museums, fascinating excursions to villages and monasteries. Local sightseeing offers an insight into the distinct culture, age old traditions and the lifestyle of the deeply spiritual and mystical Kingdom. The tours will also take visitors through some of the most picturesque landscapes of spectacular mountain ranges and lush green valleys.

Festival

The *Tshechus* that take place throughout the country in every Dzongkhag at different times of the year which can last up to four days are worth experiencing. The several local community festivals held in various villages throughout the country attracts the local populace in a spirit of festivity, celebration and deep faith, These festivals are visually stunning and will give visitors an insight into the vibrant and rich culture of the country.

Photography

Bhutan provides a wide variety of photographic experiences with vibrant landscapes, rough rushing rivers, snow clad mountains, impressive architecture, flora and fauna and colourful traditional clothes worn by the Bhutanese. The Kingdom is a paradise for photographers.

Bird Watching

Whether an ornithologist, a casual birder, or a bird photographer, Bhutan can cater to all your birding interests. With an estimated 770 species and a great variety of endangered species, Bhutan is an ideal place to see a wide variety of birds that maybe impossible or difficult to spot anywhere else.

Botanical Tours

With 7,000 vascular plants, 360 orchid species, 46 species of rhododendron and about 500 species of medicinal plants, Bhutan is a true biodiversity haven for nature lovers. To see the best of the country's flora, the beginning of the monsoon is the best time while spring is the ideal time to see flowering rhododendrons, magnolias, and other spring flowers and shrubs.

Fishing

As a Buddhist country, fishing is not common amongst Bhutanese but for visitors, fishing in the crystal clear rivers set against breathtaking landscape can be quite an experience. Fishing spots range from large rivers to crystal clear spring-fed streams at altitudes ranging from 1,200m to 3,000m. The most common varieties are the snow trout and the brown trout. The best times for fishing are in spring (February to April) and Autumn (September to October).

Mountain Biking

Mountain biking in Bhutan is said to be the best, with the country's mountainous terrain offering a fascinating adventure for mountain biking enthusiasts. The route along Bhutan's

west-east highway is an exciting one with challenges of battling a new pass over 3000m everyday. The drop from Pele La to Trongsa, a distance of 70km is said to be the longest downhill stretch in the world.

Rock Climbing

Rock climbing was first introduced in Bhutan in 1998 by the "Vertical Bhutan Climbing Club". The "Nose", a climbing rock ideally situated just above Bhutan's capital Thimphu, offers 13 different safely bolted climbing routes in difficulty degrees from 4B up to 7B in lengths between 12 and 27m. The Vertical Bhutan Climbing Club welcomes every visitor to join in. The club provides climbing equipment and training if required.

Hiking

Possibilities for day hikes are numerous all over Bhutan. There are short one or two hour walks to a strenuous hike for a whole day. Hiking is the best way to explore the beauty of Bhutan as you hike through the serene nature, wilderness and enchanting valleys with incomparable views.

Golfing

Golfing on the top of the world can be an amazing experience for avid golfers. The Royal Thimphu Golf Course is one of the highest in the world. It is a challenging nine hole (par 34) course beautifully situated behind Tashichhodzong and surrounded by mountains. The course's water hazards are man made and is strategically placed for a challenging game on the narrow fairways. A different set of tees for the back nine makes it a great double round of 18 holes (par 67).

Rafting and Kayaking

Rafting and kayaking in Bhutan is at a nascent stage but has the potential for some of the best white water sports. There are plenty of good stretches on many of the rivers ranging from class 3 to 5. The outstanding ones are the Mo Chhu, upstream of Punakha in western Bhutan, and the Ema Datse Canyon on the Mangde Chhu in central Bhutan. March till May and October till December is the ideal time for rafting in Bhutan. New and virgin rivers are still being explored.

Trekking

Trekking in Bhutan can involve treading through passes as high as 5,500m with spectacular landscape and breath-taking views of the Himalayas. There are trekking packages ranging from low altitude short three-day treks like the Druk Path to high altitude three-week treks that cover 356 kms and climbs three of the Kingdom's highest passes. During spring, summer and autumn one can enjoy the alpine meadows filled with countless varieties of flowers, birds and butterflies, the views of high mountain peaks, pristine lakes and lush high valleys.

Trekking Season

The best periods for trekking in Bhutan are October-November and March-May for all high altitude treks going over 4,000m. Some shorter treks like the Druk Path, Bumthang, Gangtey can be undertaken almost every season. In the autumn, clear warm days prevail affording the best mountain views. In the spring mixed weather patterns prevail with clear spells followed by occasional thunder showers and light rain. Spring is best because rhododendrons, magnolias and other plants are in bloom.

TOURISM MAP

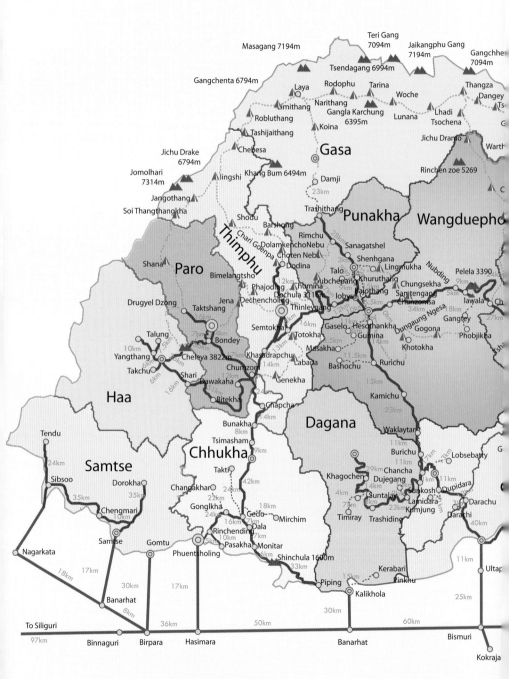

Source: Tourism Council of Bhutan, 2009

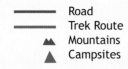

Road
Trek Route
▲▲ Mountains
▲ Campsites

Some Trekking Routes in Bhutan

Sl.	Trek Route	Entry Point	Exit Point	Camp sites
1	Jumolhari Trek 1	Drukgyal Dzong	Drukgyal Dzong	Shana, Soi Thangthangka and Jangothang
2	Jumolhari Trek 2	Drukgyal Dzong	Drukgyal Dzong	Shana, Soi Thangthangka, Jangothang, Soi Yaksa, Thombu Shong
3	Jumolhari Trek 3	Drukgyal Dzong	Dodina (Chari Goenpa)	Shana, Soi Thangthangka, Jangothang, Lingshi, Shodu, Barshong, and Dolom Kencho,
4	Bumthang Cultural Trek	Toktu Zampa	Mesithang	Nga Lhakhang, Thakung,
5	Wild East Rodungla Trek 1	Ugyen Choling	Tangmachu zam	Phokpey, Ungar, Kheni Lhakhang,
6	Wild East Rodungla Trek 2	Ugyencholing	Trashiyangtse	Phokpey, Ungar, Kheni Lhakhang, Tangmachu.zam, Minji, Pemi, Taupang, Shakshing
7	Dongla Trek	Tangmachu zam	Trashiyangtse	Minji, Pemi, Taupang, Shakshing
8	Punakha Winter Trek	Dechen Choling	Rimchu	Chumina, Dubchepang, Choeten Ningpo
9	Dagala Thousand Lakes Trek	Genekha	Simtokha	Geynizampa, Gur, Labatamba, Panka, Talakha, Chamgang
10	Gantey Trek	Phobjikha	Tikke Zam	Gogona, Khotokha
11	Samtengang Trek	Punakha	Chuzomsa	Lingmukha, Chungsekha, Samtengang
12	Chelela Trek	Chelela	Thimphu	Chonana, Jebkarpo, Lower mingula, Thong
13	Laya/Gasa Trek 1	Damji	Damji	Gasa Tsachu, Koina, Laya
14	Laya/Gasa Trek 2	Drukgyal Dzong	Damji	Shana, Thangthangka, Jangothang, Lingzhi, Chebisa, Tsherijathang, Robluthang, Limithang, Laya, Koina, Gasa Tsachu
15	Snowman Trek 1	Drukgyal Dzong	Thangbi	Shana, Soi Thangthangka, Jangothang, Lingshi, Chebisa, Tsherijathang, Roubluthang, Laya, Roduphu, Narithang, Tarina, Woche, Lhedi, Thanza, Dangey, Tsorim, Geche Woma, Phorang, Warthang, Dur Tsachu, Tshochenchen, Gorsum,

Sl.	Trek Route	Entry Point	Exit Point	Camp sites
16	Snowman Trek 2	Drukgyel Dzong	Chuserbu (Nikka Chu)	Shana, Soi Thangthangka, Jangothang, Lingshi, Chebisa, Shomuthang, Roubluthang, Laya, Roduphu, Narithang, Tarina, Woche, Lhedi, Thanza, Tshochena, Jichu Dramo, Chukarpo, Tampetsho, Maorothang
17	Dur Hot Spring Trek	Dur	Dur	Gorsum, Lungsum, Tshochenchen, Dur Tsachu
18	Druk Path Trek 1	Paro Museum	Motithang	Jele Dzong, Jangchulakha, Jimelangtso, Simkotra tsho, Phajoding
19	Druk Path Trek 2	Paro Museum	Tsheluna	Jele Dzong, Jangchulakha, Jimelangtsho,
20	Nabji Trail	Reutola	Tongtongphey	Nimshong, Nabji, korphu, Kubdra, Jangbi
21	Lingmithang – Zhemgang Trek	Limithang	Gomphu	Tshona, Silumbi, Nagor, Dalli, Bjoka, Kaktang, Gushing Trong, Mamung Trong.
22	Royal Heritage Trek	Wangdichholing Palace	Kuenga Rabten palace	Domkhar Makhathang, Jamsapang,
23	Sinchula Trek	Pangrizampa	Zomlingthang, Punakha	Sinchula, Dupshipang, Choeten Ningpo
24	Nubtsona Pata Trek	Haa	Lu-Kha	Tshokham, Wangjithang, Nubtsonapata, Rigona, Yu-Lu
25	Gangkar Puensum 1	Toto Zampa	Gorsum	Khagtang, Kuphu, Jiuthangka, Ba Marpo, Tsampa Gompa, Toley Thang, Ta She Sa (Chockomey)
26	Gangkar Puensum 2	Warthang	Warthang	Sintha, Gangitsawa, Gangkar Puensum base camp
27	Gangjula Trek	Woche	Trashithang/ Shari	Gangjula (Cheriphu), Jazeephu, Ramina
28	Rigsum Goenpa Trek	Choeten Kora	Choeten Kora	Dechen Phodrang, Rigsum Goenpa

Source: Tourism Council of Bhutan

Atsara or the jesters are a key charater at Tshechu who provide comic relief to the audience during the festival. While engaging in their antics, they also assist in maintaining order.

Jigme Wangchuk

1st Month

1
7-9
Punakha Dromche

2
15-30
Choeten Kora
Trashiyangtse

1
10-12
Punakha Tsechu

3
16-18
Bulli Mani
Bumthang

3
14-18
Tangsibi
Mani (Ura)
Bumthang

3
28-30
Gaden
Chodpa
Bumthang

3
15
Tharpaling
Thongdrol
Bumthang

2nd Month

10
11-15
Paro Tshechu
Paro

6
13-15
Chukha Tshechu
Chukha

4
8-10
Gom Kora
Tshechu
Trashigang

3rd Month

3
12-16
Ura Yakchoe
Bumthang

3
10-12
Domkhar
Tsechu
Bumthang

4th Month

3
20-21
Petsel-ling Kuchod Bumthang

5th Month

3
8-10
Nimalung Tshechu
Bumthang

3
10
Kurjey Tshechu
Bumthang

RELIGIOUS DANC

10th Month

15
7-10
Mongar
Tshechu
Mongar

14
7-10
Pemagatshel
Tshechu
Pemagatshel

4
15
Jambay
Lhakhang
Bumthang

3
15-17
Nalakhar
Tshechu
Bumthang

4
8-11
Trashigang
Tshechu
Trashigang

3
14-18
Chojam
Rabney (T:
Bumthang

8th Month

9
10-12
Thimphu Tshechu
Thimphu

5
8-10
Wangdue Tshechu
Wangdue
Phodrang

3
14-16
Tangbi Mani
Bumthang

9
5-9
Thimphu
Drupchen
Thimphu

3
10-12
Tamshingphala
Choepa
Bumthang

FESTIVAL MAP

9th Month

3
6-10
Shingkhar
Rabney (Ura)
Bumthang

3
8-11
Jakar Dzong
Tshechu
Bumthang

3
15-18
Jambay
Lhakhang Drup
Bumthang

3
16-18
Prakhar
Duchhoed
Tshechu
Bumthang

3
26-30
Sumrang
Khangsol
(Ura)
Bumthang

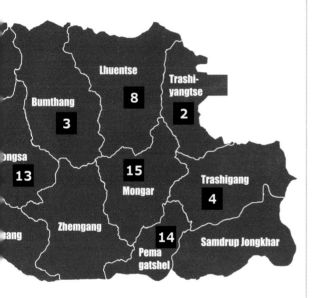

*Dates are based on the
Bhutanese Lunar Calendar*

3
9-10
Namkha
Rabney
(Tang)
Bumthang

11th Month

13
9-11
Trongsa
Tshechu
Trongsa

8
9-11
Lhuentse
Tshechu
Lhuentse

12
15-19
Nabji
Lhakhang Drup
Trongsa

3
15
Shingkhar
Metochodpa (Ura)
Bumthang

TRAVEL TIPS

Currency

The national currency is the Ngultrum (Nu). 100 Chetrum = 1 Nu. Exchange rate is approximately USD 1 = Nu. 45.50 (March, 2010). Indian Rupees circulate at par and is widely used except for the denomination of Rs 500 and Rs 1000.

American Express credit cards

VISA credit cards are accepted in few shops in the capital and important towns. American Express credit cards are accepted in few hotels and shops at a higher commission. Visitors are advised to carry traveller cheques (preferably American Express) with some cash (US Dollars).

Time Difference

Bhutan Standard Time is 6 hours ahead of GMT. There is only one time zone through out the country. The time in Bhutan is 30 minutes earlier than India, 15 minutes earlier than in Nepal, and 1 hour later than in Thailand.

Electricity

230 - 240 volts, 50 cycles A.C. The current is variable. If you do bring electrical appliances, bring along an international converter kit with a set of adapter plugs.

Plugs and Sockets

Bhutan uses the standard Indian round-pin sockets which come in variety of sizes. Most European round pin-plugs work, but their pins are usually smaller than the Indian variety and fit loosely and provides an unreliable connection. There are plenty of electrical shops in Thimphu where you can buy an adapter if you have any trouble plugging in an appliance.

Laundry

Hotels do the laundry, but very few hotels have dryers. Same day service is possible depending on the availability of sunshine. There are few dry cleaners in Thimphu and Phuentsholing.

Communication Facilities

Reliable telephone and fax services are available in all towns in Bhutan . International connections are excellent. Internet cafes are few in number and available only in a few places. However most tourist hotels have internet connection. Prepaid SIM card can be purchased and you can use your mobile phones in most of the major towns in the country.

Insurance

To protect against unforeseen accidents and mishaps, it is advisable to obtain travel insurance from your country. It should adequately cover helicopter evacuation and medical assistance.

Health Information

No vaccinations are currently required for travelling to Bhutan. However, visitors coming from an area infected with yellow fever are required to get a yellow fever vaccination and must be administered at least ten days before arrival into Bhutan. Likewise, visitors arriving from a cholera infected should get vaccinated.

Cuisine

Bhutanese delicacies are rich with spicy chillies and cheese. Continental, Chinese and Indian cuisine are served in most restaurants. In Thimphu, there are more choices with restaurants specialized solely in Chinese, Thai, Italian, Indian, Nepali and Japanese.

Shopping

The country's exquisite postage stamps, lovely hand woven fabrics, carved masks, woven baskets, wooden bowls, handmade papers, finely crafted metal objects, thangkha paintings are popular items purchased by foreign visitors. Buying and selling of antiques is strictly forbidden in the Kingdom.

Gratitudes

In general, tipping is neither compulsory nor there is any fixed amount. It is dependent on how much the individual did to make your travel more enjoyable.

Winding Roads

The roads are winding and narrow by western standards. Since Bhutan is a mountainous country it takes time to travel from place to place. To travel 127 kms it may take 5 hours.

Altitude

The maximum elevation that you can reach on a Bhutanese road is 3150m in the west and 3750m in the east. There are rare cases where individuals have suffered from altitude problems.

Clothing

While casual clothes are fine, sleeveless top, shorts and caps are strictly not permitted for entry into Dzongs, government offices and monastic festivals. To withstand Bhutan's changeable weather, it is advisable to bring travel clothes and warmer clothes for evenings.

Photography

Bhutan is a photographer's paradise. However, it is recommended to seek permission before you photograph people and places of interest.

Senior Travellers

Many visitors are senior citizens travelling in organized groups. Hotel guides and tour operators are all familiar with their needs and treat them with respect that the Bhutanese have for their elders. The primary precaution one should take is to have an ample supply of any special medicines, as they probably may not be available in Bhutan.

Smoking in public places

On 17th December 2004 , in keeping with the decision of the Bhutanese parliament, the nationwide ban on the sale of tobacco products was implemented, making Bhutan the first country in the world to do so. The maximum amount of cigarettes that can be imported for personal consumption is 200 pieces. For other tobacco products like snuff and chewing tobacco, the maximum import amount is 50 grams. For pipe tobacco, it is three tins of 50 grams each.

Smoking in public places which includes parks, discotheques, entertainment centers, sports facilities like football grounds and archery ranges, commercial centers including shops, bars and restaurants, institutions like Dzongs, hospitals, schools, and government offices, public transport carriers, public gatherings such as monastic festivals, official receptions, national celebrations, and vegetable markets is banned.

Masked dances from an integral part of religious dance festivals

Jigme Wangchuk

LIST OF TOUR OPERATORS

Absolute Bhutan Travel
'Your most trusted travel companion for Dream Holidays'
Post Box No. 698, Thimphu
Tel: + 975-2-335336
Fax: + 975-2-322007
Email: abs@druknet.bt
lilywangchuk@gmail.com
info@absolutebhutantravel.com
www.absolutebhutantravel.com
Contact: Ms. Lily Wangchhuk

All Bhutan Connection (ABC)
'Exclusive holidays for the traveller in you'
Post Box No. 668/1176, Thimphu
Tel: + 975-2-327102, 325165
Fax: + 975-2-326741
Cell: +975-17110866, 17110919
Email: bhutanconnection@druknet.bt
wangdeeabc@druknet.bt
www.abc.com.bt
Contact: Mr. Needup Wangdee,
Mr. Tshering Dhendup

Ancient Bhutan Tours & Treks
'Explore the land of living museum'
Post Box. No. 1198, Thimphu
Tel: + 975-2-326677
Fax: + 975-2-332434
Email: bhutanancient@druknet.bt
www.bhutanancient.com.bt
Contact: Mr. Pema Gyalpo

Atlas Tours & Travels
'easy journey, great experience'
Post Box No. 820, Thimphu
Tel: +975-2-325581
Fax +975-2-326453
Email: langad@druknet.bt
atlas@druknet.bt
www.bhutanatlas.com.bt
Contact: Mr. Langa Dorji

Bara Lynka Tours & Travels
'experience the magic and mystery of Bhutan'
Post Box No. 1289, Thimphu
Tel: +975-2-335392
Fax: +975-2-335389
Email: tdem@druknet.bt
www.baralynka.com
Contact: Mrs. Thinley Dem

Bhutan All Seasons Tours & Treks
'Unforgettable moments in the land of the thunder dragon'
Post Box 993, Thimphu
Fax: +975-2-321263
Cell: +975-17110720
Email: bhutanallseasons@gmail.com
www.bhutanallseasons.bt
Contact: Mrs. Kinley Yangden

Bhutan Aries Tours & Treks
'Exclusive vacations into the last paradise'
Post Box No. 238, Thimphu
Tel: +975-2-327177
Cell: +975-17600396
Email: bhutanaries@druknet.bt
www.bhutanaries.com
Contact: Mr. B.L. Gurung

Bhutan Dorji Holidays
'discover Bhutan through our eyes'
Post Box No. 550, Thimphu
Tel: +975-2-328663, 322982
Fax: +975-2-325174
Cell: +975-1712 4567, 17151515
www.bhutandorji.com
Contact: Mr. Chambula Dorji

Bhutan Dragon Adventures
'Come, explore with us this mystical country'
Post Box. No. 304, Thimphu
Tel : +975-2-336686
Fax: +975-2-336685
Email : dragonadventures@druknet.bt
karma@bhutandragonadventure.com
www.go2bhutan.com
www.bhutandragonadventure.com
Contact: Mr. Karma Gyeltshen

Bhutan Majestic Travel
'the Best Service Provider'
Post Box No. 1148, Thimphu
Tel: +975-2-334661
Fax: + 975-2-334662
Cell: +975-17111095
Email: info@bhutanmajestictravel.com
www.bhutanmajestictravel.com
Contact: Mr. Namgay Dorji

Bhutan Mandala Tours and Treks
'discover the ultimate land of happiness'
Post Box. 397, Thimphu
Tel: +975-2-324842
Fax +975-2-323675
Email: mandala@druknet.bt
www.bhutanmandala.com
Contact: Mr. Dominic Sitling

Bhutan Men–Lha Adventure
'your authentic holiday maker in the Himalayas'
Post Box. No. 1377, Thimphu
Tel: +975-2-321555
Fax +975-2-331730
Email: menl-adventure@druknet.bt
trekkingbhutan@gmail.com
www.adventurebhutan.com
www.trekkingbhutan.com
Contact: Mr. Tashi Gyeltshen

Bhutan Mountain Holiday
'the Bhutan Specialist'
Post Box No. 1013, Thimphu
Tel: +975-2-320115
Fax: +975-2-335989
Cell: +975-17113661
Email: kargyel@druknet.bt
info@bhutanmountainholiday.com
www.bhutanmountainholiday.com
Contact: Mr. Karma Gyeltshen

Blue Poppy Tours and Treks
'discover the mysteries of Bhutan'
Post Box No. 1296, Thimphu
Tel: +975-2-333 540/+ 44-20-7700 3084
Fax: +975-2-333 541/+ 44-20-7609 2029
Cell: +975-1760 3602/+44-7751-723-041
Email: choki@bluepoppybhutan.com
www.bluepoppybhutan.com
Contact: Mr. Choki Dorji

Bhutan Tourism Corporation Ltd.
'The most trusted travel companion'
Post Box. No. 159, Thimphu, Bhutan
Tel: + 975-2- 322647
Fax: +975-2-323392
Email: btcl@druknet.bt
www.kingdomofbhutan.bt
Contact: Mr. Thinley Wangchuk

Bhutan Travelers
'Travel the path less taken'
Post Box No.1298, Thimphu
Tel: +975 2 328868
Fax: + 975-2-328869
Email: wladventures@druknet.bt
www.bhutanadventure.com
www.bhutantravelers.com
Contact: Karma

Bhutan Travel Service
'Go where happiness resides'
Post Box No. 919, Thimphu
Tel: 975-2- 325785
Fax: 975-2-325786
Email: btskoko@druknet.bt
www.bhutantravel.com.bt
www.bhutantreks.com.bt
Contact: Mr. Karma Khorko,
Mrs. Tshering Choden

Bhutan Yarden Tours & Treks
'trekker's natural paradise'
Post Box No. 227, Thimphu
Tel: +975-2-334818
Fax: + 975-2-333261
Email: karma@bhutanyarden.com
www.bhutanyarden.com

Bhutan "Your Way" Tours & Travel
'Experience the enchantment'
Post Box No. 1260, Paro
Tel: +975-8-272038
Fax: +975-8-240465
Cell: +975-17641224
Email: info@bhutanyourway.com
www.bhutanyourway.com
Contact: Jamie Vaughan or
Ugyen Dorji

Big Foot Adventure Trekkers
'step into the land of amazement'
Post Box No. 1155, Thimphu
Tel: +975-2-335958, 335959
Fax: +975-2- 335960
Cell: +975-17111881
Email: bhutanbigfoot@druknet.bt
info@bhutanbigfoot.com
bhutanbigfoot@hotmail.com
www.bhutanbigfoot.com
www.bigfoottravels.com
Contact: Mr. Ashika Pradhan

Boonserm Tours & Travels
'Make it a journey to remember for life'
Post Box No. 609, Thimphu
Tel: + 975-2-322257
Fax: +975-2-323731
Cell: +975-17627369, 17607032
Email: boonserm.tours@gmail.com
www.welcome2bhutan.com
Contact: Mr. Tashi Namgay

Diethelm Travel Bhutan
"Step into an enchanted journey"
Post Box No.107, Thimphu
Tel: 975-2-323484
Fax: 975-2-323894
Email: dwpenjor@druknet.bt
www.diethelmtravel.com
Contact: Mrs. Dechen Wangmo

Druk Executive Travel
'Travel Bhutan the Executive way'
Post Box No. 1544, Thimphu
Tel: +975-2-336955
Fax: +975-2-336957
E-mail: windhor@druknet.bt
www.drukexecutivetravel.com
Contact: Mr. Kinley Namgay

Etho Metho Tours & Treks Pvt. Ltd.
'We are confident of delivering the best'
Post Box No. 360, Thimphu
Tel: +975-2-323162, 323693
Fax: +975-2-322884
Email: info@ethometho.com.bt
ethometo@druknet.bt
emtt@druknet.bt
www.bhutanethometho.com
Contact: Mrs. Dago Beda

Experience Bhutan Travel
'A journey into the hidden Kingdom'
Post Box No. 1157, Thimphu
Tel: +975 2 328961
Fax: +975 2 335398
Cell: + 975 17619485
Email: info@experiencebhutan.com
ebt@druknet.bt
www.experiencebhutan.com
Contact: Mr. Khetnath Sharma

Exotic Destinations
'For unforgettable holidays'
Post Box No. 682, Thimphu
Tel: +975-2-327405/406
Fax: +975-2-326171
Email: exotic@druknet.bt
Contact: Mr. Chencho Wangdi

Happy Holidays Tours and Treks
'A vacation you'll never forget'
Post Box No. 522, Thimphu
Tel: + 975-2- 326899
Fax: +975-2-332948
Email: tokey@druknet.bt
www.happyholidays.com.bt
Contact: Mr. Tokey Dorji

Mahakala Tours and Treks
'partake in its unique experience'
Post Box No. 393, Thimphu
Tel: 975-2-324167, 334690
Fax: 975-2-334690
Email: d-ongmo@druknet.bt
www.mahakalatravels.com
Contact: Mrs. Dechen Ongmo

Norda Expeditions & Travels
'discover the reason you'll come again'
Post Box No. 1419, Thimphu
Tel: +975-2-329116
Fax: +975-2-326818
Email: norda@druknet.bt
karmawangmo@gmail.com
www.bhutannorda.com
Contact: Mrs. Karma Wangmo

Odiyan Events
'travel with us for a journey of
life time'
Post Box. No. 689, Thimphu
Tel: + 975-2- 326835
Fax: +975-2-324926
Email: odiyan@druknet.bt
Contact: Mr. Karma Temphel

Passage to Himalayas
'Thousands of reasons. Experience
yours.'
Post Box No. 1068, Thimphu
Tel: +975-2-321726
Fax: +975-2-321727
Email: lekid@druknet.bt
Contact: Mr. Leki Dorji

Sakten Tours and Treks
'experience your precious moments'
Post Box No. 532, Thimphu
Tel : +975-2-325567
Fax :+975-2-325574
Email: sakten@druknet.bt
www.bootan.com
Contact: Mr. Tshewang Rigzin

Silver Dragon Tours and Treks
'The Complete Himalayan Experience'
Post Box No.1312, Thimphu
Tel: + 975-2-328122
Fax: + 975-2-328121
Email: silverdragon@druknet.bt
www.tourismbhutan.com
Contact: Mr. Palden Tshewang

Sky Travels
'be amazed in the enchantment'
Post Box 1052, Thimphu
Tel: +975-2-326944
Fax :+975-2-323651
Email: skybhutan@yahoo.com
sky@druknet.bt
www.bhutansky.com
Contact: Mr. Tshering Jamtsho

Snow Lion Adventure Travels
'experience the legends'
Post Box. No.796, Thimphu
Tel: + 975-2- 323511
Fax: +975-2-322481
Email: skarmtt@druknet.bt
www.bhutansnowliontours.com
Contact: Mr. Nim Dorji

Sophun Tours & Treks
'Explore more than the usual. Experience the
mystic country'
Post Box No. 317, Thimphu
Tel: +975-2-328557
Fax: +975-2-321319
Cell: +975-17615023
Email: sophun@druknet.bt
sophunbhutan@gmail.com
sophuntravels@yahoo.com
www.bhutantripinfo.com
www.sophuntravels.com.bt
www.sophuntravels.com
Contact: Mr. Kesang Namgyel

Yangphel Adventure Travel
'your trusted holiday partners in Bhutan'
Post Box No. 236, Thimphu
Tel: + 975-2-323293
Fax: + 975-2-322897
Email: md@yangphel.com
www.yangphel.com
Contact: Mr.Karma Lotey,
Ms. Karma Choden

YANA Expeditions, Inc.
'Travel as Guests, Not as Tourists'
Post Box No. 1211, Thimphu
Tel: +975-2-339779, 332329
Fax: +975-2-331583
Cell: +975-17119779
Email: yana@druknet.bt
md.yana@gmail.com
www.YANATravel.com
www.DiscoverBhutan.com

LIST OF PREMIUM HOTELS

Uma Paro

COMO Hotels and Resorts' Uma Paro offers luxury in the heart of the rugged wilderness of Bhutan. Dine in style at the *'Bukhari'* restaurant, or indulge in the holistic COMO *Shambhala* Retreat for Asian-inspired treatments and yoga.

Post Box 22, Paro
Tel: +975 8 271597
Fax: +975 8 271513
res.paro@uma.como.bz
www.uma.como.bz

Terma Linca

Nestled in a private oasis of panoramic tranquility lies an elegant stretch of Bhutanese architectural gems strung together to exemplify the spirit of Terma Linca. Framed by lush paddy fields and snow-fed waters of the Wangchhu, Terma Linca is situated merely five kilometers away from the urban expanse of Thimphu.

Terma Linca's 30 rooms cocooned in this resort overlook the river that is magnificently framed by wall to wall windows and each room echoes the silent serenity and stillness. It has a fine spa and a well equipped banquet hall.

Post Box 2009, Thimphu
Tel: +975 2 351490, 351491
Fax: +975 2 351629
termalinca.th@druknet.bt
termalinca.com

Taj Tashi
Its 66 rooms offer a majestic view of the mountains surrounding the Thimphu valley while cradling the guest with every modern comfort and facility- from the luxurious spa and the indoor heated pool to elegant meeting facilities and gourmet dining.

Post Box 524, Thimphu
Tel: +975-2-336699
Fax: +975-2-336677
tajtashi.thimphu@
tajhotels.com
www.tajhotels.com

Amankora
Combining *'aman'*, Sanskrit for peace, with *'kora'* or circular pilgrimage in Dzongkha, the Bhutanese language, Amankora is a series of lodges that covers Bhutan's central and western valleys of Paro, Thimphu, Punakha, Gangtey and Bumthang.

Post Box 831, Thimphu
Tel: +975 2 331 333
Fax: +975 2 331 999
amankora@amanresorts.com
www.amanresorts.com

Zhiwa Ling Hotel
The 45-room **Zhiwa Ling Hotel** combines the sensibilities of a fine Bhutanese guesthouse with the best of 21st Century technology. It has elaborate hand-carved wooden cornices and masterful stonework coexist beautifully with cutting-edge telecommunication systems and Swedish under-floor heating.

Paro
Tel: +975 8 271277
Fax: +975 8 271456
info@zhiwaling.com
www.zhiwaling.com

LIST OF RECOMMENDED HOTELS AND RESORTS

THIMPHU

✦ **Hotel Jumolhari**
'a boutique hotel'
Post Box 308
Tel: + 975 2 322747
Fax: + 975 2 324412
Cell: 975 7619540
E-mail: hoteljumolhari@druknet.bt
Web: www.hoteljumolhari.com

✦ **Hotel Phuntsho Pelri**
'Return home with glowing memories'
Post Box No: 159
Tel: +975 2 334970/1/2
Fax: +975 2 334974
Cell: +975 77212821
E-mail: phuntshopelri@druknet.bt
Web: www.btclhotels.com
Contact: Mr. Nawang Jigme
(Asst. Manager)

✦ **Hotel River View**
'Overlooking the capital in a majestic setting'
Near Old India House, Dechen Lam,
Post Box No 309, Thimphu
Tel: +975 2 325029/30/31/32
Fax: +975 2 323496
Email: hotelriverview@druknet.bt
riverview@druknet.bt
Web: www.skykingdomadventures.com
Contact: Mr. Rinzin Samdrup
(General Manager)

✦ **Wangchuk Group of Hotels and Resorts**
'Where Bhutanese charm and hospitality awaits you'
Post Box No. 507
Tel: +975 2 365174, 365262
Fax: +975 2 365164/326323
Cell:+ 975 17110822
E-mail: htlwangchuk@druknet.bt
Web: www.wangchukhotel.com
Contact: Mr. Chencho Namgay

✦ **Hotel Kisa**
'designer boutique hotel'
Post Box No: 1478
Tel: + 975 2 336494
Fax: + 975 2 336395
Cell: +975 17115580, 17117769
Email: bhutankisa@gmail.com
Web: www.hotelkisa.com
Contact: Ms. Indira Maya *(Manager)*

✦ **Peaceful Resort**
'A mythical experience awaits'
Tel: +975 2 337012, 337013
Fax: +975 2 337015
Cell: +975 17719010, 77719010
Email: coolraajrai@ymail.com
peacefulresort@druknet.bt
Web: www.bhutanpeacefulresort.com
Contact: Mr. Kul Raj Rai
(General Manager)

✦ **Jambayang Resort**
'A home awaits you amidst a serene environmen
Post Box No. 583
Tel: + 975 2 322349
Fax: +975 2 323669
Cell: 975 17111754
E-mail: jamyangs@druknet.bt
Web: jambayangresort.com.bt
Contact: Mr. Dhendup Tshering *(Proprietor)*

✦ **Hotel Dragon Roots**
'In the heart of the town with service par excellen
Post Box No: 952
Tel: + 975 2 332820/1/2
Fax: + 975 2 332823
Cell: + 975 17110490
E-mail: droots@druknet.bt
Contact: Mr. Sangay Dorji *(Proprietor)*

✦ **Yeedzin Guest House**
'Comfort beyond expectations'
Post Box No: 438
Tel: +975 2 322932, 325702
Fax: +975 2 324995
Cell: +975 17110810/ 17610017
skype: jimmy20097
E-mail: yeedzin@druknet.bt
Contact: Mr. Laxuman Rai *(Manager)*

PARO

✦ Hotel Olathang
'indulge in grandeur, glide in comfort'
Post Box No: 1214
Tel: +975 8 271304, 271305
Fax: +975 8 271454
Cell No: +975 17752617
Contact : Mr.Tshering Dhendup
E-mail: ohotel@druknet.bt
Web: www.btclhotels.com

✦ Hotel Gangtey Palace
'a blend of service and comfort.'
Post Box. No 1218
Tel: +975 8 271301, 272004
Fax: +975 8 271452
Cell: + 975 17111462
Email: chukie@gangteypalace.com,
hgpp@druknet.bt
Web: www.gangteypalace.net
Contact: Chukie-Om Dorji (*Proprietor*)

✦ Janka Resort
'...a charming family hotel '
Luni Nemjo
Tel: +975 8 272352/240685
Fax: +975 8 272314
Cell: +975 17114351
E-mail: jankaresort@druknet.bt
Web: www.jankaresort.com
Contact: Mrs. Kinley Dema (*GM*)

✦ Dechen Hill Resort
'You'll forget your home'
Tel: +975 8 271392/3/4
Fax: +974 8 272492
Cell: +975 17110254
Email: dchncot@druknet.bt
Web: www.dechenhillresort.com
Contact: Mr. Sushil Kumar Manchanda
(*Manager*)

✦ Hotel Holiday Home
'Next to the wings of the dragon'
Post Box No. 707
Tel: +975 8 2721101/2
Fax: +975 8 272103
Cell: +975 17110517
E-mail: hhhparo@druknet.bt
Contact: Mr. Ugyen Wangchuk (*Proprietor*)

✦ Thri-Shing Yeowang Villa
'amidst apple orchard, with spectacular view of the lush paddy fields'
Cell: +975 17601030, 17646592
Fax: +975 8 240997
Email: yedennamgyel@hotmail.com
tinkar2006@gmail.com

✦ Tashi Namgay Resort & Spa
'Relax in serene atmosphere'
Tel: + 975 8 272319
Fax: + 975 8 272217
E-mail: reservations@tnr.bt
Web: www.tnr.bt
Contact: Mrs. Dawa Dem (*Proprietor*)

✦ Pelri Cottage
'Discover the pure enchantments of Bhutan'
Tel: +975 8 271683
Fax: +975 8 272472
Email: peril@druknet.bt
Web: www.pelricottages.com
Contact: Mr. C.D. Gyeltshen/Mr. Peter

✦ Hotel Jor-Yangz
'Your Home Away From Home'
Post Box No. 1224
Tel: +975 8 271747/272498
Fax: 975 8 271557
Cell: 975 17111291
E-mail: joryangz@druknet.bt
Web: www.joryangzhotel.com.bt
Contact : Mrs. Sonam, Gem Dhendup
(*Proprietor*)

✦ Rinchenling Lodge
'Discover the meaning of hospitality'
Post Box No. 1234
Tel: +975 8 271111
Fax: +975 8 271454, 271771
Cell: 975-17606619, 17110927
E-mail: nawang@druknet.bt
Contact: Mr. Phub Dorji (Proprietor)

✦ Namsey Chhoeling Guest House
'Stay in comfort, with style'
Tel: +975 8 272080, 240620
Fax: +975 8 240621
Cell: +975 17111226
E-mail: namseyresort@druknet.bt

PUNAKHA

✦ **Dochula Resort**
'Enjoy spectacular view of the Himalayas'
Post Box No. 1007
Tel: +975 3 380404, 380406
Fax: +975 2 336304, 380405
Cell: +975 17111165, 17635633
E-mail: namgay_budhar@hotmail.com
Web: www.dochularesort.com
Contact: Mrs. Namgay/Mr. Ugyen Dorji
(Proprietor)

✦ **Damchen Resort**
'A hotel with a difference, an ideal place to rest or explore... '
Post Box No. 120
Tel: +975 2 584367/368
Fax: +975 2 584375
Cell: +975 17843459
E-mail: damchenresort@druknet.bt
Web: www.damchenresort.com
Contact: Mr. Rajesh Chettri *(Manager)*

✦ **Meri Puensum Resort**
'Experience Bhutanese hospitality at the highest'
Post Box No. 135
Tel: +975 2 584195, 584237
Fax: +975 2 584236
Cell: 975 17777771, 17656565
E-mail: mpuensum@druknet.bt;
meripuensum@gmail.com
Web: www.meripuensum.com.bt
Contact: Mrs. Sonam Choden
(Proprietor)

✦ **Zangto Pelri**
'Your preferred place of stay'
Tel: +975 2 584125, 584615, 584427
Fax: +975 2 584203
Cell: +975 17110322
E-mail: hotzang@druknet.bt
Contact: Mr. Lapchu Tshering

WANGDUE

✦ **Dragon's Nest Resort**
'Serene setting overlooking the peaceful river.'
Post Box No. 1235
Tel: +975 2 480522
Fax: +975 2 480503
Cell: +975 17114347
E-mail: nest@druknet.bt
Web: www.dragonsnesthotel.com
Contact: Mr. Sharma *(Manager)*

✦ **Hotel Y.T.**
'Perfect holiday setting with perfect hospitality'
Tashi Kuenga Norbuling
Post Box No. 1247
Tel: + 975 2 376012
Fax: +975 2 376029
Cell: 975 17110657, 17614911
E-mail: hotely@druknet.bt
Contact: Mr. Yeshey Tenzing *(Proprietor)*

✦ **Hotel Tashiling**
'Take good memories home'
Post Box No. 1250
Tel: +975 2 481403/481676
Fax: +975 2 481682
Cell: +975 17603705
Contact: Mr. Kezang *(Proprietor)*

GANGTEY

✦ **Dewachen Hotel**
'The answer to a perfect gateway in Bhutan'
Tel: +975 2 442550
Fax: +975 2 272638, 442626
Cell: + 975 17974887
E-mail: manager@dewachenhotel.com;
reservation@dewachenhotel.com
Web: www.dewachenhotel.com
Contact: Mr. Lotay *(Manager)*/
Mrs. Sonam Dema

TRONGSA

✦ **Chendebji Resort**
'peaceful and relaxing'
Post Box No. 1007
Tel: +975 3 380404/380406
Fax: +975 2 336304, 380405
Cell: +975 17111165, 17635633
E-mail: namgay_budhar@hotmail.com
Web: www.dochularesort.com
Contact: Mrs. Namgay/Mr. Ugyen Dorji
(Proprietor)

✦ **Yangkhil Resort**
'Homely and serene'
Post Box No. 566
Tel: +975 3 521417/8
Fax: +975 3 521420
Cell: +975 17113867
E-mail: yangkhilresort@druknet.bt
Contact: Mrs. Sonam Chenzo *(Proprietor)*

✦ **Phuenzhi Guest House**
'a perfect holiday home'
Post Box No. 185
Tel: 975 3 521197
Fax: +975 3 521356
Cell: 975 17627156
E-mail: puenzhi@druknet.bt
Contact: Mr. Tobgay Tshering *(Proprietor)*

MONGGAR

✦ **Druk Zhongkhar Hotel**
'The peaceful haven of the dragon'
Tel: + 975 4 641587
Fax: + 975 4 641590
Cell: + 975 17111684:
E-mail: tungtung@druknet.bt
Contact: Mr. Kinley Jamtsho (Proprietor)

✦ **Wangchuk Hotel**
'Serene atmosphere'
Tel: +975 4 641522
Fax: +975 4 641291
Cell: + 975 17110882
E-mail: htlwangchuk@druknet.bt
Web: www.wangchukhotel.com
Contact: Mr. Chencho Namgay
(Proprietor)

TRASHIGANG

✦ **Druk Deothjung Hotel**
'A perfect quiet stay'
Tel: +975 4 521214, 521145
Fax: +975 4 521269
Cell: +975 17119909
E-mail: drukdeothjung@druknet.bt
Contact: Mrs. Jambay Yudon *(Proprietor)*

PHUENTSHOLING

✦ **Lhaki Hotel**
'We treat you with special care all the way'
Post Box No. 187
Tel: +975 5 257222, 257444
Fax: +975 5 251185
Cell: +75 17610923, 77610923
E-mail: lhakihotel@druknet.bt
Contact: Mr. Namgay Wangchuk
(General Manager)

✦ **Hotel Sinchula**
'Your perfect host'
Post Box No. 326
Tel: +975 5 252589
Fax: +975 5 252772
Cell: +975 17110452
E-mail: hotelsinchula@yahoo.com
Web: www.hotelsinchula.com
Contact: Ms. Sangay Zam *(Proprietor)*

SAMDRUP JONGKHAR

✦ **Friends Hotel**
'Rejuvenate your senses'
Tel: +975 7 251544
Fax: +975 7 251318
Cell: +975 17614708
Contact: Mr. Deepak Pradhan
(Proprietor)

BUMTHANG

✦ Hotel Wangduechholing
'For a blissful stay'
Post Box No: 107
Tel: +975 3 631369
Fax: +975 3 631959
Cell: +975 1775028
E-mail: hotelwangduechholing@druknet.bt
Web: www.btclhotels.com
Contact: Mr. Ngawang Leksha
(Asst. Manager)

✦ Hotel Peling
'An experience of peace and tranquility'
Post Box No: 120
Tel: +975 3 632020
Fax: +975 3 632011
Cell: +975 17725675
E-mail: hotelpeling@druknet.bt
Web: www.hotelpeling.com.bt
Contact: Mr Jamyang Tenzin (Manager)

✦ Chumey Nature Resort
'relax in the heartland of nature'
Padma's i Denzin Geytsa
Fax: +975 3 16342001
Cell: +975 17111625, 17114836
E-mail: info@chumeynatureresort.com
Web: www.chumeynatureresort.com
Contact: Mr.Chime Dorji (Proprietor)

✦ Wangdicholing Resort
'A home in the heart of nature'
Tel: + 975 3 631452
Fax: +975 3 631278
Cell: +975 17860426
E-mail: wangdicholingresort@druknet.bt
Contact: Mr. Pema Namgyel (Manager)

✦ Swiss Guest House
'Truly International'
Post Box No. 115
Tel: +975 2 631144/45
Fax: +975 3 631918
Cell: +975 17111926
E-mail: swissguesthouse@druknet.bt
Contact: Mr. Tshering Wangchuk
(Proprietor)

✦ Gongkhar Guest House
'Get pampered with our service'
Tel: +975 3 631288
Fax: +975 3 631345
Cell: +975 17671035
E-mail: tsheringgongkhar@yahoo.com
Contact: Mr. Tshering Dorji (Proprietor)

✦ Hotel Home
'Feel at home with our hospitality'
Tel: +975 3 631444, 631666
Fax: +975 3 631450
Cell:+ 975 17612962
Email: hotelhomebtn@yahoo.com

✦ Jakar Village Lodge
'Rated fourth best hotel in Bhutan by
Trivago Top Hotel and 21st best hotel in
Asia for bed and breakfast'
Post Box No: 105
Tel: +975 3 631242
Fax: +975 3 631377
Cell:+ 975 17636477
Email: gyeldup@druknet.bt
Web: www.wix.com/jakarvillagelodge/
bhutan
Contact: Mr. Gasey Lhendup (Proprietor)

✦ Mountain Lodge
'family owned hotel since 1996'
Tel: +975 3 631255
Fax: +975 3 631275
Cell: +975 17670456, 17676676
E-mail: mtnlodge@druknet.bt
Contact: Mr. Thinley Namgyal
(Proprietor)

✦ Rinchenling Lodge
'We serve you with our best'
Tel: +975 3 631147
Fax: +975 3 631103
Cell: +975 17670400
E-mail: jampel@druknet.bt
Contact: Mr. Jampel Ngedup (Proprietor)

✦ **River Lodge**
'truly Bhutanese experience '
Tel: +975 3 631287
Fax: +975 3 631668
Cell: +975 17791460, 17677252
E-mail: pemadawa@druknet.bt
Web: www.drukriverlodge.com
Contact: Mr. Pema Dawa (*Proprietor*)

✦ **Udee Guest House**
'Feel the taste of your comfortable home'
Tel: + 975 3 631139
Fax: +975 3 631309
Cell: + 975 17631213
Email: udee@druknet.bt
Contact: Mr.Ugyen Dorji (*Proprietor*)

✦ **Yugharling Resort**
'A Place of Tranquility and Serenity'
Tel: + 975 3 631948
Fax: 975 3 631644
Cell: 17601932
Email: yugharling@druknet.bt
Web: www.yugharling.com
Contact: Mr.Tempa Chophel (*Proprietor*)

BHUTAN'S DIPLOMATIC MISSIONS ABROAD

INDIA
The Royal Bhutanese Embassy
Chandragupta Marg,
Chanakyapuri,
New Delhi 110021, India
Tel: +91 11 26889230,
26889809, 26889807
Fax: +91 11 26876710
Telex: 3162263 DRUK IN
E-Mail: bhutan@del2.vsnl.net.in
Website: http://www.bhutan-info.org

THAILAND
The Royal Bhutanese Embassy
375/1 Soi Ratchadanivej
Pracha-Uthit Road
Samsen Nok, Huay Kwang
Bangkok 10320, Thailand
Tel: +66 2 2744740/1/2
Fax: +66-2 2744743
E-Mail: bht_emb_bkk@yahoo.com

BANGLADESH
The Royal Bhutanese Embassy
House No. 12, CEN Road # 107
Gulshan Two, Dhaka 1212
Bangladesh
Tel: +880 2 8826863, 8827160
Fax: +880 2 8823939
E-Mail: bhtemb@bdmail.net

BELGIUM
The Royal Bhutanese Embassy
Avenue Jules Cesar 70
1150 Brussels, Belgium
Tel: +32 2 7619570
Fax: +32 2 7619577
E-Mail: Brussels@mfa.gov.bt

KUWAIT
The Royal Bhutanese Embassy
Consul General
Qurtuba Area, Block No. 4
Jaddah No. 7, Street 1, Villa 5
P.O.Box 1510, Safat 13016, Kuwait
Tel: +965 5331506, 2516640, 2516650
Fax: +965 5338959, 2516650
E-Mail: bhutankuwait@hotmail.com
E-Mail: butanemb@kems.net

UNITED STATES
Permanent Mission of the Kingdom of Bhutan to the United Nations
Two United Nations Plaza, 27th Floor,
New York, NY 10017, U.S.A.
Tel: +1 212 826 1919, 826-1990/1
Fax: +1 212 826 2998
E-Mail: pmbnewyork@aol.com

SWITZERLAND
Permanent Mission of the Kingdom of Bhutan to the United Nations
17-19, Chemin du Champ d'Anier
1209 Geneva Switzerland
Tel: +41 22 7990890
Fax: +41 22 7990899
E-Mail: mission.bhutan@ties.itu.int

BHUTAN'S HONORARY CONSULS ABROAD

AUSTRALIA
Honorary Consul of Bhutan
Ms. Catherine Harris PSM,
Post Box 57,
78 Louisa Road, Birchgrove,
NSW 2041, Australia
Email: Charris@harrisfarm.com.au

FRANCE
Honorary Consul of Bhutan in Paris
Dr. Francoise Pommaret
2, Rue d'Enghien, 75010 Paris, France
Tel: +33 1 4483 9565
Fax: +331 4523 4177
Email: Fpommaret@aol.com

GERMANY
Honorary Consul of Bhutan in Southern Germany,
Dr. Wolfgang Pfeiffer,
Bahnhofsplatz 4
74321 Bietigheim-Boissingen, Germany.
Tel: +49 7142 53232
Fax: +49 7142 54655
Email: Dr.W.Pfeiffer@t-online.de

HONG KONG & MACAO
Honorary Consul of Bhutan in Hong Kong & Macao
Dato Dr. Cheng Yu - Tung,
New World Development Co. Ltd.
32/F, New World Tower
16-18, Queen's Road. C., Hong Kong
Tel: +852 28443117, 28443111
Fax: +852 25247652
Email: joycecheung@nwd.com.hk

REPUBLIC OF KOREA
Honorary Consul of Bhutan,
Mr. Han Young Kim,
123-5 Nonhyun-Dong,
Kangnam-ku, Seoul,
Republic of Korea
Tel: +82 2 3444 5961
Fax: +82 2 3444 4384
Email: hykmes@hanafos.com

SRI LANKA
Honorary Consul of Bhutan,
Mr. Abbas Esufally,
Level 06, Hemas House
No 75, Braybrooke Place
Colombo-02, Sri Lanka.
Tel: +94 11 2313131
Fax: +94 23 00003
Email: bhutan.consul@hemas.com;

THE NETHERLANDS
Honorary Consul of Bhutan in the Netherlands
Mr. Cornelis Klein,
Koningin Marialaan 176
2595 GE Den Haag, The Netherlands
Tel: +31 70 7786215
Fax: +31 +6 45247468
Email: connelisklein@hotmail.com

UNITED KINGDOM
Honorary Consul of Bhutan in London,
Michael Rutland, Esq., OBE
2, Windacres, Warren Road,
Guildford GU1 3HG, United Kingdom
Tel: +44 1483 538189
Fax: +44 1483 538189
Email: mrutland@aol.com

BHUTANESE FRIENDSHIP SOCIETIES AND ASSOCIATIONS

AUSTRALIA
Tim Fischer,
Chairman
Australia-Bhutan Friendship Association
Post Box 8154, Birallee,
Wodonga, Vic, 3689, Australia

AUSTRIA
Dr. Claus Walter,
Austrian-Bhutan Society (ABS)
A-1230 Vienna,
Endemanngasse 6-18/2/39, Austria
Tel: +43 1 888 73 82/53120-2870
Fax: +43 1 53120 2879
Email: bhutanaustria@yahoo.de
Claus.walter@bmbwk.gv.at

DENMARK
Ms. Trine Dich,
Danish-Bhutanese Friendship Association
Valbirkvej 7,
2900 Hellerup, Denmark
Tel: +45 3961 9932, 3528 3432
Fax: +45 3528 3709, 3961 9942
Email: revald@post9.tele.dk

FINLAND
Mr. Juhani Dukpa,
Finland-Bhutan Society
Paivansateentie 7,
13500 Hameenlinna, Finland
Tel: +358 3 6184747, 674 2498
Fax: +358 3 6184797
Email: yeti@mail.htk.fi
dromen@dlc.fi

FRANCE
Dr. Francoise Pommaret,
Les Amis du Bhoutan
2 rue d'Enghien,
75010 Paris, France
Tel: +33 1 45234177
Email: amisbhutan@aol.com

GERMANY
Prof. Manfred Garner,
Bhutan-Himalaya Society
Propsteischlob Johannesberg,
36041 Fulda, Germany
Tel: +49 661 9426104
Fax: +49 661 942 5233
Email: bhg.gerner@web.de
Bhg.hartmann@t-online.de

Ambassador (rtd.) Herald N. Nestroy,
Executive Chairman
Pro Bhutan Association
Carl-Keller-Weg 1
79539 Lörrach, Germany
Tel: +264 61 258971
Email: h.n.nestroy@proBhutan.com

Dr. Werner Haring,
President
Pro Bhutan Association
Carl-Keller-Weg 1
79539 Lörrach, Germany
Tel: +49 7621 86454
Email: dr.w.haring@proBhutan.com
www.probhutan.com

GREECE
Mr. Eleni Petroutsou
President
Greece-Bhutan Friendship Association
Athens, Greece
Email: e.petroutsou@gmail.com

ITALY

Prof. Maddalena Fortunati
Amici del Bhutan - Italia
Via Bronzetti 6
46100 Mantova, Italy
Tel: +3933 55 25 24 06
Email: madda2000@hotmail.com

JAPAN

H.E. Mr. Sakutaro Tanino, *President,*
Japan-Bhutan Friendship Association
12-6-5F Gobancho, Chiyoda-Ku, Tokyo
102-0076, Japan

Mr. Daisaku Komatsu, *President,*
Kobe-Bhutan Friendship Association
C/o Kobe Chikagai Co., Ltd.
Kobe Kotsu Centre Building
1-10-1, Sannomiya-Cho,
Chou-ku Kobe 650-0021, Japan

Mr. Yasuo Miyazawa, *President,*
**Yokohama-Bhutan Friendship
Association**
Homest Plaza Tokaichiba (East Bldg) 202
801-8 Takaichiba, Midori
Yokohama 226, Japan

Dr. Kazuto Iwama, *President,*
Hokkaido Bhutan Association,
Faculty of Agriculture,
Hokkaido University, Kita 9, Nishi 9,
Kita-ku, Sapporo +81 60 8589, Japan

NETHERLANDS

Mr. Albert van der Schaaf
Stiching Friends of Bhutan
Korte Poten 7
2511 EB Den Haag, The Netherlands
Tel: +31 70 3569971, 54662877
Email: avanderschaaf@planet.nl
zonder@planet.nl

SPAIN

Mr. Sergi Vega Rosello
Bhutan Society of Spain
Rocafort 29 Planta Balxa B
08015 Barcelona, Spain
Tel: +34 93 423 78 87
Fax: +34 93 426 05 54
Email: bhutansocietyspain@yahoo.com

SWEDEN

Ms. Ruth Hylander-Tshering
The Jumolhari Trust
C/o Ms. Carin Nygren
Stallgatan 20,
SE-933 32 Arvidsjaur, Sweden
Tel: +46 960 21605
Email: carin.nygren@alfa.telenordia.se
foto.anders.bergman@telia.com

Mr. Arne Georgzen
Swedish Bhutan Society
C/o Mr. Anders Bergman
Toretorpsv. 27
SE-812 92 G-Hammarby, Sweden
Tel: +46 290 510 83
Fax: +46 290 510 83
foto.anders.bergman@telia.com

SWITZERLAND

Mr. Ernst Reinhardt, *Chairman*
Society Switzerland-Bhutan
C/o ecoprocess
Post Box CH-8022 Zurich, Switzerland
Tel: +4143 344 8989
Fax: +4143 344 8990
Email: ersnt.Reinhardt@ecoprocess.ch
info@bhutan-switzerland.org

UNITED KINGDOM

Lord Wilson of Tillyorn, *President,*
Sir Simon Bowes Lyon, *Chairman,*
Bhutan Society of the United Kingdom
Unit 23, 78 Marylebone High Street,
London, W1U 5AP, UK
Tel/Fax: +975 2 361185
Email: info@bhutansociety.org
mrutland@aol.com

BHUTAN-INDIA AND INDO-BHUTAN FRIENDSHIP & YOUTH ASSOCIATIONS

BHUTAN-INDIA FRIENDSHIP ASSOCIATION (BIFA), BHUTAN

BIFA, THIMPHU
H. E. Lyonpo Ugyen Tshering
Vice President

Dasho Penjore, *Secretary General*

BIFA, PHUENTSHOLING
HRH Ashi Deki Yangzom Wangchuck
Vice President

Mr. Thinley Dorji, *Secretary General*

BIFA, GELEPHU
Mr. Gyeltshen Dukpa, *Vice President*

INDO-BHUTAN FRIENDSHIP ASSOCIATION (IBFA), INDIA

IBFA, NEW DELHI
Dr. Bhishma Narain Singh, *President*,
C-83 Upkar Apartments
Mayur Vihar. Ext. Phase 1
New Delhi - 110091
Tel: +91 11 2712322

IBFA, CHANDIGARH
Dr. Anmol Rattan Sidhu, *President*,
#1313 Sector 34-C, Chandigarh
Tel: +91 172 2604903
Fax: +91 172 2660498

IBFA, KOLKATA
Mr. Amit Kumar Sen, *President*
63, Jodhpur Park, Kolkata - 700 0678
Tel: +91 33 24733231/4558

IBFA CHENNAI
Mr. M.C.H. Krishnamurthi Rao,
President,
Titanium Equipment & Anode Mfg.
Co.Ltd.,
Team House, GST Road, Vanalur,
Chennai 600048
Tel: +91 44 22750325, 25126092 (R)

IBFA SILIGURI
Mr. R.S. Baid, *President*,
Cinderella Hotel, Sevoke Road - 5
Siliguri

IBFA ASSAM
Mr. Dillip Baruah, *President*,
C/o Upada Apartment,
R.G. Baruah Road, 12 Byelane,
Near AIDC Post Office, Guwahati
Tel: 2457705 (R)
Cell: +91 9435045643

IBFA BANGALORE
Mr. Vinay Kumar Poddar, *President*,
C/o C M Academic
No.118, Second Main Road, 5 Cross,
Chamarajapet, Bangalore - 560018
Tel: +91 80 22262355/6
Tel: +91 80 22261524

IBFA ARUNACHAL PRADESH
Mr. Omak Apang, *President*,
Hill Top Colony, ESS Sector, Itanagar,
Papum Pare District,
Arunachal Pradesh-791111
Tel: +91 360 2217419
Cell: +91 9436043577

INDO BHUTAN YOUTH ASSOCIATION, MUMBAI
Mr. Rajiv Samant,
President

DIPLOMATIC MISSIONS AND INTERNATIONAL ORGANIZATIONS IN BHUTAN

EMBASSY OF INDIA
India House Estate,
Thimphu Bhutan
Tel: +975 2 322280/322612
Fax: +975 2 323195/325341
Phuentsholing, Liaison Office
Tel: +975 5 252632
Website: http://www.eoithimphu.org

EMBASSY OF BANGLADESH
Plot No. HIG-3, Upper Chubachu,
Thimphu, Bhutan.
P.O.Box 178, Thimpu Bhutan
Tel: +975 2 322 539
Fax: +975 2 322 629
Email: bdoot@druknet.bt

THAILAND
Royal Thai Consulate Office
Honorary Consul of Thailand
Thimphu Bhutan
Telephone : +975 2 323978
Fax : +975 2 323807
Email: royalthaiconsulate@druknet.bt

AUSTRIA
Austrian Development Cooperation,
Austrian Coordination Office (ACO),
Post Box No. 307, Thimphu, Bhutan,
Tel. +975 2 324495, 324287, 323053
Fax +975 2 324496
Email: thimphu@ada.gv.at

DENMARK
Liaison Office of Denmark
P.O. Box 614
Thimphu Bhutan
Phone: +975 2 323331
Fax: +975 2 322813
Email: pbhrpk@um.dk
Website: www.missionthimphu.um.dk

JAPAN
JICA/JOCV Bhutan Office
Post Box No. 217
Thimphu, Bhutan
Tel: +975 2 322030, 323218
Fax: +975 2 323089
E-mail: jicajvbt@druknet.bt
Website: http://www.jica.go.jp/bhutan

NETHERLANDS
SNV Bhutan
Post Box No. 815, Thimphu, Bhutan
Phone: +975 2 322732, 322900
Fax: +975 2 322649
Email: snvbh@druknet.bt
Website: http://www.snv.org.bt/

SWITZERLAND
Helvetas/SDC Coordination Office
Post Box No.
Thimphu Bhutan
Tel: +975 2 322870, 323209, 327103
Fax: +975 2 323210
Email: helvetas@druknet.bt
Website: http://www.helvetas.org.bt/

UN AGENCIES AND INTERNATIONAL NGO'S IN BHUTAN

Food and Agriculture Organization
United Nations House,
Post Box No. 162, Thimphu, Bhutan
Tel: +975 2 323932, 322315
Fax: +975 2 323006
E-mail: fao-bt@fao.org
Website: www.fao.org

United Nations Development Program
United Nations House,
Post Box No. 612, Thimphu, Bhutan.
Tel: +975 2 322424,322315
Fax: +975 2 322657
E-mail : fo.btn@undp.org
Website: www.undp.org.bt

United Nations Population Fund
United Nations House,
Thimphu, Bhutan.
Tel: +975 2 232242
Fax: +975 2 325264
E-mail: fo.btn@unfpa.org
Website: www.unfpa.org

United Nations Children's Fund
Post Box No. 239, Thimphu, Bhutan
Tel: +975 2 331369, 331370
Fax: +975 2 323238
E-mail: thimphu@unicef.org
Website: www.unicef.org/bhutan

World Food Program
United Nations House,
Thimphu, Bhutan.
Tel: +975 2 322424, 323007
Fax: +975 2 323988
E-mail: WFP.Thimphu@wfp.org
Website: www.wfp.org

World Health Organization (WHO)
Post Box No. 175, Thimphu, Bhutan.
Tel: +975 2 322864
Fax: +975 2 323319
E-mail: wrbhu@druknet.bt
Website: www.who.org.bt

Bhutan- Canada Foundation
Post Box 201, Thimphu, Bhutan
Tel/Fax: +975 2 322109
Email: Canada@druknet.bt
Website: www.bhutancanada.ca

The Bhutan Foundation
Nazhoen Pelri Youth Center
Post Box 255, Thimphu, Bhutan
Tel: +975 2 335613
Fax: +975 2 335614
www.bhutanfound.org

Save the Children, USA
Post Box No. 281, Thimphu, Bhutan
Tel: +975 2 323419, 325599
Fax: +975 2 322290
Email: post@savethechildren.org.bt

WWF Bhutan Program Office
Post Box No. 210, Thimphu Bhutan
Tel: +975 2 323528, 323316
Fax: +975 2 323518
www.wwfbhutan.org.bt

LITERARY & COFFEE TABLE BOOKS ON BHUTAN

1. Treasures of the Thunder Dragon: A Portrait of Bhutan, *Her Majesty Ashi Dorji Wangmo Wangchuck*

2. Of Rainbows and Clouds: *Her Majesty Ashi Dorji Wangmo Wangchuck*

3. Jewel of Men: a collection of poetry, *Tarayana Foundation*

4. 'As I am so is My Nation', *Lyonpo Thakur S. Powdyel*

5. Facts about Bhutan - The Land of the Thunder Dragon, first edition, *Lily Wangchhuk*

6. Within the Realm of Happiness, *Kinley Dorji*

7. 'Seeing with the Third Eye: growing up with Angay in rural Bhutan,' *T. Sangay Wangchuk*

8. Coming Home, *Pema Euden*

9. The Restless Relic, *Karma Tenzin*

10. Druk Yul Decides, *Gyambo Sithey & Dr. Tandi Dorji*

11. Bold Bhutan Beckons, *Tim Fischer and Tshering Tashi*

12. Mammals of Bhutan, *Tashi Wangchuk*

13. The Hero with a Thousand Eyes, *Karma Ura*

14. The Ballad of Pemi Tshewang Tashi: A Wind Borne Feather, *Karma Ura*

15. Deities, Archers and Planners in the Era of Decentralization, *Karma Ura*

16. The Bhutanese Development Story, *Karma Ura*

17. Folktales of Bhutan, *Kunzang Choden*

18. Bhutanese Tales of the Yeti, *Kunzang Choden*

19. Dawa: The Story of a Stray Dog in Bhutan, *Kunzang Choden*

20. The Circle of Karma, *Kunzang Choden*

21. Chilli and Cheese - Food and Society in Bhutan, *Kunzang Choden*

22. History of Bhutan based on Buddhism, *C.T. Dorji*

23. A Political and Religious History of Bhutan (1651 – 1906), *C.T. Dorji*

24. Blue Annals of Bhutan, *C.T. Dorji*

25. Speaking Statues, Flying Rocks, *Sonam Kinga*

26. Impact of Reforms on Bhutanese Social Organization, *Sonam Kinga*

27. Changes in Bhutanese Society: Impact of Fifty Years of Reforms, *Sonam Kinga*

28. Birds of Bhutan, *Yeshey Dorji*

29. Portraits & Landscapes, *Ugyen Wangchuk*

30. Wild Rhododendrons of Bhutan, *Rebecca Pradhan*

31. An Illustrated Guide to Orchids of Bhutan, *Dhan Bahadur Gurung*

32. BHUTAN, World's Largest Book, *National Geographic Society*

33. Immortal Lines, *Bhutan Times*

34. Dzongs of Bhutan, *Bhutan Times*

35. Sacred Monasteries and Religious Sites of Bhutan, *Bhutan Times*

36. Seeds of Faith Vol I, *KMT Publishers*

37. The Legacy of a King, *Tourism Council of Bhutan*

38. 100 Years of Monarchy, *Rabsell Media Services*

39. The King of Destiny, *Rabsell Media Services*

40. Bhutan and the British, *Peter Collister*

41. Bhutan & Tibet, *Samuel Turner*

42. Bhutan towards a grass root participatory polity, *Bhabeni Sen Gupta*

43. Bhutan, Himalayan Mountain Kingdom, *Francoise Pommaret*

44. World Lonely Planet Guide to Bhutan, *Stan Armington*

45. Driving Holidays in the Himalaya: Bhutan *Koko Singh*

46. Beyond the Sky and the Earth, *Jamie Zeppa*

47. Bhutan, Kingdom of the Dragon, *Robert Dompnier*

48. Colours of Bhutan, *Robert Dompnier*

49. Bhutan- Mountain Fortress of the Gods, *Christian Schichigruber/Francoise Pommaret*

50. Bhutan Kingdom in the Himalaya, *Sangay Acharaya*

51. Bhutan Kingdom of the Dragon, *Robert Dompnier*

52. The Raven Crown, *Michael Aris*

53. Views of Medieval Bhutan, *Michael Aris*

54. Textile Arts of Bhutan, *Susanne Bean*

55. Bhutan a Kingdom in the Sky, *M.S Kohli*

56. Bhutan The Land of Thunder Dragon, *John Berthold*

57. Bhutan A Trekker's Guide, *Bart Jordans*

58. The Dragon's Gift: Sacred Arts of Bhutan, *Serindia*

59. Land of Serenity, *Mathieu Richard*

60. Enchanted by Bhutan, *Yoshiro Imaeda*

USEFUL WEBSITES

ACTS OF BHUTAN
http://www.bhutan.gov.bt/
government/acts.php

BHUTAN OFFICIAL WEB PORTAL
http://www.bhutan.gov.bt

CORONATION
http://www.bhutan2008.bt

DRUKNET, BHUTAN INTERNET SERVICE PROVIDER
http://www.druknet.bt

GOVERNMENT PUBLICATIONS
http://www.bhutan.gov.bt/
government/publications.php

NATIONAL ASSEMBLY OF BHUTAN
http://www.nab.gov.bt

RULES AND REGULATION
http://www.bhutan.gov.bt/
government/rulesAndRegulations.php

CONSTITUTIONAL BODIES

CONSTITUTION OF BHUTAN
http://www.constitution.bt

ANTI CORRUPTION COMMISSION
http://www.anti-corruption.org.bt/

ELECTION COMMISSION OF BHUTAN
http://www.ecb.gov.bt

ROYAL CIVIL SERVICE COMMISSION
http://www.rcsc.gov.bt

ROYAL AUDIT AUTHORITY
http://www.raa.gov.bt

POLITICAL PARTIES

DRUK PHUENSUM TSHOGPA
http://www.dpt.bt

PEOPLE'S DEMOCRATIC PARTY
http://www.pdp.bt

GOVERNMENT AGENCIES/AND AUTONOMOUS BODIES

BHUTAN TELECOM
http://www.telecom.net.bt/

BHUTAN INFORMATION COMMUNICATIONS AND MEDIA AUTHORITY
http://www.bicma.gov.bt/

BHUTAN POST
http://www.bhutanpost.com.bt

BHUTAN POWER CORPORATION
http://www.bpc.com.bt

BHUTAN ELECTRICITY AUTHORITY
http://www.bea.gov.bt/

CENTRE FOR BHUTAN STUDIES
http://www.bhutanstudies.org.bt

DRUK HOLDINGS & INVESTMENT
http://www.dhi.bt

DRUK GREEN POWER CORPORATION
http://www.dgpc.bt

GROSS NATIONAL HAPPINESS COMMISSION
http://www.pc.gov.bt
http://www.grossnationalhappiness.com

MINISTRY OF AGRICULTURE & FORESTS
http://www.moa.gov.bt

MINISTRY OF HOME AND CULTURAL AFFAIRS
http://www.mohca.gov.bt

MINISTRY OF ECONOMIC AFFAIRS
http://www.mti.gov.bt/

DEPARTMENT OF TRADE
http://www.trade.gov.bt/

DEPARTMENT OF INDUSTRY
http://www.mti.gov.bt/industry/
industry.htm

DEPARTMENT OF GEOLOGY AND MINES
http://www.mti.gov.bt/dgm/dgm.htm

MINISTRY OF EDUCATION
http://www.education.gov.bt/

MINISTRY OF FINANCE
http://www.mof.gov.bt/

MINISTRY OF FOREIGN AFFAIRS
http://www.mfa.gov.bt

MINISTRY OF HEALTH
http://www.health.gov.bt/

MINISTRY OF INFORMATION AND COMMUNICATIONS
http://www.moic.gov.bt/

DEPARTMENT OF INFORMATION TECHNOLOGY & TELECOM
http://www.dit.gov.bt/

MINISTRY OF LABOUR AND HUMAN RESOURCES
http://www.molhr.gov.bt/

DEPARTMENT OF HUMAN RESOURCES
http://www.molhr.gov.bt/DHR/

DEPARTMENT OF EMPLOYMENT
http://www.employment.gov.bt

MINISTRY OF WORKS AND HUMAN SETTLEMENT
http://www.mowhs.gov.bt

DEPARTMENT OF ROADS
http://www.dor.gov.bt/

DEPARTMENT OF URBAN DEVELOPMENT & ENGINEERING SERVICES
http://www.dudh.gov.bt/

NATIONAL HOUSING DEVELOPMENT CORPORATION
http://www.nhdc.gov.bt/

NATIONAL COMMISSION FOR WOMEN AND CHILDREN
http://www.ncwcbhutan.net

NATIONAL PENSION AND PROVIDENT FUND
http://www.nppf.org.bt

OFFICE OF ATTORNEY GENERAL
http://www.oag.gov.bt

ROYAL CIVIL SERVICE COMMISSION
http://www.rcsc.gov.bt

ROYAL MONETARY AUTHORITY
http://www.rma.org.bt

TOURISM COUNCIL OF BHUTAN
http://www.tourism.gov.bt

THIMPHU CITY CORPORATION
http://www.tmc.gov.bt

DZONGKHAGS/DISTRICTS

http://www.bumthang.gov.bt

http://www.chukha.gov.bt

http://www.dagana.gov.bt

http://www.gasa.gov.bt

http://www.haa.gov.bt

http://www.lhuentse.gov.bt

http://www.mongar.gov.bt

http://www.paro.gov.bt

http://www.pemagatshel.gov.bt

http://www.punakha.gov.bt

http://www.samdrupjongkhar.gov.bt

http://www.samtse.gov.bt

http://www.sarpang.gov.bt

http://www.thimphu.gov.bt

http://www.trashigang.gov.bt

http://www.trashiyangtse.gov.bt

http://www.trongsa.gov.bt

http://www.tsirang.gov.bt

http://www.wangduephodrang.gov.bt

http://www.zhemgang.gov.bt

JUDICIARY

Royal Court of Justice
http://www.judiciary.gov.bt

INSTITUTES

ROYAL UNIVERSITY OF BHUTAN
http://www.rub.edu.bt/

COLLEGE OF SCIENCE AND TECHNOLOGY
http://www.rbit.edu.bt

ROYAL INSTITUTE OF MANAGEMENT (RIM)
http://www.rim.edu.bt/

SAMTSE COLLEGE OF EDUCATION
http://www.niesamtse.edu.bt/

PARO COLLEGE OF EDUCATION
http://www.nieparo.edu.bt

SHERUBTSE COLLEGE, KANGLUNG

DISTANCE TEACHER EDUCATION
http://www.dtepniesamtse.edu.bt

ROYAL BHUTAN INSTITUTE OF TECHONOLOGY
http://www.rbit.edu.bt

ROYAL THIMPHU COLLEGE
http://www.rtc.bt

MEDIA

BHUTAN BROADCASTING SERVICE
http://www.bbs.com.bt

BHUTAN TIMES
http://www.bhutantimes.bt

BHUTAN OBSERVER
http://www.bhutanobserver.bt

BHUTAN TODAY
http://www.bhutantoday.bt

CENTENNIAL RADIO
http://www.centenialradio

KUENSEL, BHUTAN'S NATIONAL NEWSPAPER
http://www.kuenselonline.com

KUZOO SOCIETY
http://www.kuzoo.net/

RADIO VALLEY
http://www.radiovalley.bt

NGOS - NATIONAL & INTERNATIONAL

THE BHUTAN FOUNDATION
http://www.bhutanfound.org

RENEW
http://www.renew.org.bt

YOUTH DEVELOPMENT FUND
http://www.bhutanyouth.org

TARAYANA FOUNDATION
http://www.tarayanafoundation.org

NWAB
http://www.nwabbhutan.org.bt

ROYAL SOCIETY FOR PROTECTION OF NATURE
http:// www.rspn-bhutan.org

SAVE THE CHILDREN
http://www.savethechildren.org/countries/asia/bhutan

WWF, BHUTAN
http://www.wwfbhutan.org.bt

FINANCIAL INSTITUTIONS

ROYAL INSURANCE CORPORATION OF BHUTAN (RICB)
http://www.ricb.com.bt

BANK OF BHUTAN (BOB)
http://www.bobltd.com.bt

BHUTAN NATIONAL BANK
http://www.bnb.com.bt

BHUTAN DEVELOPMENT FINANCE CORPORATION LTD
http://www.bdfcl.com.bt

OTHERS

ASSOCIATION OF BHUTANESE TOUR OPERATORS
http://www.abto.org.bt/

BHUTAN CHAMBER OF COMMERCE AND INDUSTRY
http://www.bcci.com.bt

BHUTAN-INDIA FRIENDSHIP ASSOCIATION
http://www.bifa.org.bt

BHUTAN CULTURAL TRUST FUND
http://www.ctf.gov.bt

BHUTAN HEALTH TRUST FUND
http://www.bhtf.gov.bt/

CONSTRUCTION ASSOCIATION OF BHUTAN
http://www.cab.org.bt

CONSTRUCTION DEVELOPMENT BOARD
http://www.cdb.gov.bt

DRUK AIR CORPORATION
http://www.drukair.com.bt

MENJONG CHOTHUN TSHOGPA(MCT)
http://www.menjong.org

ROYAL INSURANCE CORPORATION OF BHUTAN
http://www.ricb.com.bt

VAST
http://www.vast-bhutan.org

VOLUNTEERS IN BHUTAN
http://www.vib.org.bt

JDWNRH HOSPITAL
http://www.jdwnrh.gov.bt

STATE TRADING CORPORATION OF BHUTAN LIMITED
http://www.stcb.com.bt

DIPLOMATIC MISSIONS AND INTERNATIONAL ORGANIZATIONS IN BHUTAN

EMBASSY OF INDIA
http://www.indianembassythimphu.bt

HELVETAS-BHUTAN
http://www.helvetas.org.bt/

JICA-BHUTAN
http://www.jica.go.jp/bhutan

LIAISON OFFICE OF DENMARK
http://www.missionthimphu.um.dk/en

SNV-BHUTAN
http://www.snv.org.bt/

VOLUNTEER SERVICE ABROAD
http://www.vsa.org.nz/

UN AGENCIES

FAO
http://www.fao.org

UN AGENCIES
www.unct.org.bt

UNITED NATIONS DEVELOPMENT PROGRAMME, BHUTAN
http://www.undp.org.bt/

UNICEF- BHUTAN
http://www.unicef.org/bhutan/

UNFPA
http://www.unfpa.org

WORLD FOOD PROGRAMME (WFP)
http://www.wfp.org

WORLD HEALTH ORGANIZATION (WHO)
http://www.who.org.bt

Conversational Dzongkha for Travellers

Greetings

Greetings/ Hello :
Kuzoozangpo La
(Response is also
Kuzoozangpo La)

Welcome
Joen pa Leg So

How are you ?
Ga Day Bay Zhu Yoe Ga?

I'm fine
Nga Leg shom Bay Rang Yoey

Good Wishes
Tashidelek!

Thank You
Kaadinchhey La

Introductions

What is your name? (for elders or with respe(
Na gi Tshen Ga Chi Mo ?

What is your name? (for peers)
Chhoey gi Ming Ga chi Mo ?

My Name is .....
Ngegi Ming .... Ein.

Where are you from ?
Chhoey ga te lay mo ?

How old are you ?
Kay Lo gadem chi Ya si?

Good Bye
Log Jay Gay.
(Meaning we
will meet again)

ཀུ་གཟུགས་བཟང་པོ་ལགས།
(Greeting each other: Kuzoozangpo La)

Travel Talk

Where does this road lead to?
Lam di ga thay jow mo ?

Is it far ?
Tha ring sa in-na?

Here : *Na/Nalu*

There : *Pha/Phalu*

Where? : *Ga tey?*

Which? : *Gadee?*

In front of : *Dongkha*

Next to : *Bolokha*

Behind : *Japkha*

Shopping Conversation

What time does it open ?
Chutsho gademchi lu go pchiu mo?

What time does it close?
Chutsho gademchi lu go dam mo?

What is this?
Ani ga chi mo?

How much is it?
Dilu gadem chi mo?

That's too much
Gong bom may

Eating and Drinking

Waiter! : *Wai Chharo!*
(literally meaning friend)

Waitress! *: Wai Bumo!*
(literally meaning girl)

Please Have/Eat: *Zhey*

Water : *Chhu*

Hot Water : *Chhu Tshe*

Milk Tea : *Na Ja*

Butter Tea : *Su Ja*

Get me ...... : *........ Nang*

No more, Thanks : *Me Zhu*
(while making a gesture of moving one's hand in front of the mouth)

It was tasty : *Zhim bay*
(while making a gesture of moving one's forefinger in front of the cheek)

Telephone Tete-a Tete

Hello:
Kuzoozangpo La

Who is speaking ?
Ga Sung Mo La ?

I'm .... Speaking
Nga .... Zhu Do la

Yes, Yes
Ong, Ong

Yes in Affirmative
Ein Ein La

Roger/Signing off:
Las La. Laso La

Emergency Essentials

I'm ill : *Nga nau may*

Where is the toilet?
Chhapsa ga tey in-na?

Where is the hospital
Menkhang ga tey in na?

Guest Contribution by: Shankar
Art by : Tshewang Tenzin
www.learndzongkha.com

A Glossary of Dzongkha Terms

Ashi	:	Honorific title used by women of the Royal or aristocratic family
Avalokitesvara	:	Bodhisattva of compassion.
Bodhisattava	:	Enlightened beings.
Bon	:	Religion with shamanistic and animist practices that predated Buddhism in the Himalayan region
Chathrim	:	Act, rules and regulations
Chhu	:	River or water
Chitshog	:	Parliament
Chiwog	:	Group of villages.
Choesham	:	An altar, shrine room
Choeten	:	Stupa, usually containing sacred relics
Choetho Thrimkiduensa	:	High Court
Dasho	:	A title given by His Majesty the King to people who have been recognized for their services to the country
Desi or Deb	:	Title given to temporal ruler of Bhutan from 1851-1905
Dochok Gothrip	:	Title given to the Leader of Opposition.
Drangpon	:	Judge
Dratshang	:	Central Monastic Body
Driglam Namzha	:	Age old etiquette and code of conduct
Dromchoe	:	Annual religious festival held at Punakha and Thimphu Dzongs dedicated to the Protecting Deities of Bhutan
Druk	:	Thunder Dragon
Druk Gyalpo	:	Formal title for reference to His Majesty the King of Bhutan literally meaning the King of Bhutan.
Druk Yul	:	Dzongkha name for Bhutan. It means "Land of the Thunder Dragon" or "Land of the Drukpas"
Drukpa Kagyu	:	The sect of Buddhism that is the official state religion of Bhutan
Duar	:	Indian word meaning doorway or gate, which refers to the traditional entrances to Bhutan from the Bengal and Assam plains of India.
Dungkhag	:	Sub Division of a District.
Dungkhag Thrimkiduensa	:	Sub-Divisional-Court
Dungpa	:	Head of Sub-Divisions.
Dzong	:	Fortress-like structure that serves as the headquarters of a district administration and the residence of the Monk Body
Dzongda	:	District Administrator
Dzongkha	:	The national language of Bhutan (literally means language of the Dzong)
Dzongkhag	:	District
Dzongkhag Thrimkiduensa	:	District Court
Dzongkhag Tshogdu	:	District Council
Dzongkhag Yargye Tshogchung	:	District Development committee

Gewog	: County, consisting of a block of villages
Gewog Tshogdu	: County Committee
Gewog Yargye Tshogchung	: Block Development Committee.
Gho	: Men's traditional attire, a long-sleeved robe, worn knee-length and fastened at the waist
Goenpa	: Monastery
Gup	: Head of a County
Guru Padmasambhava	: The Indian saint who brought Buddhism to Bhutan in the 8th century also known as Guru Rinpoche.
Gyalyong Tshogde	: National Council
Gyalyong Tshogdu	: National Assembly
Je Khenpo	: Chief Abbot of Bhutan, also Head of the Monastic Body
Kabney	: Ceremonial scarf worn by men
Keyra	: Hand woven fabric belt to fasten a women's kira
Khuru	: A game of darts.
Kira	: Traditional ankle-length dress worn by women
Koma	: A pair of silver brooches, which fastens the women's kira at the shoulder
La	: Mountain pass
Lama	: Buddhist priest who is a religious master
Lhakhang	: Buddhist temple
Lhengye Zhungtshog	: Cabinet
Lodroe Tshogde	: Royal Advisory Council
Lyonchhen	: Title for Prime Minister
Lyonpo	: Title for a minister
Mangmi	: Elected representative of the county,also the deputy Gup
Namthar	: Life stories of great people or hagiography
Nyentho Thrimkiduensa	: Supreme Court
Penlop	: Governor of a region consisting of several districts.
Rabdey	: District Monastic Body
Rinpoche	: Title given to reincarnated lamas
Thrimchee Lyonpo	: Title given to the Chief Justice
Thrimzhung Chhenmo	: The 'Supreme Law', which is a comprehensive code of categories of criminal offences and the appropriate penalties that were approved by the National Assembly in 1957
Thrizin	: Title for Chairperson of the National Council
Thromde Tshogde	: Municipal Committee
Thrompon	: Municipal Administrator
Tshechu	: Religious dance festival held in honour of Guru Padmasambhava
Tshokpon	: Title for Speaker of the National Assembly
Yenlag Thromde	: Satellite town
Zhabdrung	: Title given to Ngawang Namgyal and his successive reincarnations. Literally means "he at whose feet one submits"

BIBLIOGRAPHY

1. *Annual Education Statistics,* Ministry of Education, Royal Government of Bhutan, 2009.

2. *Annual Health Bulletin,* Ministry of Health, Royal Government of Bhutan, 2009.

3. *Bhutan At A Glance,* National Statistical Bureau, Royal Government of Bhutan, 2009.

4. *101 Sacred Places & Monasteries,* Bhutan Times, 2009.

5. *National Accounts Statistics,* National Statistics Bureau, Royal Government of Bhutan (2000- 2008), October 2009.

6. *Dzongkhag Population Projections (2006-2015),* National Statistics Bureau, Royal Government of Bhutan, June 2008.

7. *Bhutan Trade Statistics,* Department of Revenue & Customs, Ministry of Finance, Royal Government of Bhutan, May 2008.

8. *Tenth Five Year Plan (2008 – 2013) Vol. 1, Main Document,* GNH Commission, RGoB, February 2008.

9. *Annual Report, 2006-2007,* Royal Monetary Authority of Bhutan, January 2008.

10. *Century of Progress in Health, Annual Health Bulletin,* PPD, Ministry of Health, RGoB, 2008.

11. *Gross National Happiness, Its Assumptions and Applications* (Concept Paper), Karma Galey, 2008.

12. *The Constitution of the Kingdom of Bhutan,* Royal Government of Bhutan, 2008.

13. *Bhutan, Information Brochure,* Department of Tourism, 2007.

14. *Bhutan, Land of the Thunder Dragon,* Department of Tourism, 2007.

15. *Statistical Yearbook of Bhutan,* National Statistics Bureau, Royal Government of Bhutan, 2007.

16. *General Statistics, 2007,* PPD, Ministry of Education, RGoB Ninth Edition, 2007.

17. *The Local Governments' Act of Bhutan,* 2007.

18. *Immortal Lines, Speeches of the 4th Druk Gyalpo Jigme Singye Wangchuck*, Bhutan Times, 2007.

19. *Annual Report, International Tourism Monitor*, Department of Tourism, 2006.

20. *Fact Sheet, Population and Housing Census 2005*, Office of the Census Commissioner, RGoB, 2005.

21. *Good Governance Plus*, Royal Government of Bhutan, 2005.

22. *A History of Bhutan* (A supplementary text for class XI), Ministry of Education, Royal Government of Bhutan, 2005.

23. *Renewable Natural Resources Sector Project Profiles*, PPD, Ministry of Agriculture, April 2005.

24. *Bhutan, Himalayan Mountain Kingdom*, Francoise Pommaret, 2005.

25. *Window on Bhutan*, Royal Bhutanese Embassy, New Delhi 2003 and 2005.

26. *Bhutan in Focus*, Royal Bhutanese Embassy, New Delhi, 2004.

27. *Bhutan National Human Development Report*, Planning Commission Secretariat, Royal Government of Bhutan, 2000.

28. *Driglam Namzhag, (Bhutanese etiquette) A Manual*, National Library, Thimphu April 1999.

29. *World Lonely Planet Guide to Bhutan*, Stan Armington, 1998.

30. *Bhutan and the British*, Peter Collister, Reprint 1996.

31. *An Introduction to Traditional Architecture of Bhutan*, Department of Works, Housing and Roads, Royal Government of Bhutan, 1993.

32. *A History of Bhutan*, Department of Education, Ministry of Social Services, Royal Government of Bhutan, 1992.

33. *Bhutan, Himalayan Kingdom*, Royal Government of Bhutan, 1979.

34. *History of Bhutan*, Education Department, Bikram Jit Hasrat.

INDEX

INDEX

INDEX

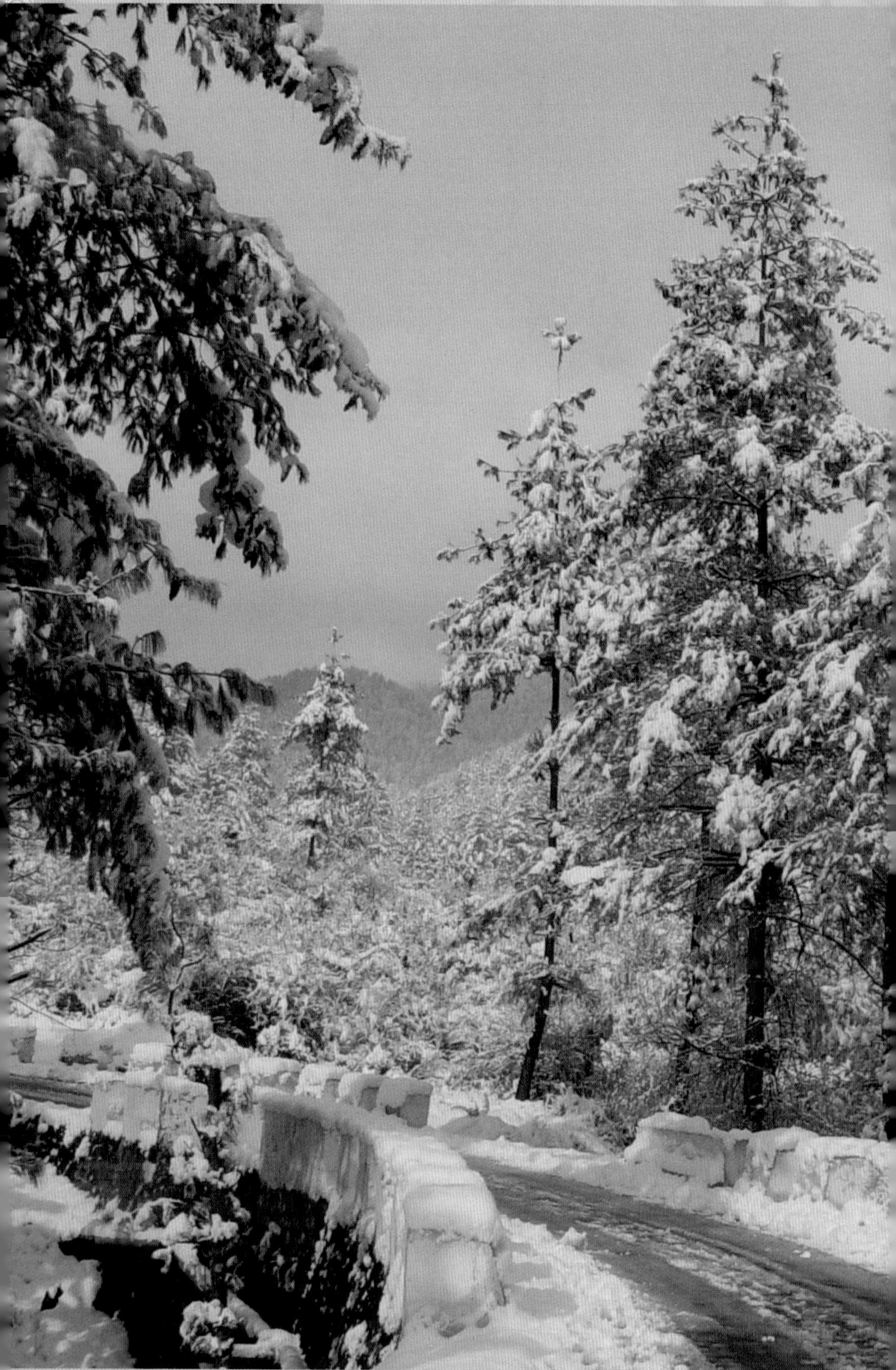

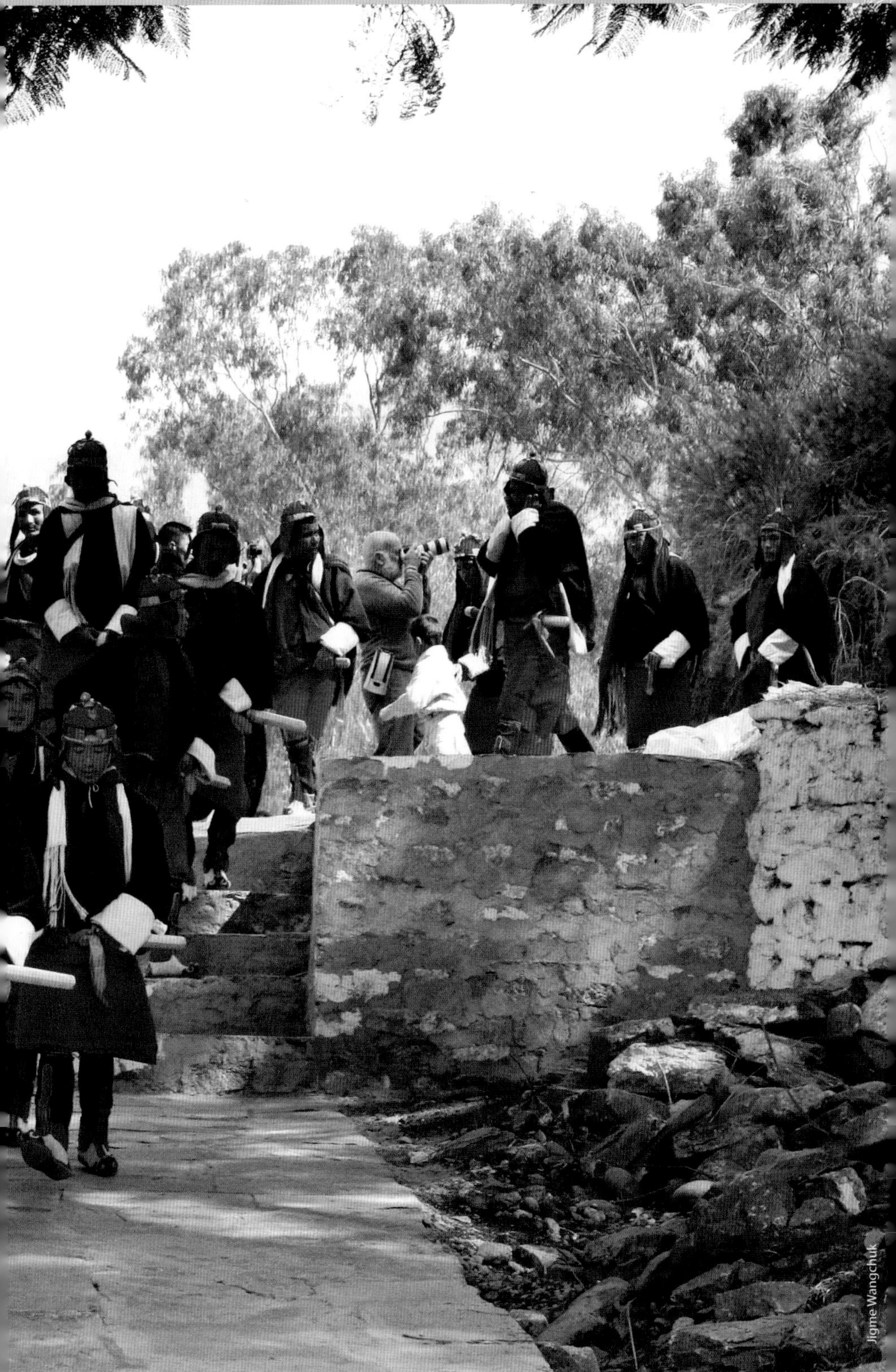

Jigme Wangchuk

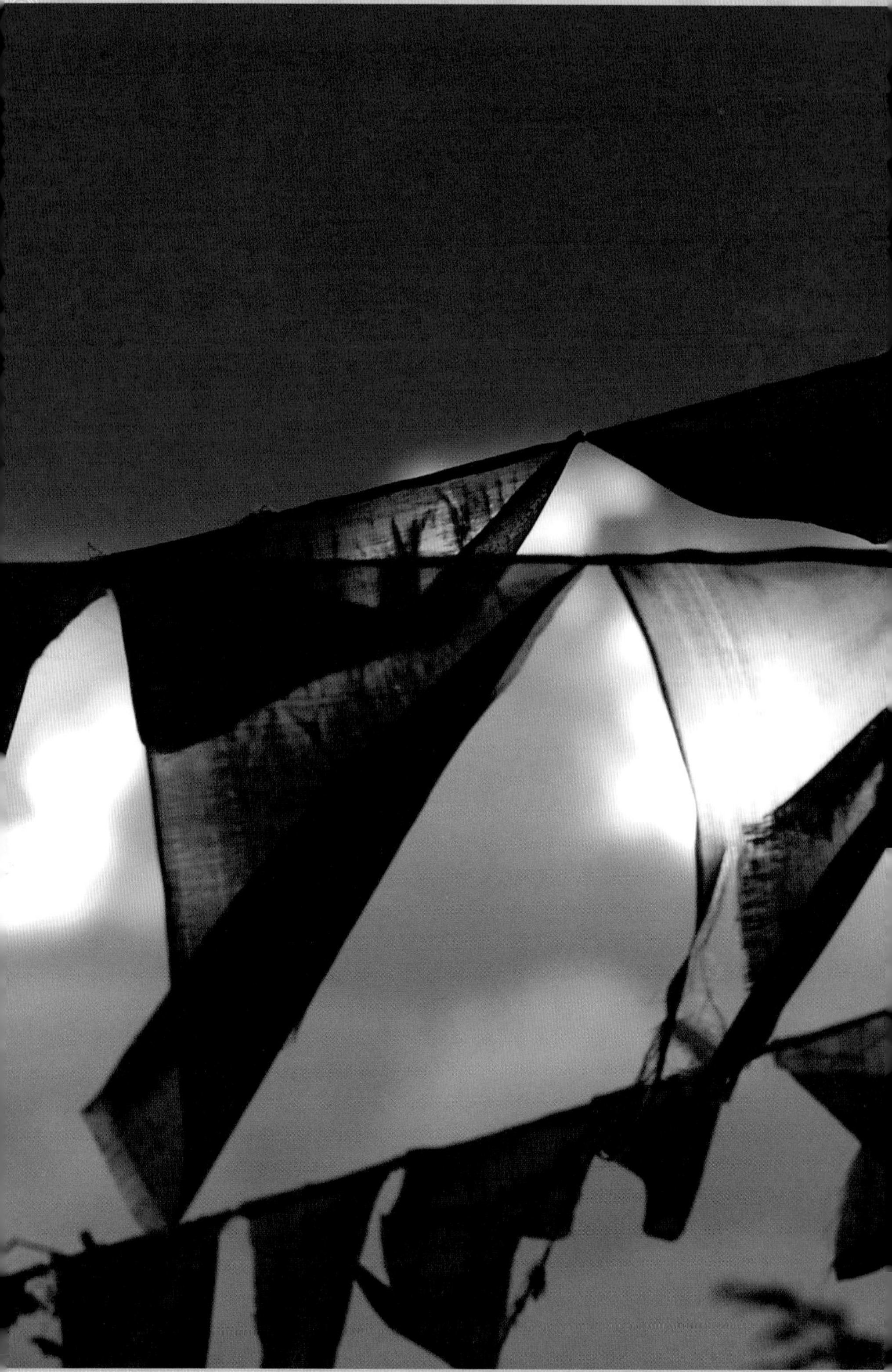

Ian Bell

Leki Dorji

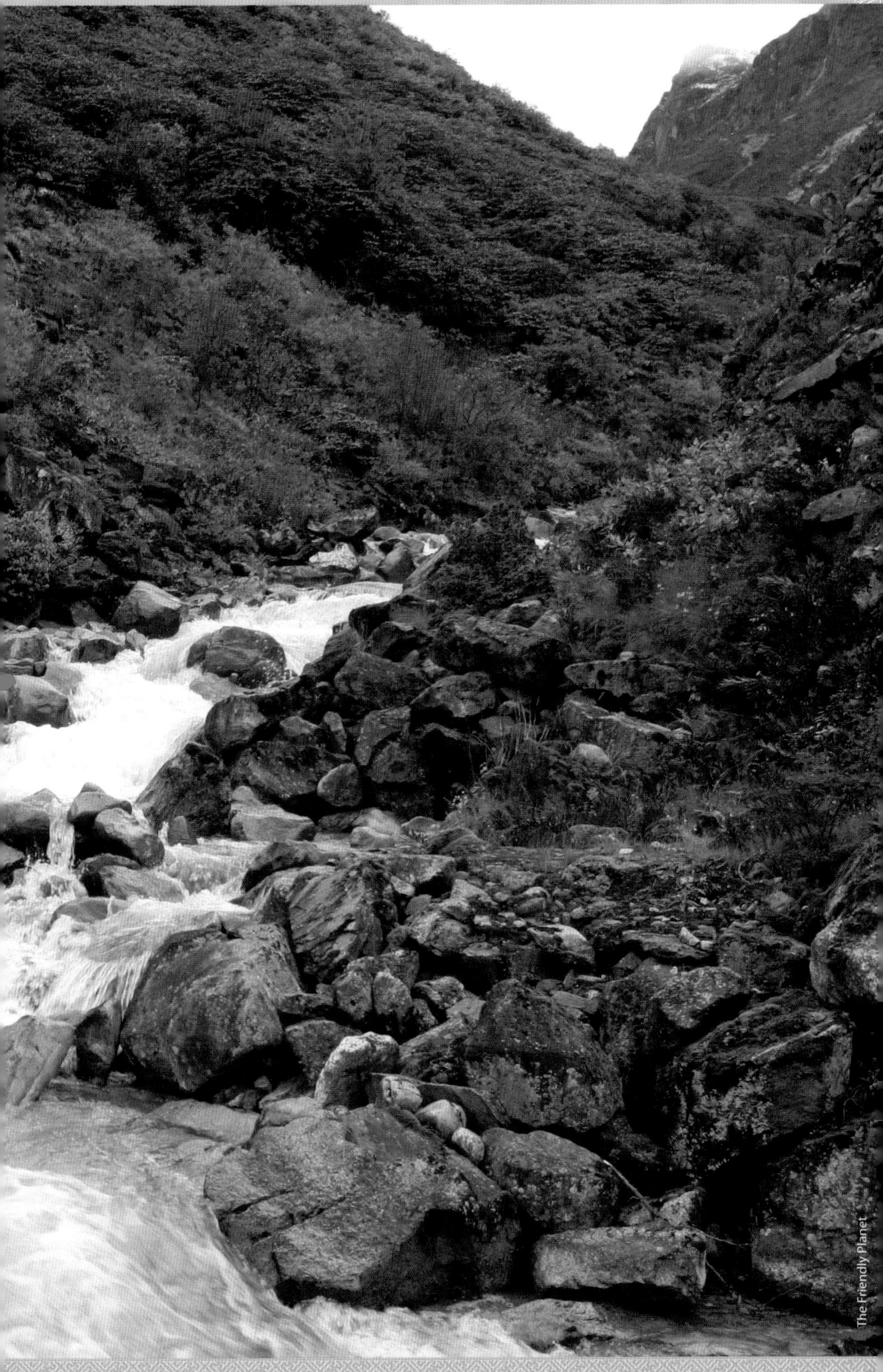

The Friendly Planet

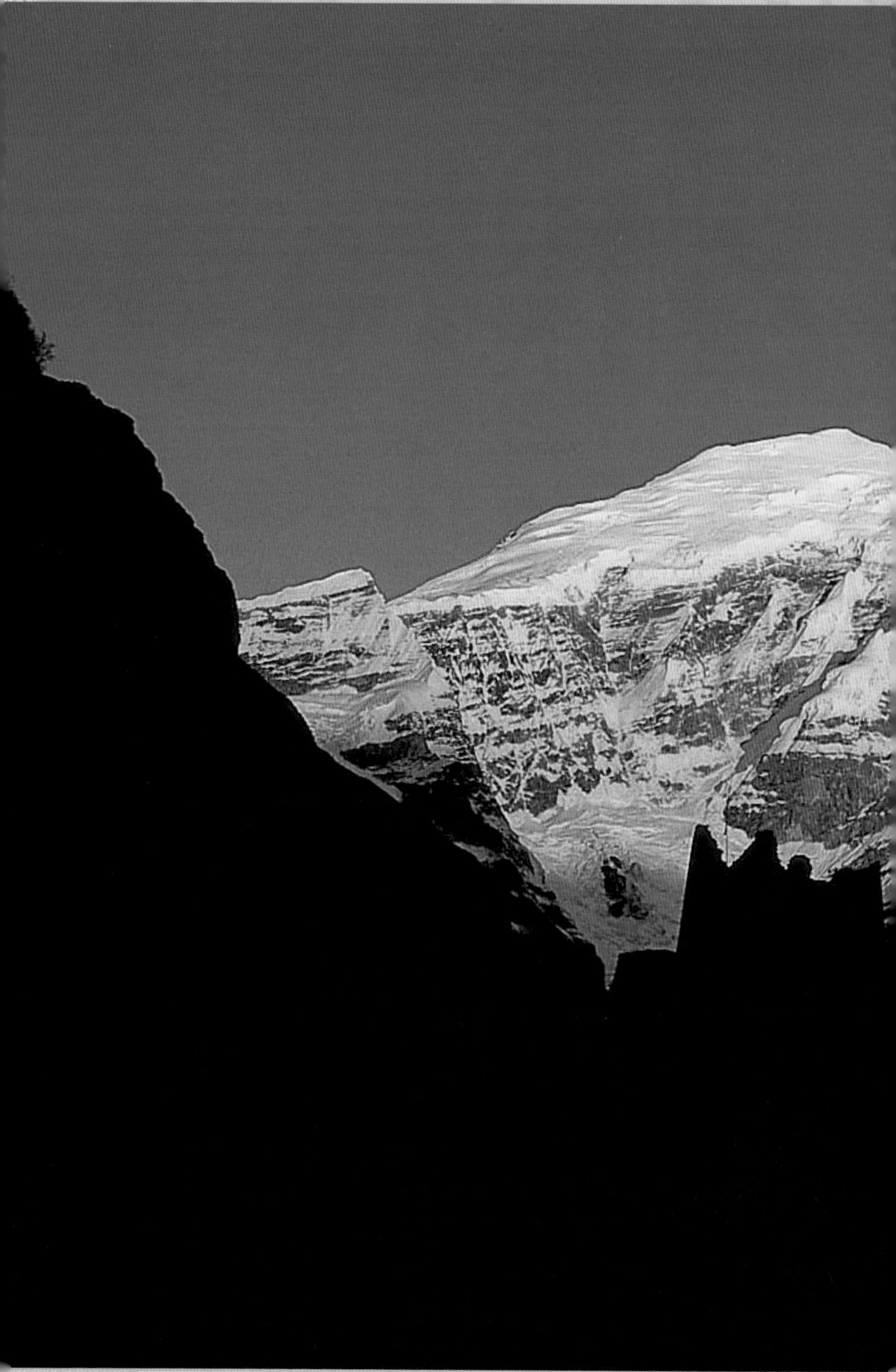